Business School Essentials for Call Center Leaders

By
Maggie Klenke

Contributing Author
Penny Reynolds

THE CALL
CeNTER
SCHOOL

Business School Essentials
for Call Center Leaders

Copyright© 2004 by The Call Center School

Printed in the United States of America by
The Call Center School Press
First printing 2004

Library of Congress Catalog Card Number: 2004110942

ISBN 0-9744179-1-2

THE CALL
CeNTER
SCHOOL

The Call Center School Press is a division of The Call Center School. The Call Center School provides a variety of consulting and educational services to call center professionals. For additional information on The Call Center School products and services, call 615-812-8400 or visit www.thecallcenterschool.com.

TABLE OF CONTENTS

CHAPTER 10: REPORTING AND COMMUNICATIONS

CHAPTER 11: MANAGING STAFF PERFORMANCE

CHAPTER 12: BUSINESS PROCESS IMPROVEMENT

CHAPTER 13: RISK MANAGEMENT

CHAPTER 14: LEADERSHIP CHARACTERISTICS

Preface

Business School Essentials for Call Center Leaders is a book designed to provide managers and leaders with the requisite knowledge and skills to be successful in today's evolving call center environment. It is a compilation of lessons learned from over twenty years of consulting with hundreds of call centers and interacting with thousands of call center professionals in our training programs.

Many of the 14 topics are ones taught in business programs at the bachelors' or masters' level. Each of the 14 topics is explored at a strategic level with sufficient detail to explain the fundamental concepts and applications. It is not intended as a definitive treatise on these topics as each topic could fill a book of its own. What is unique about this book is that each of these business school topics has been explained with its application to the specialized environment of the call center.

Every attempt has been made to make the processes and concepts easy to understand and apply, with simple language and real-world call center examples utilized throughout. Readers should look for ways to apply the knowledge and skills gained from these pages to their own call center operation. While reliance on legal, financial, and technical professionals is encouraged, demonstrating knowledge of the terminology and important issues in these topic areas will expand career possibilities and increase one's confidence in the workplace.

This book is a companion guide to The Call Center School's award-winning educational series entitled the *Masters Series in Call Center Leadership*. It also serves as a primer and detailed reference to those executives and leaders preparing for call center industry certification. Moreover, the how-to information in this text in essential to anyone managing the critical operations of the modern call center.

Acknowledgements

I would like to thank Penny Reynolds, co-founder of The Call Center School, for her contributions in writing Chapters 1, 4, 6, 9, 11, and 12 of this book, and for her tireless editing throughout to make the concepts succinct and readable. In addition, Pamela Trickey, our other co-founder and partner, has contributed content and shouldered a large share of the teaching responsibilities to allow writing time. To a large extent, this book is the combined effort of us all.

Thanks also go to the many individuals who have shaped and enhanced my knowledge and career over the years. During my years with Mountain Bell, I served as a service representative, an outside plant foreman (when women were first entering this role), and as an account executive. Gloradon Larkin was instrumental in encouraging thorough research and accuracy. At United Banks of Colorado, I had the opportunity to serve as Director of Telecommunications and managed my first call center team. Thanks to Mark Frohlich for giving me the opportunity to expand that role well beyond the traditional boundaries.

The real strength of my experience came during the years at TCS Management Group under the guidance of James Gordon and Dr. Robert Hayes. Their support and constant push for excellence was instrumental in my exposure to many of the concepts in this book. I would also like to thank Robert Burrow for his technical and business advice over the many years that we have worked together. He is one of a rare breed of incredibly technical people who can explain concepts to those who aren't, and can apply technology effectively to enhance a business. Clearly without all of these people, this book would not have been possible.

Last, but surely not least, I would like to thank my husband Dale for his support and belief in all of my ventures and projects over more than 30 years of our marriage. Not all of these have been roaring successes, but his faith has been unwavering. Without him, much of my career would not have been possible.

Dedication

To Jennifer and Corwyn

About the Author

As a founding partner of The Call Center School, Maggie Klenke develops and teaches courses on a wide variety of topics and speaks at many industry conferences and association meetings. She leads the firm's consulting practice that specializes in call center operational assessments, workforce planning, acquisition and implementation of call center technologies, and strategic planning. She specializes in the workforce management, leadership, business management, and technical topics of The Call Center School's training curriculum.

Klenke has spent over thirty years in the telecommunications and call center industry, beginning a career with a telecommunications provider in the 1970s. Prior to starting The Call Center School, Klenke was the Vice President of Consulting Services for TCS Management Group, and was instrumental in starting the Call Center University program.

Her articles can be found in a wide variety of online and print media and she serves on the editorial boards of the International Journal of Call Centre Management and CRM Magazine. She is a member of Women in Technology International (WITI) and was among the first to receive the CIAC Call Center Management Consultant certification. Klenke graduated with honors from Loretto Heights College.

CHAPTER 1:
THE BUSINESS OF CALL CENTERS

Introduction

A call center is defined as a place where contacts are made and received. It is often the "front door" to a business and is the place where most crucial customer interactions take place. Therefore its effective and efficient operation is a key ingredient to the overall success of enterprise.

There are many different types, sizes, and functions of call centers handling all sorts of customer contacts. This chapter will explore the history and evolution of call centers and discuss their most important functions within the business world today.

Origins and Evolution

Definition

The definition of a call center in its simplest form is "a place where calls are made and received." The definition increasingly includes mention of the handling of various types of interactions in addition to telephone calls. Therefore, some individuals and organizations use the term "contact center" to refer to the place where these transactions take place.

The terms "call center" and "contact center" are used interchangeably, with "call center" being the most commonly used. The term "call center" is more easily understood and for now best represents the proportion of interactions that are indeed carried out by telephone versus other contact channels such as email or web chat. Even with the explosive growth of the Internet and email transactions, telephone calls will continue to be the primary means of customer communications in the first decade of the 21st Century.

In addition to defining a call center as a place for customer interactions, it is important to denote what else makes an entity a call center and not just a place where telephone calls are answered. A call center is typically defined as an operation where more than one person is responding to handle the contacts, and also where the interaction can be handled by anyone within a group. In other words, the call requires a capability and not a specific individual to handle it.

For example, a travel agency where customers call directly into their favorite travel agent would not constitute a call center. In this situation, callers would likely find their agent of choice busy on another call and have to wait or leave a message, while other agents who could just as easily handle the call sat idle. Where there are strong relationships between individuals or sales commissions involved, the concept of a call center may not be the best solution. If the agency instead had customers call a number and then directed them to any one of a group of individuals who could address their need, the agency would have a call center. The benefits would be better utilization of their travel agents and a quicker response time to customers, even though the personal relationship between the customer and the travel agent would be minimal.

Now that the term "call center" has been defined, the following timeline explores how the telephone and call center industry has evolved into what makes up the call center in the 21st Century.

Evolutionary Steps

In his book, *A Call From the 21st Century*, Paul Anderson outlines the evolution of modern communications devices from the 19th century telegraph to the sophisticated digital networks of today. In summary, these events were as follows:

1840s – Invention of the telegraph. Samuel Morse invented the first instrument to transform information into electrical form and transmit it over long distances. The telegraph, invented in the 1840s, used "Morse Code" to send individual letters in a message by a key and sounder device. This form of communications was used for almost 150 years, until officially discontinued by Western Union in 1991. The telegraph played a significant role in business by enabling companies to communicate information in minutes rather than days.

1870s – Invention of the telephone. The telephone was a by-product invention by Alexander Graham Bell in 1876 in his work to create a microphone for the deaf. Bell's "electrical speech machine" led to the creation of the first telephone exchange in Connecticut in 1878. By 1880, there were nearly 60,000 telephones in existence, including long-distance communications capabilities between Boston and New York City. By the turn of the century, over six million telephones were in use.

1890s – Invention of the radio. Guglielmo Marconi produced the first wireless telegraph system that used electromagnetic waves for long-distance communications in 1895, and by 1899 the first wireless message was broadcast across the English Channel. In the 30 years that followed, more advanced radio communications was made possible by the development of the electron tube, which permitted the detection of high-frequency radio waves and the ability to amplify radio and sound waves. This technology development was the first step in enabling the cellular telephone communications of today.

1920s – Invention of the television. In 1929, David Sarnoff invested $50 million in television experiments that resulted in a full demonstration of television at the **1939** World's Fair and the beginnings of RCA. While the early development of television was slow due to war efforts and government bureaucracy in the 1940s, growth accelerated in the 1950s, with television having a profound effect in mass communications capabilities.

1950s – Invention of the minicomputer. The first integrated circuit was invented in 1959, enabling the development of smaller, more efficient, and less expensive minicomputers. The major computer manufacturers began offering a wide range of computer capabilities and peripheral devices in the 1960s, which were widely used by businesses for accounting, payroll, inventory control, and billing.

1980s – Growth of personal computing and communications. In the 1980s, the personal computer (PC) evolved from being a device primarily used for stand-alone word processing and spreadsheets to a means of communications. With the growth and proliferation of PC modems along with a dramatic increase in processing power, a new age of communications began with the computer as a communications device. Through today's desktop computers, a wide variety of data, print, sound, and video can be transmitted easily throughout the world.

It is interesting to note that these evolutionary communications developments have occurred every 25–30 years, with each having an approximate 150-year life span. So even with the increasing capabilities of digital communications, this mode of communications is only a few decades old in comparison with the telephone, which is a 125-year old global cultural institution. If this pattern holds true, the telephone is not destined to go away for another 15–25 years, meaning the primary communications channel within the call center will likely remain the telephone, at least throughout the first decade of the 21st Century.

In addition to the evolution of communications devices, there have been significant business and regulatory events that have driven business communications and the formation of call centers. Some of these milestones are outlined below:

1930s – Formation of Federal Communications Commission (FCC). The FCC was formed by the Communications Act of 1934 to regulate communications activities across interstate borders. The FCC has been the primary force throughout the last century in forming telecommunications policy related to transmission issues as well as competitive issues among communications suppliers.

1960s – Carterphone decision. In this Supreme Court Decision in 1968, an entity was allowed to connect mobile phones to AT&T land lines. This decision opened competition for premise-based telecommunications suppliers. A host of competitors began to supply end-user telephone equipment and compete with AT&T.

1960s – Toll-free services introduced. In a move that would have a profound effect upon the development of call centers, AT&T introduced its first toll-free service in 1967, enabling customers to call into an organization at a cost to the receiving company and not the individual caller. This service grew rapidly in popularity and usage, with seven million toll-free calls placed in the first full year of availability in 1968, and increasing to eight billion calls per year by 1988. With the cost burden removed, more and more customers became accustomed to doing business by telephone.

1970s – Increased long-distance competition. In 1971, the FCC allowed a non-AT&T company (MCI) to install a long-distance link between St. Louis and Chicago. MCI followed this link by installing lines in other heavy traffic routes both with microwave links and reselling AT&T facilities. MCI was soon followed by Sprint, SBS, and United Telecom in provision of alternative long-distance services.

1970s – Implementation of automatic call distribution(ACD). If a call center is defined by the distribution of calls to a group of individuals, then the first official call center came into being in 1973 when Continental Airlines installed technology from Rockwell Collins that would answer and distribute calls in a pre-planned manner. This first ACD installation was soon followed by others in the airline and reservation business with ACDs from Rockwell and Teknekron.

1980s – Divestiture of AT&T. In a suit filed in 1974 and settled in 1982 by Judge Harold Green, AT&T was forced to divest either its long-distance services or regional Bell Operating Companies. The regional Bell Operating Companies were divested, meaning AT&T could no longer provide local telephone service in addition to long-distance.

1980s – Increased ACD choices. Throughout the 1980s, other vendors joined Rockwell and Teknekron as ACD suppliers. Stand-alone ACD systems became available from Aspect and Telcom Technologies, and traditional telephone switch providers like AT&T (now Avaya), Northern Telecom (now Nortel), and Rolm (now Siemens) entered the ACD market with PBX add-on capabilities to supply ACD functionality. ACD services also became available on a "lease" basis from the local Bell operating companies.

1990s - 800 number portability. An FCC ruling in 1993 made 800 numbers "portable" so that companies could purchase any 800 number from any long-distance carrier and not from just the carrier that "owned" a certain set of numbers. This ruling had significant impact for call centers in initial selection as well as decisions to switch long-distance service providers. The 800 area code was quickly filled and additional area codes were added to handle the toll-free calling traffic.

1990s – Growth of call center technologies. Throughout the 1990s, many technologies were developed to enable the call center to perform more effectively. These technologies included call routing and distribution, automated dialers, interactive voice response, workforce management, quality monitoring, contact management, and a wealth of others.

These developments and milestones bring the call center into the 21st Century, which will be described in the following section.

Present Day Definitions

The present day call center can be defined in a number of ways. It can be defined by the type of contact handled (inbound versus outbound), the type of center (in-house versus outsourced), the primary functions performed (customer service versus sales), the geographic scope (single versus multi-site), and financial structure (revenue generating or not). The following outlines the most common definitions of call centers today using these five definitive categories:

Types of Contacts

The types of call center contacts can be categorized into these definitions:

Business to Business. The primary contacts for this call center are other business entities. For example, the call center may take calls from a business that wishes to order company insurance or benefits for its employees. Likewise the center may place outbound calls to sell printer or copier supplies to another business.

Business to Consumer. The primary contacts for this center are individuals. This type of center may take calls from individual customers placing a catalog order or making a hotel reservation, or provide support to someone using the company's product or service. On the outbound side, the center may place calls to individuals to raise funds or sell a specific product aimed at the individual consumer.

Internal. The primary contacts for this center are the company's own employees. The center may be an internal help desk for technical issues or may be a hot-line for employee benefit and compensation issues. All calls are internal communications.

Types of Call Centers

The types of call centers are generally divided into these four categories:

Inbound Call Center. This type of center responds to incoming calls and inquiries related to that organization's customers.

Outbound Call Center. This type of center's primary business is placing outbound calls to its customers or prospects.

Blended Call Center. This type of center takes both incoming calls and places outbound calls. The term "blended call center" also refers to the types of contacts being handled. A blended inbound center might handle contacts that include incoming telephone calls along with emails or web chats. Likewise, a blended outbound center might communicate through outbound calling as well as email or fax communications.

Outsourced Center. An outsourced call center is one that handles calls on behalf of another organization. Its primary business is initiating or receiving other companies' customer or prospect calls.

Primary Functions

The primary functions of a call center can generally be categorized into one of the following six categories:

Customer Service. The function of a customer service center is to provide assistance regarding a company's or organization's products or services. Examples include utility customer service, tracking assistance for overnight carrier, consumer hotline for food product company, and credit card service centers.

TeleSales. The function of a sales center is primarily to generate revenue through the sale of the company's goods and services through either inbound calls, outbound calls, or both. Examples include hotel reservations, catalog sales, direct television advertising orders, and newspaper classified advertising or subscription centers.

Technical Support. The function of these centers is to provide assistance in using a company's products. Examples may include computer hardware support, software help desk, or specialized support desk for use of medical technology products.

Dispatch. The function of a dispatch center is to take an inbound call and in turn engage a resource to address the problem or customer need. Examples may include taxi or transportation dispatch, package pickup and delivery, 911 emergency assistance, or vehicle roadside services.

Collections. The function of these centers is to contact customers with the primary purpose of collecting money or funds. Examples include credit card collection centers, mortgage collection, and specialized collection agencies.

Research. The function of a research center is not to sell or support a product, but to conduct research for the company or outside organizations. Examples include market research firms and political polling organizations.

Any of these roles could be performed for the company as a whole, as a service provided to another department internally (such as marketing or product management), or as a service sold to another company. Some call centers perform a mix of these functions and may serve a variety of these "customers" at the same time.

Geographic Scope

Another way to define a call center is by its geographic scope as outlined in the following definitions:

Internal. An in-house center is one that serves only internal customers such as an internal help desk or human resources central hotline.

Local. A local call center may only serve customers in a limited geographic area due to the scope of the business. For example, a local taxi or bus service will likely only take calls from the immediate area where its customer base resides and all calls may be local, not long-distance calls. Similarly, a furniture business with three local stores may take calls from a three-county area and receive both local and limited long-distance calls.

Regional. A regional call center may provide a product or service to customers beyond a local area, but limited by regional boundaries. For example, most local telephone companies provide service in a specific regional area and their customer service or sales centers may cover several states with local and long-distance calls coming into the call center.

National. These centers take calls from the entire country, with toll-free services making geography transparent. Examples include reservation centers, catalogs, and various product support centers.

International. These centers take calls that extend beyond national borders in scope.

Certainly, with the growth of the Internet, contacts can easily be made with customers all over the world and many of these email and web contacts are handled by the call center. With the growth of international outsourcing (often referred to as "off-shoring"), contacts between a company and its customers within a single country may well be routed to an international location for handling.

Another distinction that may be defined as geographical in nature is the number of call center sites that exist and the degree to which these centers are linked together. Call centers may operate as stand-alone, single-site entities. Others may be one of the company's multiple call centers. In a multi-site call center scenario, each call center may operate independently, or may be networked with other centers in providing services to customers.

Financial Structure

A final way to categorize a call center operation is to determine its financial structure. Call centers tend to fall into one of these categories:

Profit Center. Call centers that generate revenue, such as a catalog center, reservations center, or telesales center are generally viewed and defined as profit centers. The revenues may accrue to other departments (such as the branches in banks), or they may be accrued in the call center's budget. The revenues they generate more than pay for the overall cost of the operation.

Cost Center. Call centers that generate no direct revenue of their own are often viewed as "cost centers." While this is a common categorization approach, it is not one that truly reflects the value of the call center operation. Even though a call center may not generate direct revenue, most have a significant impact on the business that far outweighs their cost. These benefits include contribution to customer retention, market research and feedback, and numerous other benefits that will be outlined later in this section.

Current Demographics

Scope of Business

Given the far-reaching definition of what makes up a call center, it is difficult to ascertain precisely how many call centers truly exist. Since a two-person office that shares phone responsibilities could meet the broad definition of a call center, there could be literally hundreds of thousands of these type operations.

However, since being a call center typically implies having technology to answer and distribute calls, the number of "official" call centers is therefore lower. In turning to general business research firms such as DataMonitor, Frost & Sullivan, International Data Corporation (IDC), and others, an estimate of the number of call centers in existence is generally based on the proliferation of call distribution technology and network services. Using these sales as the basis for extrapolation, the following numbers are "best estimates" of the size and scope of the call center industry.

There were approximately 70,000 sites using call center related technologies in the

United States in 1998, growing to 75,000 call centers in 2000. At current growth rates, it is estimated that there will be 78,000 call centers by end of 2003 and over 80,000 by end of 2005.

The United States is home to more call centers than any other country, but the call center market is growing rapidly in other parts of the world as well. According to a recent study from DataMonitor, it is estimated that Canada had 7,500 call centers in 2000 with estimates of 9,000 centers to be in place by end of 2003. There were approximately 13,000 call centers in Europe in 2000 with expectations of 25,000 by the end of 2005. Australia had almost 4,000 call centers in 2002 and Latin American countries had 1,500 call centers, with substantial growth expected in both areas from 2003–2005. The Asia-Pacific region is the newest region to experience call center growth, with over 4,500 call centers in place at the end of 2002.

Labor Force

With such a large number of call centers in place, the call center profession is obviously one that employs large numbers of employees. Indeed, based on studies from The Call Center School using U.S. Bureau of Labor Statistics, it is estimated that approximately four million frontline agent positions are active today.

Approximately 2.6 million of these positions are filled by full-time staff and the remaining 1.4 million positions are shared by part-time staff (about 2.4 million persons). These five million persons employed by call centers by the end of 2003 represent approximately 1.8% of the total United States population and about 3.5% of the working population.

Economic Impact

The call center industry plays an important role in today's economy, not just by employing so many workers, but by enabling trade and commerce. According to studies by the Gartner Group published in the Harvard Business Review, more than 70% of business transactions take place over the telephone and 80% of these transactions occur in a call center setting.

Roles in the Enterprise

The call center can play many roles within the organization. The call center may be the primary focus of the business in many organizations, such as in a catalog operation. In others, the center may play a smaller role in the operation, but be nonetheless critical to the success of the business.

Some of these roles are outlined below.

Customer Service

Perhaps the most significant role the call center plays is providing service to customers so they remain customers of the organization. Research studies show that it costs seven times more to acquire a new customer than to retain an existing one. Providing satisfactory service to customers and addressing all needs, concerns, and problems via the call center plays a significant role in customer loyalty and retention.

Revenue Generation

The call center can serve as a sales channel exclusively (as in a telemarketing or reservations environment), or can serve to support a more traditional sales process. The call center can serve as a central point for maintaining contact and sales information, enabling the company to turn more inquiries into leads, and more leads to sales.

Cost Reduction

It is not easy to quantify the cost of doing business without a call center. But the role that the call center plays in centralizing calls into one place can reduce overall staffing costs compared to calls being handled by disparate groups of employees. There may also be opportunities to reduce long-distance costs as calls are funneled into one place to take advantage of economies of scale of telephone operations. In many cases a centralized call center may replace several "storefronts" to handle customer service or complaints for an organization, thereby reducing both real estate and staffing costs.

Market Research

The call center likely plays a bigger role in customer interaction than any other part of the business. Nowhere else is there more opportunity to hear the voice of the customer. The call center can gather data on customer demographics, product usage, buying trends, most wanted features and services, etc. This information can enable the company to provide more targeted marketing and focus product development in areas most likely to provide the biggest return on investment.

Customer Surveys

The call center can be an effective vehicle for conducting customer satisfaction surveys. While many companies use paper-based or electronic-based mail surveys to query their customers on a variety of topics, the return rate on these surveys is generally low. There is a greater opportunity via the call center to gather more recent and pertinent information about the customer experience, with a higher percentage of customers participating and more valid information available from a "real time" experience.

Branding Support

The call center can and should be a vehicle for an organization to further establish and solidify brand image. For example, if an organization is known for its efficiency and speed of service, the call center can demonstrate these characteristics in its service standards and operations. Another may be known less for speed and more for going the extra mile in customer service, while a third call center may be focused on delivering the utmost in quality and experience. Other companies may use their call centers to demonstrate their superiority in technology and innovation, while others use them as an extension of their fun or entertaining image.

Quality Control

With its direct communications link with customers, the call center can serve as a feedback mechanism to manufacturing or product development. Segmenting call types and noting reasons for calls can assist in targeting product quality or production problems. This same sorting of calls can help provide feedback on user interface issues such as product usability, documentation, or distribution channels.

Public Relations

The call center can serve as a front-line communications vehicle for customers, employees, and media when there is a significant news release or company news event. Many organizations rely on the call center to serve as the "company's voice" for questions and concerns on a daily basis as well as during periods of change.

The role(s) that a call center plays within an organization will be closely linked with the center's mission and goals. The "best-of-class" call centers all have a mission statement that explains the center's purpose and most of these describe the value the center provides to the organization as a whole. This mission statement is important in defining what the call center's purpose and goals will be and should be communicated clearly to everyone in the call center.

Summary

A call center is defined as a place where calls and contacts are made and received. There are many different types, sizes, and functions of call centers handling many different types of contacts. There are nearly 80,000 call centers in operation today in the United States alone, employing nearly five million people. These call centers serve many roles within an organization, serve as an extension of a company's brand, and play a significant role in a company's success. Because of its increased role in the success of an organization, the call center is gaining much visibility, making call center management a legitimate and desirable career for the 21st Century.

CHAPTER 2: STRATEGIC PLANNING

Introduction

A strategic plan is an important document in the establishment and operation of an effective call center. It defines the role and mission of the center within the enterprise and sets the stage for all the decisions that will need to be made concerning personnel, technology, processes, services, and so on. The plan links the call center to the company as a whole and to the clients it serves both internally and externally. It sets the stage for several years into the future as well as outlining short-term requirements for the next budget cycle. The process can be challenging the first time, but it is well worth the effort. The good news is that after the first plan has been completed and approved, annual updates will be relatively easy.

Preparing a strategic plan is often thought of as the role of the senior management team and the board of directors. After all, this is where the company's mission statement and overall approach to the market are defined. But every department within a company should have a strategic plan and the call center is no exception. Each departmental plan should link to the overall corporate plan, of course, but each department has its own role to play and can do it better if the directions are clear.

A strategic plan is comprised of seven specific segments starting with the broadest and leading to the most specific plans for the coming budget cycle. The seven segments are:

1. Mission & Vision Statement
2. Internal Environment Analysis
3. External Environment Analysis
4. Assumptions
5. Objectives
6. Strategies
7. Tactics and Goals

Assuming that there is a readily accessible and current strategic plan for the overall enterprise, this is the appropriate starting point for the call center director or manager to begin planning. The role and mission of the company dictates the role and mission of the call center to a large extent. However, many organizations do not have a well-documented plan for the company, and others may have no plan at all. That does not relieve the call center leader of the responsibility of developing a departmental plan, but it does mean that the starting point will require some research and gathering of consensus regarding the role and mission of the center.

Call center management should research the competitive situation of the company and determine what position senior management is taking to meet it. A recent annual report should be carefully reviewed along with other documents prepared for stockholders to get a clear overview of overall business objectives. Call center management should interview senior management to identify long-range views, plans for major organizational or infrastructure changes, and any corporate restructuring such as expansion or consolidation of operations. This information can serve as the basis of the call center plan, but it will need to be validated or adjusted at some point after senior management goes through the review process.

The call center plan must link to the enterprise plan. For example, if the enterprise plan is to "maintain position as the low cost provider of services in this product sector," then the call center plan might include a plan to "maximize the technologies and offerings for self-service options to minimize the cost of support." But if the enterprise plan is to "provide unique and valuable products and service that meet the specific needs of each client," then self-service options in the call center may not be a good choice. Instead, the call center plan may "identify unique product requirements through customer interactions and record them for use in product development and customization efforts." In an enterprise that has positioned itself in the marketplace to "provide superior service that maximizes customer delight," the call center plan might "implement customer contact strategy that maximizes accessibility and quality of customer interactions." The whole focus of the call center is quite different depending on the company's overall strategy and position in the market.

Mission and Vision Statement

The mission statement defines the purpose of the organization. Why does the call center exist? How will the call center conduct itself in its relationship with its stakeholders (typically customers, employees, and management/shareholders)? What products will be offered and what customer needs will be met? It might define which disciplines are included and how the department interfaces with customers, suppliers, and other departments in the company. It should state clearly (generally in one paragraph) why the call center exists and what the enterprise seeks to gain by its existence. It is advisable to keep this statement fairly broad in order not to artificially limit the scope of the call center's future.

The vision statement creates an image of the end result that the call center is focused on achieving. What will the long-term goals produce? What will the call center be in the future? Values or ethics statements may also be included in this statement.

Defining the call center's role in the enterprise is a challenge, but it is essential to moving from a cost item to a valued organizational asset. Call center organizations that develop and then live by a values and vision statement distinguish themselves by their professionalism, high expectations, and constant questioning. And their managers are able to make effective cases for budget dollars.

Part of the process of defining the mission and vision statements is to define a customer contact strategy. Will the center offer access 24 hours a day, 7 days per week or some shorter hours of operation? Will the emphasis be on having a live person available to handle calls or directing customers into a self-service option? Perhaps the focus will be different for different kinds of customers depending upon their value to the organization.

How the call center will be positioned in the gathering, storage, analysis, and use of customer data is often defined in the mission statement. Will the call center be responsible for gathering demographic data on customers to support market segmentation processes? Perhaps the call center will gather customer reactions to products/services to support product development efforts.

The personnel strategy that the center will employ may be defined in the mission statement, too. Statements about personnel development to foster growth within the company and treating staff with respect and dignity often find their way into mission statements. But companies who wish to outsource wherever feasible and minimize staffing costs may position themselves differently than those that are looking for the best long-term, full-time personnel to staff the center.

Another strategy that may be included here is one addressing technology. One company may be quite conservative and only employ proven technologies that demonstrate a clear return on investment. Another may be more innovative and encourage the call center to experiment with leading-edge technologies to maintain a leadership position against competitors.

Below are two examples of mission statements that take quite different approaches to align with the enterprise position:

The ABC call center provides customers access to support and information on demand, with speed and accuracy that ensures customer and associate delight. The center gathers data for marketing research and product development that supports the company's efforts to become the vendor of choice in the marketplace, using proven technologies as appropriate.

The XYZ technical support center responds to customer requests for technical assistance on software products balancing the need for speed, accuracy, and cost-effectiveness. Availability and fees are designed to encourage customers to use self-service options but also maximize customer retention. The call center identifies new technologies to be integrated into the delivery process to maximize service and minimize customers' need for assistance.

Internal Environment

The next part of the plan is intended to define the current situation, including strengths and weaknesses. Analysis of such things as workload volume, service result metrics, sales results, quality control measures, agent satisfaction, data supplied to other departments, and overall customer satisfaction measures should be included. Confine the internal sections to those things that are contained within the call center and its relationships with other parts of the organization.

Staff turnover should be analyzed, along with the reasons that departing employees give for leaving, and hiring strategies reviewed to determine how well they are filling the needed positions. Review employee development and promotional plans to determine if the call center is a "dead end" or a springboard to other opportunities in the company. If coordination with other departments is a key role, explore how well it is being done today and if this is an area that needs improvement. Where major enterprise-wide technology rollouts are planned, explore the timing of the impact on the center, impacts on training and system downtimes, and any other issues that might impact the center or customers. Check the contingency and disaster recovery plan and determine the state of readiness for such situations.

Some examples of internal environment analysis findings include:

- *The 3-year trend of cost per transaction has been increasing at 4% annually.*

- *The call center operates in three cities with each site supporting a specific group of states on a 24 x 7 basis.*

- *Turnover of staff has averaged 57% per year for the last three years.*

- *The company web site does not include the option to access an agent via web chat or call back.*

- *Product development feedback from customer calls has resulted in four new enhancements in the last two years.*

The most common complaint heard from call center professionals about interdepartmental coordination is that the marketing department does not keep them informed about upcoming plans that will affect the call center's workload. This is not a failure of the marketing department so much as it is a failure of call center management in recognizing that the marketing department is a client and one that needs to be involved in the planning processes. It does the company little good to spend massive dollars on a marketing campaign to increase customer inquiries, only to have those inquiries turned away at the call center because the two departments did not talk to one another.

Such communications issues may be addressed by positioning the call center strategically as a provider of services to marketing. This means having a service level agreement in place with a forecast of workload and agreements about services to be provided and fees to be charged. Formalizing the relationship can go a long way to building a process that works for both departments.

External Environment

This section of the strategic plan explores the opportunities and threats that develop outside of the company. These include the competitive market, regulatory issues, competition for agents in the area, overall impact of the economy on the company and call center, supplier stability and pricing plans, and so on. If new regulations or laws are likely to have an impact on operations, analyze the impact and the likelihood of the regulations' adoption and timing. Look for ways the center can impact the competitive position of the company, through better service or more sales. Analyze the suppliers used by the call center to identify any that might need to be replaced, and others who have offerings that may not have been thoroughly exploited.

Examples of external environment analysis results include:

- *Competitors are weak in the Northeast region, making this area a good target for added outbound sales effort.*

- *A major competitor has recently offered a real-time web chat capability on the web site and reports increased sales as a result.*

- *Recent Do Not Call legislation will limit the company's ability to use this method to reach new prospects.*

- *The number of local call centers has raised the labor saturation level to a point where competition for staff is intense, driving up both salary costs and turnover rates.*

Combined with the Internal Environment Analysis, this part of the plan is often called the SWOT Analysis (Strengths, Weaknesses, Opportunities, and Threats).

Strategic Assumptions

It is important to clearly state any assumptions used in the plan and any that have resulted from the internal and external analysis. These assumptions will set the basis for future plans and might include such things as growth rate of workload, regulations anticipated in the future, and demands that will be made on the center by upcoming company-wide initiatives such as CRM. It is important to tie these assumptions back to the environmental analysis where ever possible.

Some examples of assumptions include:

- *Upgrades to agent desktop hardware to support the CRM rollout will be $xxx in the next year's budget.*

- *Expenses for toll-free network services will remain steady for the next three years.*

- *No more than 15% of current agents have the skills to handle web chats.*

Once the plan is completed through the assumptions, it is a good idea to review it with someone at the executive level for a "reality check." If there are any errors or major omissions in the SWOT analysis, or if an assumption is suspect, adjustments should be made at this point, since all subsequent steps in the process depend upon these statements being accepted as truth. Senior managers are not always willing to share major upcoming initiatives with the rest of the team too early, but if it is clear that the call center plan is basing its direction on a false premise, generally enough information will be shared to ensure that the plan is valid even if the full details are not ready for disclosure. For example, if a major site is being shut down and consolidated into other operations, or expansion to a new market is pending, it could have a significant impact on the call center plans. Once the plan thus far is generally approved as solid, the process can move to the more specific plans.

Objectives

The objectives are the department's goals over the next two to five years, so they are generally broad and long range. They must express the ends that are sought rather than the means by which they will be achieved. The connection between the objectives and the issues defined in the internal and external analysis must be clearly stated. If a high agent turnover rate is identified as a weakness, the objective might be to reduce turnover by some percentage each year, or to achieve the industry average. If the opportunity identified is that competitors have a reputation for inattentive service, the objective might be to improve service levels and customer satisfaction scores as a competitive advantage.

Some examples of objectives include:

- *Maintain less than 2% annual increase in cost per transaction.*
- *Increase quality of customer information gathered in the call center to support marketing initiatives.*
- *Increase customer self-service utilization by 5% per year.*
- *Reduce agent turnover to no more than 30% annually within three years.*

Strategies

Strategies indicate the ways in which the objectives will be met. For example, a strategy might call for standardizing the management of the several call centers in the organization if internal analysis reveals fragmented management and widely varying processes are yielding adverse results. A strategy might also focus on consolidation of centers or creating a virtual network to address the same situation. In some cases, the strategy will be in its formative stages and the first steps will need to include a feasibility study or ROI analysis. In other cases, the strategy will be quite clear and the steps to achieve it can be just as obvious.

The important distinction here is that these strategies are not ends in themselves, but the means to the ends identified in the objectives. Plans for new technology deployment, process realignment, and/or outsourcing plans could be included as strategies without naming specific vendors and products. Organizational realignment or shifting of workload could be either general or very specific strategies as well.

Examples of strategies include:

- *Create a multi-site network connection among the three existing call centers to create a virtual network to achieve economies of scale and reduce labor cost.*
- *Create a marketing department liaison position in the call center to develop and manage demographic data gathering processes and balance marketing needs with call center operational efficiency requirements.*
- *Train all agents on cross-selling opportunities to increase revenues.*

Tactics and Goals

This part of the strategic plan includes the actual measurable activities for the next 12 to 18 months. These particular projects are the ones that will need to be funded in the next budget cycle. Each tactical step should include a specific time period by which it is forecast to be completed, and should be very specific, achievable, and give management some idea of the time and resources that will be necessary to make it happen. Include every project that is reasonable since it may be difficult to explain requests to spend resources on projects not included in the plan, but be careful not to over commit since achievement of the results could affect credibility and career opportunities.

Examples of tactics and goals include:

- *Conduct a feasibility study on virtual network operations by June 2006, including estimate of cost to implement and projected benefits.*
- *Establish the marketing liaison position and select a call center staff member for the position by March 2006.*
- *Develop an agent incentive program by March 2006.*

Once the plan is completed, the flow of thought from mission statement to specific projects and tactics should be obvious. Each goal links to a strategy to achieve a specific objective. Each objective is based on the assumptions drawn from the internal and external analysis, and works to achieve the role and mission of the call center and the organization. Generally, each project is related to others and each is necessary in some way to the ones that follow it. Sometimes a graphic can make it easier to communicate the linkages between the goals and the timetables, and it is important to make the plan as free of terminology and jargon as possible so that people unfamiliar with call center operations will understand it easily.

It is also important to remember that the plan must be fluid and flexible. It should be updated on a regular basis, at least annually before the budget process, to define the goals to be funded for the next year. Circumstances change, technology evolves, competitors come and go, and the economy shifts. The plan must reflect these changes.

Summary

Preparing and presenting a strategic plan to senior management can be intimidating, especially if this is a new way of viewing the call center and its functions. But one of the major gains for the call center in the process is that the true contribution of the call center will be better understood by not only senior management, but also by the people who work in the center.

If the mission statement, internal and external analyses, and the assumptions have all been reviewed and approved by a member of senior management prior to the completion of the rest of the plan, there should be little discussion over these sections in the actual presentation. However, if there is some disagreement among the members of the management team, (generally a good reason why there is no documented enterprise plan), then this process can foster much discussion. This discussion should not be viewed as negative, even if it delays the approval of the remainder of the process while the executives try to reach consensus on direction. The company will be in a better position for having faced the issues and the call center will be remembered for its pivotal role in the process.

It is a rare case when senior management reviews a departmental plan and totally agrees with everything that call center management has planned. The suggested timing of some initiatives may conflict with other priorities, the plan may not be aggressive enough, or some other situation may have developed. These types of alterations are to be expected. This kind of planning is often an iterative process, but the dialog that accompanies it is well worth the time and energy.

In call centers where a strategic plan has been documented and approved independently of the budgeting process, approval of projects at budget time will be easier. Senior management does not need to judge each project solely on its own individual merits against competing requests for scarce resources. They can see how each project fits in the overall scheme and the effect it would have on the plan not to fund it. The call center does not spend valuable resources doing business plans for projects with little potential for approval. And the position of the call center in the organization is clear and interdepartmental challenges will be minimized.

CHAPTER 3: FINANCIAL MANAGEMENT

Introduction

Finance is the art and science of managing money. All call center managers need to understand basic financial concepts and be able to read and interpret financial information. For the call center manager, managing money means knowing how to develop a budget for the department, and spending money in the call center budget according to the plan. Obtaining money for capital projects requires knowledge of the company's processes and the standard calculations of net present value, payback period, and return on investment. When managers are knowledgeable about financial management, they can negotiate for their department's budget in terms that senior management will relate to and accept. If managers do not have firsthand knowledge of the purpose, underlying assumptions, and interpretation of the budgeting process, they will be at a disadvantage within the company and promotional opportunities will be limited.

This chapter is focused on the numbers associated with money flowing into and out of the call center. It is important for call center managers to understand the implications of spending their budget dollars in one category versus another. Focusing on both the planned and actual numbers is essential to maintain control of the center's financial health. This includes the ongoing daily costs and revenue as well as the special funding involved with acquiring a new technology or service.

In addition to the annual operating budget (planned income and expenses for the year), most call centers acquire new technology and fund new initiatives with capital dollars. Developing an effective business case and receiving approval for the use of these funds can spell the difference between an up-to-date center and one mired in old technologies and practices. However, capital budgeting (allocation of planned money for acquisitions outside of the operating budget) for projects is frequently applied poorly.

This chapter will provide an overview of financial reports and how to interpret them, along with the process for developing and managing an annual budget, and how to apply a step-by-step process of financial decision-making.

Overview of Financial Reports

There are standards and rules that have been established in the accounting profession that are called generally accepted accounting principles (GAAP). The term "generally accepted" means that these principles have "substantial authoritative support" from the two standard-setting bodies, the Financial Accounting Standards Board (FASB) and the Securities and Exchange Commission (SEC). International standards fall under the International Accounting Standards Committee (IASC).

There are four major types of financial statements that can be utilized to evaluate financial performance. The accountant prepares the four statements in the following order because numbers calculated in each are transferred to the following ones:

- Income statement
- Retained earnings statement
- Balance sheet
- Cash flow statement

Income Statement

The first financial statement to consider is an income statement. The income statement is sometimes known as the profit and loss statement and shows the revenues and expenses and resulting profit or loss generated in a given time period. The formula for the income statement is 'Revenue minus Expenses = Profit or Loss.' The income statement reports the company's or department's profit or loss over a period of time.

An income statement typically includes the following items:

- Sales revenue
- Cost of goods sold
- Operating expenses
- Other revenues and gains (from non-operating transactions)
- Other expenses and losses (from non-operating transactions)
- Income tax expenses
- Earnings per share (net income earned by each share of common stock)

A sample income statement is provided below:

Revenue		$15,000,000
Expenses		
Salaries expense	$8,000,000	
Rent expense	$200,000	
Advertising expense	$125,000	
Utilities Expense	$52,500	
Total Expenses		$8,377,500
Net Income		$6,622,500

Retained Earnings Statement

The second type of financial statement is a retained earnings statement. It summarizes the changes in retained earnings for a specific period of time. The net income from the company's income statement for a period is added to the beginning balance on the retained earnings statement. When there is a net loss, the loss is deducted from the prior balance of retained earnings. If dividends are paid out to stockholders, these are deducted leaving the net earnings retained in the business. A sample retained earnings statement is shown below.

Retained earnings, Sept. 1, 20xx	$3,450,000
Add: Net Income	$6,622,500
Total	$10,072,500
Less Dividends Paid	$1,200,000
Retained earnings, Sept. 30, 20xx	$8,872,500

Balance Sheet

The third type of financial statement is a balance sheet. The balance sheet describes the financial condition of a company at a particular time. It does so by listing all of the company's assets, liabilities, and owner's equity. Cash, property, and inventory are examples of assets and these are listed first on the statement. Liabilities are financial obligations such as debts, claims, or expected losses. Equity is the difference between total assets and total liabilities and represents the value to the stockholders. The total assets must equal the total liabilities and stockholders' equity. The balance sheet will tell what the company owns (assets), what the company owes (liabilities), and what the company is worth to its owners (equity).

A balance sheet typically breaks down the data into subgroups and this is referred to as a classified balance sheet. Typical subgroups are standard and these include:

- Assets
    - o Current Assets
    - o Long-term Investments
    - o Property, Plant, and Equipment
    - o Intangible Assets
- Liabilities and Stockholders' Equity
    - o Current Liabilities
    - o Long-term Liabilities
    - o Stockholders' Equity

These sections help the financial statement user to determine such things as the availability of assets to meet debts as they come due and the claims of short- and long-term creditors on the total assets.

Assets		
Cash		$10,385,000
Accounts Receivable		$875,000
Supplies		$1,850,000
Equipment		$3,240,000
Total Assets		$16,350,000
Liabilities & Stockholder s Equity		
Liabilities		
Accounts payable		$565,000
Stockholders Equity		
Common Stock	$6,912,500	
Retained Earnings	$8,872,500	$15,785,000
Total liabilities and stockholders equity		$16,350,000

Cash Flow Statement

The fourth type of financial statement is a cash flow statement. Cash flow is the cash that a company generates and uses over a period of time. A cash flow statement summarizes all cash movements into and out of a company over a given time period. The statement of cash flows reports the cash effects of a company's operations during the period, its investing transactions, its financing transactions, the net increase or decrease in cash during the period, and the cash amount at the end of the period. Significant financing and investing activities that do not affect cash are not reported in the body of the statement of cash flows. However, they are typically reported in a separate schedule at the bottom of the cash flow statement or in a supplementary schedule to the financial statements.

The cash flow statement typically includes the following subcategories of elements:

- Operating activities
- Investing activities
- Financing activities

A sample cash flow statement is shown below:

Cash flows from operating activities		
Cash receipts from revenues	$13,450,000	
Cash payments for expenses	($8,377,500)	
Net cash provided from operating activities		$5,072,500
Cash flows from investing activities		
Purchase of equipment		($2,125,000)
Cash flows from financing activities		
Sale of common stock	$3,250,000	
Payment of cash dividend	($1,200,000)	$2,050,000
Net Increase in cash		$4,997,500
Cash at beginning of period		$5,387,500
Cash at end of period		**$10,385,000**

Business managers need to be familiar with all these types of financial statements, and since the call center can be viewed as a business within a business, call center leaders should be comfortable with creating and interpreting these reports to evaluate the performance of their department and that of the company. Financial results will help the call center manager to understand how the center's performance affects the overall performance of the company. In some cases, it may be necessary to adjust department objectives once the financial results have been reviewed.

There are a number of useful ratios that can be used in the analysis of financial statement. These include:

- Price-earnings ratio – The ratio of the market price per share to the earnings per share. This ratio reflects an investor's assessment of a company's future earnings potential.

- Current ratio – The current assets divided by current liabilities is used to determine the company's ability to pay its maturing obligations and meet unexpected needs for cash. When expressed as a ratio, it is current ratio, but when expressed as a dollar amount, it is called working capital. This is calculated by subtracting current liabilities from current assets.

- Acid-test ratio – This is a measure of immediate short-term liquidity and it is calculated by dividing the sum of cash, temporary investments, and net receivables by current liabilities.

- Profit margin ratio – also called rate of return on sales. It measures the percentage of each dollar of sales that results in net income. Divide net income by net sales for the period to calculate this ratio.

- Receivables turnover ratio – This measures the liquidity of receivables and is calculated by dividing net credit sales (net sales less cash sales) by the average net receivables.

- Inventory turnover ratio – This measures the number of times on average the inventory is sold during the period. It is computed by dividing cost of goods sold by average inventory.

- Return on assets – The return on assets is calculated by dividing net income by total assets. This is a good overall measure of profitability. If the rate of return on assets is low, the company many not be using its assets effectively.

- Return on common stockholders' equity – This is the rate that shows how many dollars of net income were earned for each dollar of owner investment. Divide net income by common stockholders' equity to calculate this rate.

- Debt to total assets ratio – This measures the solvency of the company and the ability of the company to survive over a long period of time. Divide total debt by total assets to calculate this ratio.

Operating Budgets

The purpose of preparing a budget is for a company or department to set its financial goals and objectives for the year ahead. Some companies use a bottom-up approach to create a budget. Using this method, managers prepare the budgets for their departments and then pass them up to senior management for review, discussion, possible modification, and approval. A bottom-up approach motivates managers to participate in the budgeting process and encourages them to set targets and be innovative. It also enables managers to recognize and prioritize the call center's needs more effectively. It is more complex for senior management who must consolidate multiple departmental budgets into an overall company budget, sorting out the priorities and conflicts to keep the total within the necessary boundaries.

Other companies prefer to use a top-down approach. With this method, senior management sets the targets and the overall budget figures for each department, including the call center. This approach is simple, consistent, quick, and decisive, but leaves little room for the call center manager to lobby for special circumstances and additional funding and may over-fund another department.

Budgeting Approaches

There are five commonly used methods for creating a budget. Each method is based on either the top-down or bottom-up approach, or a combination of both.

Zero-based budgeting. This method uses a bottom-up approach, which involves maximum involvement and commitment from the call center manager. With zero-based budgeting, call center management ignores the figures of previous years and creates a budget based on expectations for the coming year instead. This requires justification of every budget line item rather than just carrying forward old numbers with an appropriate adjustment factor. The idea is to eliminate budgetary items that no longer make sense and focus the priorities on the things that matter today.

Fixed budgeting. This method is the least commonly used budgeting method. It uses a top-down approach, and is designed to remain unchanged for the year regardless of the level of activity in the company.

Incremental budgeting. With this method, the budget is based on the previous year's figures and inflated or decreased by a certain percentage for inflation/contraction. This method is based on a top-down approach and is relatively simple and inexpensive to implement. However, it does not accommodate shifts in priorities or significant changes in operations.

Rolling budgeting. For a rolling budget, managers break down the annual budget into quarterly periods. At the end of the first month of each quarter, managers review the actual situation. If necessary, costs for the next quarter are adjusted to enable the manager to stay within the budget set for the year. With this approach, senior managers can often divert resources from one department to another without the typical problems of ownership found with other budgeting methods. This method uses a blend of both the bottom-up and top-down approaches.

Flexible budgeting. This method is the most commonly used. A flexible budget is designed to adjust the permitted cost levels to suit the level of activity attained by analyzing costs into fixed and variable elements. As a result, managers can revise the variable portions of their annual budget figures in light of the actual level of activity they achieve. This method of budgeting uses a blend of both the bottom-up and top-down approaches. However, it requires vigilant attention to the details on a month-to-month basis.

Regardless of the method used, budgeting helps the company to plan ahead and monitor performance on an ongoing basis. It ensures sound financial planning for the company's activities. During the budgeting process, the budget for the call center is typically reviewed along with those of other departments before integrating into a total plan to achieve the company's targets. A formalized call center budget helps the manager to identify targets, estimate resource needs, manage resources, and make decisions affecting daily operations.

In developing an operating budget, the operating expenses need to be divided into subcategories. Each expense or cost in the operating budget can be considered a fixed or variable cost. Fixed costs do not change in total regardless of the volume or level of activity. Call center facilities charges are fixed costs because they generally remain the same month to month. Variable costs vary in total with changes in volume or level of activity. Examples of variable costs would be monthly labor costs or telephone usage charges that will vary depending upon call volume. Services obtained from outside organizations could fall into either fixed or variable categories, and materials such as office supplies may change some, but not in direct proportion to the volume of activity.

In creating an annual operating budget, each total fixed cost or expense can be divided by 12 to create monthly budgets. Most call centers have peaks and valleys for variable expenses so a true 12-month division of the expenses may not be possible for these items. Business growth may also need to be accommodated within the annual budget along with forecast changes in the economic conditions that could affect inflation or other costs.

The table below shows the starting point for a typical operating expense budget for the call center.

Operating Expense	J	F	M	A	M	J	J	A	S	O	N	D	YTD
Headcount *													
FT Wages													
FT Merit													
FT Bonus													
PT Wages													
TP Wages													
Overtime													
Facility Expense													
Utilities													
Security													
Rent													
IT/Telecom													
Telephone													
Computers													
Maintenance													
Training													
Instructor													
Travel													
Classroom													
Materials													
Advertising													
Office Supplies													
Shipping/Postage													
Recruiting/Hiring													
Consulting													
Taxes/Insurance													
Depreciation													
Miscellaneous													
Total Operating Expense													

* FT = Full-time employee, PT= Part-time employee, TP = Temporary or contract employee

Controlling the Budget

As a means of keeping the budget on track, call center managers should check their actual figures against the target figures in the budget plan at least monthly. This means that they will be able to identify problems such as overspending before the effects are irreversible. If a huge surge in call volume has occurred or a vendor has unexpectedly increased its charges, the impact will become apparent quickly so that an appropriate adjustment can be made. Routine tracking can help the call center manager to monitor finances and take the necessary corrective actions to stay within the annual budget or to request more funds based on an unexpected increase in business.

At the end of each month, call center management should look at the actual expenses compared to what was in the budget. Then, the variance, or difference, should be calculated. The variance can be calculated as a dollar or percent variance. The dollar variance is found by subtracting the original budget figure from the actual expenditures. These figures can be misleading because what appears to be a large amount over or under budget can actually be a small percentage. That's why it is important to calculate the percentage variances as well. To calculate the percentage variance for each item, the dollar variance is divided by the original budget figure for the month.

If established targets are not met, it is critical to discover the reasons and be able to account for them. An important point to remember is that there may be nothing wrong with unfavorable budget variances, provided call center management can justify them to senior management. If the variances cannot be justified, then corrective action needs to be taken.

Budget Adjustments

Should there be a need to request additional funding for the budget, the call center manager should be prepared to answer the following questions:

• Why is additional funding required?

• Were expenses higher than planned?

• How will the additional funding be used?

• How will this increase benefit the call center and the company as a whole?

To achieve credibility and results when it comes to requesting additional funding, the responses to these questions should be specific, quantitative answers, and should be expressed in financial terms. This means developing and providing data to convince senior management that the benefits of the proposed request outweigh the risks.

Operating Budget Components

While each call center will have some unique requirements based on the industry or type of business, the following four components will be found in nearly every call center's list of budgetary items:

• Personnel

• Services

• Supplies

• Facility

Each of these must be considered in detail as the budget is developed.

Personnel

Staffing costs must include the frontline agents, as well as supervisors, managers, and support staff to reflect the total staff picture. Some will be full-time employees and others part-time. Contractors and personnel supplied by staffing agencies as temporaries must also be accounted for in the plan. Both salaries and benefits are typically included in the call center's budget even though the benefits may be actually contracted for and paid for out of the human resources department.

The budget must include the cost to recruit, hire, and train the new staff planned during the year, including the cost to replace those lost due to turnover. Raises in salaries, bonuses, and incentives are also part of the personnel costs.

Services

A wide range of possible costs can be found under services, including the cost of consultants, trainers, or other outside labor that is charged to the center but not directly related to the handling of the workload. Sometimes the IT and telecommunications costs are allocated internally and the call center's portion of these costs will show up in the call center's budget.

Supplies

This is the section in which paper, pencils, printer toner, and other consumables will be noted. Capital expenditures for things like chairs and furniture would generally not be included as these are not consumable. The center may send out brochures or other items and these might be included in this budget area as well.

Facility

This part of the budget may include a single number that is allocated by the facilities department to cover all costs. However, it may also have the details of power, space rental, security and other facilities-related charges.

Capital Budgeting

Capital budgeting involves the process of generating, evaluating, and selecting projects for long-term financial gain. Some of these projects may require new purchases while others are related to replacement decisions. Call center equipment may need to be replaced to keep up with evolving market and customer demands. There are several types of capital budgeting decisions that a company might consider. They include cost reduction projects, replacement of assets, and obtaining new facilities (or expanding existing ones).

Capital budgeting needs to conform to the company's cash position, financing strategy, and projected growth rate. Projects should be selected based on the company's long-range planning and should take into consideration corporate strengths and weaknesses. Consideration should also be given to the time, cost, and the cost-justification of the project.

After a project has been approved and completed, the project managers should calculate the actual results. The purpose of the post-project assessment is to evaluate the original calculations in the business case assessment. Were the original calculations and assumptions correct? What factors were identified during the course of implementing the project that impacted the original calculations? During the implementation of the project, these calculations can also be used as a means of promoting the financial benefits to the organization, customers, and partners.

Main Components

Capital budgets are used to cover the cost of items that are not part of the operating budget. The items may be purchased, leased, or even rented, but the costs are incremental to those planned for ongoing expenses. Capital budgets may also include an element of revenue and/or cost savings to justify the expenditure.

In the call center, the most frequently considered items for the capital budget are technology and equipment purchases. For example, the center may be expanding and need more cubicles, furnishings, computers, and telephones. Or the center may believe that implementing an IVR technology is needed to provide customers with a 24 x 7 self-service option and to reduce staffing costs to handle calls. These acquisitions would be handled under the capital budget process.

Financial Decision Making

Types of Models

Cost justification, or the calculation of savings/benefits, can be accomplished several ways. There are several commonly used strategies to determine if a project will yield an adequate return. While other methods such as internal rate of return (IRR) and return on assets (ROA) calculations are sometimes used, the three most common methods are:

- Net Present Value (NPV)
- Payback Period
- Return On Investment (ROI)

Net Present Value (NPV)

The calculation of the discounted projected cash flows of an investment derives the Net Present Value (NPV). Present value is a concept that is intuitively appealing, simple to compute, and has a wide range of applications. It allows comparison and aggregation of cash flows that occur at different points in time. Cash flows can be either positive or negative in any given period. Cash flow in the future is generally worth less than a similar cash flow today because people generally prefer present consumption to future consumption, inflation decreases the value of currency over time, and any uncertainty or risk associated with the future cash flows reduces the value. The process by which future cash flows are adjusted to reflect these factors is called discounting, and the magnitude of these factors is reflected in the discount rate. The higher the discount rate is, the lower the present value will be for future cash flows.

When comparing two potential projects or options within a project, the timing of the cash outflows and inflows might be quite different. For example, a firm might have a choice of purchasing a software tool with one large up-front payment versus using an application service provider (ASP) with a usage-based pricing plan. In the purchase, a large sum will be spent initially, but ongoing costs will be low. In the ASP plan, the initial costs will be lower or zero, but the ongoing costs will be higher. Comparing the total effect of these costs and any returns expected from the project requires that all the costs and returns be converted into a common point in time and that is the role of the NPV analysis.

The formula for NPV is as follows:

$$NPV = \frac{CF_1}{(1+R)^1} + \frac{CF_2}{(1+R)^2} + \frac{CF_3}{(1+R)^3} + ...+ \frac{CF_n}{(1+R)^n}$$

Legend:

- **CF** - The net cash flow for each year that the NPV is to be applied. The net cash flow represents the difference between the annual costs of the proposed environment and the annual costs of the existing environment.

- **R** - The discount rate or investment yield rate for the organization at the time the NPV is being calculated. Other options for choosing a discount rate include the cost of capital and the return rate of alternative projects.

- **N** - The total number of years for which the NPV calculation is to be applied. The calculation is performed for each year being considered.

Present Value of $1

Period	4%	5%	6%	8%	9%	10%	11%	12%	15%
1	.96154	.95238	.94340	.92593	.91743	.90909	.90090	.89286	.86957
2	.92456	.90703	.89000	.85734	.84168	.82645	.81162	.79719	.75614
3	.88900	.86384	.83962	.79383	.77218	.75132	.73119	.71178	.65752
4	.85480	.82270	.79209	.73503	.70843	.68301	.65873	.63552	.57175
5	.82193	.78533	.74726	.68058	.64993	.62092	.59345	.56743	.49718
6	.79031	.74622	.70496	.63017	.59627	.56447	.53464	.50663	.43233
7	.75992	.71068	.66506	.58349	.54703	.51316	.48166	.45235	.37594
8	.73069	.67684	.62741	.54027	.50187	.46651	.43393	.40388	.32690
9	.70259	.64461	.59190	.50025	.46043	.42410	.39092	.36061	.28426
10	.67556	.61391	.55839	.46319	.42241	.38554	.35218	.32197	.24719
11	.64958	.58468	.52679	.42888	.38753	.35049	.31728	.28747	.21494
12	.62460	.55684	.49697	.39711	.35554	.31863	.28584	.25668	.18691
13	.60057	.53032	.46884	.36770	.32618	.28966	.25751	.22917	.16253
14	.57748	.50507	.44230	.34046	.29925	.26333	.23199	.20462	.14133
15	.55526	.48102	.41727	.31524	.27454	.23939	.20900	.18270	.12289
16	.53391	.45811	.39365	.29189	.25187	.21763	.18829	.16312	.10687
17	.51337	.43630	.37136	.27027	.23107	.19785	.16963	.14564	.09293
18	.49363	.41552	.35034	.25025	.21199	.17986	.15282	.13004	.08081
19	.47464	.39573	.33051	.23171	.19449	.16351	.13768	.11611	.07027
20	.45639	.37689	.31180	.21455	.17843	.14864	.12403	.10367	.06110

The NPV shows the value of $1 one or more years from the date of the calculation. A dollar in today's currency is worth $1. However, $1 one year from now is worth less than $1 today because of the time value of money. For example, assuming that the discount rate is 10%, then $1 today is worth $1.10 one year from now. However, $1 one year from now is worth $0.91 in today's dollars because the interest earned on the $0.91 over the course of a year at the investment's yield rate of 10% would be $0.09. Adding the interest earned during the year, $0.09, to the net present value, $0.91, equals $1 one year from now. A table showing the present value of a dollar over 20 years at rates of 4% to 15% is provided.

The example below shows the calculation of NPV on an investment of $130,000 for a new Integrated Voice Response (IVR) system. The company has forecast savings in agent labor costs to this self-service method, but will have to pay a maintenance fee each year for the system. There is a positive net cash flow each year, which increases as more customers are anticipated to use the system over time. This example assumes a 10% discount rate.

	Cash Flow	PVIF @ 10%	PV for Each Year
Year 1	$ 35,000	0.909	$ 31,815
Year 2	$ 60,000	0.826	$ 49,560
Year 3	$ 70,000	0.751	$ 52,570
Year 4	$ 70,000	0.683	$ 47,810
Net Present Value			$181,755

The total NPV of the savings over 4 years is $181,755 but the $130,000 initial investment is made in present value dollars and reduces the total return to $51,755. This is still a solid return that would justify the expenditure in an organization where the "hurdle rate" is 10%. The savings and return depend upon the length of the analysis period. If a 3-year analysis is done, the savings ($133,945) will barely pay for the investment, but if the analysis is done for more than four years, it will look even better than the savings shown here. Therefore, the sensitivity of the timeframe for the analysis is an important consideration.

NPV is often used to compare two ways of paying for a solution such as a purchase or a lease. Since the outflows will vary between the two payment methods, but the savings are likely to be similar, the NPV is a good way to see the impact of paying less up-front and more each year for the lease alternative. In the analysis below, the lease costs have been analyzed.

	Cash Flow	PVIF @ 10%	PV for Each Year
Year 1	$ 15,000	0.909	$ 13,635
Year 2	$ 17,000	0.826	$ 14,620
Year 3	$ 20,000	0.751	$ 15,020
Year 4	$ 20,000	0.683	$ 13,660
Net Present Value			$ 56,935

Now the call center is in a good position to compare the two financing options over a 4-year period. The NPV of the purchase is $51,755 and the NPV of the lease is $56,935. If all other factors are equal (and they rarely are), the lease appears to be the better financial decision. However, once again the timeframe of the analysis is important. The net return for each additional year is quite different from the purchase to the lease, and the purchase NPV will outpace the lease NPV in the following year.

Payback Period

The payback is the number of months or years it takes to recover the initial investment. For example, if the initial investment is $450.000 and the cost savings anticipated from the investment are $45,000 per month, then the payback period is ten months. Most companies require a payback period of less than three years to consider a technology acquisition, but as economic climates change and the competition for capital dollars shifts, so does the payback period required to win approval of funding. The payback formula is as follows:

$$\text{Payback period} \quad = \quad \frac{\text{Initial Investment}}{\text{(NPV of Saving/Years}_n)}$$

In the example below, the payback period is calculated for the same IVR purchase as explored above in the NPV section. The initial investment is $130,000 and the payback period seeks to determine at what point in the future that the returns are equal to that $130,000.

	NPV	Cumulative NPV
Year 1	$ 31,815	$ 31,815
Year 2	$ 49,560	$ 81,375
Year 3	$ 52,570	$133,945
Year 4	$ 47,810	$181,755

If the company must recover $130,000, it is clear that it won't happen until some time in the third year. At the end of year two, $81,375 has been recovered in savings, and by the end of Year 3, it is more than $130,000. To determine the exact month of payback, subtract $81,375 from the initial $130,000 to determine the remaining balance to be recovered ($48,265) during the third year. Then divide the $52,570 recovered in all of Year 3 by twelve months to determine how much is gained per month ($4381). Finally, divide the $48,265 by the monthly amount of $4381 and the payback is in the 11th month of Year 3. In this example, the total payback is at 35 months

(24 months for the Years 1 and 2 and 11 more in Year 3).

It is not uncommon to see payback period analyzed without calculating the NPV of the cash flows and just using the actual dollars. This is an incorrect process and will produce a faster payback assumption than will actually be experienced. In the example above, the payback without NPV will be 30 months rather than 35 months as calculated with NPV considerations.

Return on Investment (ROI)

The most commonly used cost justification approach involves calculating Return on Investment (ROI). The ROI calculation evaluates the NPV of projected cash flows derived from the project divided by the initial investment. This assesses the benefit of the project over the initial cost. For example, if the NPV of savings on the project are estimated at $1.5 million and the initial investment is $1 million then the ROI is $150%. The ROI formula is as follows:

$$ROI = \frac{NPV \text{ of Savings}}{\text{Initial Investment}} \times 100$$

In the IVR investment example, the ROI would be calculated by dividing the NPV of $181,755 by the initial investment of $130,000 to yield a 1.4 or 140% return on investment.

Capital Budgeting Assumptions

Development of any of the financial calculations mentioned above requires that all of the financial impacts of the project be estimated and included in the analysis. This includes the initial investment and the recurring costs. Non-financial considerations may also be included such as improved information access, higher customer satisfaction, and other items that are difficult to quantify. Striking a balance between the financial measurements and the qualitative analysis is crucial in both winning support and in the ultimate success of a project.

It is common to leave out the soft-dollar returns because they are hard to calculate. Common soft dollar returns include such things as improved customer satisfaction and the resulting increases in customer retention, or improved employee satisfaction and resulting reductions in turnover. It is perceived that soft-dollar calculations aren't reliable representations of actual ROI. They may also be left out because including the soft dollars can drive the ROI so high as to make the returns unbelievable.

Some kinds of savings can be interpreted as either soft or hard dollars. For example, if using a speed dial code versus manually dialing saves five seconds per call, multiplying the five seconds times the average wage rate of sales people dialing calls, times the total number of dialed calls should provide an estimate of the soft dollar savings. But it is not clear that the five seconds that have been saved will be redeployed to the company's benefit, and that is where the doubts start. On the other hand, if this same kind of time savings was applied in a call center, such as might occur with a CTI application that pops up a screen on the agent's desktop, these savings would probably be viewed as hard dollars. That is because the AHT of each call is a firm productivity measure and the system will force more calls to the agent to fill the added time, so the gains will likely be realized. Even in this CTI screen pop example, there are potential soft dollar savings in the form of improved customer and employee satisfaction. It is likely because agents don't have to enter the account numbers or listen to customers complain about having to repeat information, and if these assumptions are valid, some reasonable calculation of the impact that will have on the company could be included in the analysis. The trick is in determining when these returns will occur and how the dollars will be recovered for use elsewhere. These questions cannot be answered with certainty, but the assumptions can still be used in the ROI analysis. The assumptions should be stated with some indication of how realistic these numbers could be, and a range of low to high expectations can make them more credible as well.

Gathering the data for the ROI analysis requires some research. Some of the data will be available from internal sources including such items as:

- Total number of customers
- Annual gross revenue
- Average value of a contact
- Customer acquisition rate
- Customer acquisition costs
- Retention rate
- Total number of employees (in the call center if appropriate)
- Turnover rates (both internal transfers and departures)
- Average salary and benefits costs
- Call volume received, handled, and abandoned
- Abandon percentage
- Blockage percentage
- Percent of calls answered within service goal
- AHT (broken down into talk and after-call work)
- Occupancy percentage
- The company's planning horizon to be used for the ROI analysis
- The company's discount rate

Other data will need to be gathered from external sources. This includes the system costs, maintenance fees, network charges, and other cost items associated with the acquisition under analysis. Some of the reference accounts of the vendor may also be able to help support assumptions about returns from the actual results they have experienced. More generic information may be available from case studies, benchmarking data, or consultants who have accomplished a similar project elsewhere. When all else fails, a pilot project may be the best way to project meaningful assumptions before a broader rollout of the proposed solution.

Summary

Understanding financial reports, operating budgets, and handling capital budget requests are key skills for anyone in a management role. This is the language of senior management and it is essential for the call center manager to be able to communicate effectively on these topics in conversations with senior management as well as with the staff in the call center.

CHAPTER 4: STAFF PLANNING

Introduction

Deciding how to staff the call center is the first and most important operational step. Once the strategic plan is in place and the role and mission clearly defined, the decisions about whether to hire staff for an in-house center or seek some other alternative will be possible. The staffing plan will drive all other decisions about facilities, technology, and processes. Organizing the staff into a cohesive team will set the stage for a successful operation.

Staffing Alternatives

A critical step in developing a call center operation is to decide how it will be staffed. Since about three-fourths of call center costs are related to labor costs, this decision is fundamental to the operation of the business. How a business chooses to get people in place to handle its customer interactions will have an impact on every other function within the center, including site selection and facility design, forecasting and scheduling, performance management, technology acquisition and management, facilities management, human resources administration, and risk management.

The four main options for call center staffing include:

Outsourcing. Outsourcing involves contracting out some or all of the contacts to another company to handle. Outsourcers may handle the calls at their own facilities or may supply the personnel and equipment to handle calls at the client's facility.

In-House Staffing. This option is the traditional staffing model in which the business operates and staffs its own call center.

Telecommuting. This option is one in which the business supplies its own staff to handle the calls, but some or all of the staff are not physically located at the call center site.

Contract Staffing. This option, also called in-sourcing, involves having an on-site call center, but contracting out to a staffing agency to supply the staffing and perhaps some of the support or management personnel.

Each of these options is explored in the sections that follow.

Outsourcing

Outsourcing is the practice of contracting out some or all of a business function to a company that specializes in that particular function. In call center outsourcing, businesses contract with other companies to answer or place some or all of its calls or other types of contacts rather than handling those contacts in-house.

The main reason that businesses outsource call center functions is to avoid the resource drain and costs associated with initial set-up and ongoing operation of a function that is typically not the core competency of the business. Developing and running a call center is expensive and many companies find they can accomplish the call handling operation more cost-effectively by outsourcing it than trying to do it in-house.

Outsourcing can be an alternative solution to building a dedicated in-house call center or it can be used to supplement a company's call center operation. It can be a particularly attractive option for start-up companies or for businesses unsure what their call center needs will be. Outsourcing allows the company to buy call center services as they need them without investing in expensive equipment, software, facilities, or labor. The benefits are the same for established companies that may choose to focus on their core business and outsource the calling handling to the experts, or for companies that have one call center, but do not wish to open another to meet growth requirements.

In cases where a company decides to outsource the IT support function, it is common for the internal help desk call center to be outsourced as well. When an existing call center operation is outsourced, the company may decide to take advantage of the already acquired systems, furniture, and equipment by transferring those assets to the outsource provider who will use the company's facility and supply the staffing needed. The company's call center staff is typically transferred to the payroll of the outsourcer in this type of arrangement.

Outsourcing Benefits

There are many benefits to be considered in using an outsourcer to handle inbound or outbound calling. Some of these benefits are discussed below.

Reduced Costs

While an in-house call center must bear the cost of site selection, building, operating, staffing, and maintaining technologies and facilities, outsourcers can amortize these costs over many clients. The client benefits by paying for only the services directly needed, resulting in cost efficiencies. Outsourcers are also able to reduce labor costs by sharing programs with different companies, so that clients are not paying for idle time. Known as a "shared agent" arrangement, this concept enables companies to benefit from the high occupancy in an outsourced call center, bringing down the staff-to-workload ratios in the center and resulting in a lower cost-per-call that can be passed along to the client.

While the "shared agent" arrangement helps to drive up occupancy and drive down costs, some companies prefer a "dedicated agent" contract. Here agents are assigned to one contract only and specialize in only that company's products and services. This is often the preferred arrangement when calls are more complex and difficult to handle, such as in a technical support environment.

Flexibility

Inbound calls arrive in peaks and valleys and traditional call centers are therefore by nature inefficient. During periods of low call volumes, agents may be idle and equipment is not utilized. In an outsourced call center, multiple clients' calls tend to smooth out the peaks and valleys meaning a greater utilization of equipment and staffing resources. And given the large size of most outsourcing operations, there are typically more staff and phone lines available to handle even the biggest of spikes in call volume due to marketing or advertising campaigns. An in-house center may have difficulty dealing with unanticipated increases in volume due to insufficient telecommunications capacity or labor resources.

Outsourcers can also be used just to handle the peaks of call volume that an internal center cannot handle. Businesses can contract with them just for disaster recovery purposes, for peak time overflow situations, for after-hours, for certain types of calls, for seasonal increases, and so on. They provide the flexibility for a company to send just what it is not prepared to handle. In some unusual cases, the outsourcer is contracted to handle a guaranteed load of calls each day and the company handles the peaks. For example, this may be done in companies that utilize the product testing and development staff to handle calls right after a new product is released, but pulls them off the phones when the call volume returns to normal to focus them on development of the next product.

Well-Trained Staff

Internal call centers tend to focus most of their training on specific products and services, with not as much emphasis on general call-handling skills or knowledge of call center operations. Outsourcers spend much more time training agents to be generalists on the front-end so they are prepared to adapt quickly to a particular customer's needs. Training may be more comprehensive in nature, resulting in better overall quality of the call handling process.

Management Expertise

Running a call center means having a management and supervisory staff with essential knowledge and skills about call center operations. And for larger centers, skilled support staff such as workforce planners and schedulers, quality specialists, trainers, and technology specialists will need to be in place. Many internal call centers find it difficult to hire or to develop this expertise in-house quickly and ensure everyone stays up to speed on the best practices, skills, and knowledge. Outsourcers have these specialists on staff and perform these various functions on a daily basis to keep skills and knowledge finely tuned.

Speed to Market

Outsourcers can get a call-handling function up to speed much more quickly than an in-house operation. The key to their quickness is in their contractor status. When bidding on a job, the outsourcer has to have the site, labor, and equipment ready to begin delivery on the agreed date. The site and equipment are ready to go and the outsourcer may have staff either immediately available or on-call for the next assignment.

Data Collection Expertise

Outsourcers are equipped to capture and manipulate many different types of information related to customer calls. Experience in working with multiple businesses and campaigns helps equip the outsourcer with the expertise and technology to convert raw data more easily into useful information.

Cost Tracking

Outsourcers can detail costs per transaction and costs per hour since their billing procedures are set up that way. For most outsourcers, the profitability relies on being able to manage the margin between their costs and the price to the client, so understanding their costs is a core capability. The total cost of the operation shows on the outsourcer's bill each month and can be tracked easily. In-house operations tend to have hidden costs, making it difficult to track and manage the financial aspects of the operation and evaluate profitability and overall effectiveness.

Specialized Expertise

Because many outsourcers specialize in providing services to certain industries only, a company may find a high level of focused expertise with an outsourcer. The outsourcer may bring years of collective experience in a specific industry to a customer that could benefit from a broader perspective and understanding of the competitive environment. For example, a new banking call center may benefit from using an outsourcer who has experience handling the credit card processing for many different banks. The outsourcer may understand the processing and servicing of accounts better than the bank, where credit card processing is just one of the many functions being handled by an internal center.

Quality Monitoring

Due to the nature of most service level agreements, rigorous call monitoring is typically done to ensure the customer's calls are being handled in a professional, quality manner. The most sophisticated equipment is typically in place and supervisors and quality specialists are highly trained in monitoring and coaching techniques. Daily performance assessment is part of the agreement with most clients and is therefore done more often and more thoroughly than in an in-house center where supervisors may not have the time to devote sufficient time and attention to it. Provisions are also made to allow the customer to monitor calls remotely, if desired.

State-of-the-Art Technology

Most outsourcers invest in state-of-the-art technology to meet their many customers' demands. Investment in the latest technology is an expensive option for in-house call centers, while outsourcing centers are able to spread the cost of the technology investment across multiple projects and customers. The outsourcer typically has a set of technology specialists on hand whose job is simply to stay on top of the technology and apply it effectively for their customers.

Testing Capabilities

An outsourcer is often better at conducting a test of a new program or campaign than an internal center might be. Internal call centers may find it difficult to find the staffing resources and/or the technology required to trial a new call type or program. By using an outsourcer, a company can determine the viability of a program very quickly with little to no capital outlay or hiring of new staff.

High Performance Levels

Since there are so many different outsourcer options in the call center industry today, it is very competitive among outsourcing companies. This high level of competition typically results in high levels of performance if the outsourcer is to survive in the business. Outsourcers can be held to higher levels of performance than perhaps internal call centers, since the customer can simply take away business if performance standards are not met. Internal call centers may take longer to respond to customer demands and there is typically not as much of a significant consequence if performance levels are not met for some period of time.

Round-the-Clock Operations

Despite growing customer expectations, many companies cannot afford to operate their call center seven days a week, twenty-four hours a day. The small number of calls that arrive in non-peak hours make it prohibitively expensive to operate at certain hours. Therefore, availability to customers during those times is limited to self-service options for many call centers. An outsourcer can provide this service for a company at a much lower cost per call and help the business maintain round-the-clock availability.

Global Presence

Many outsourcers have centers in multiple countries and specialize in bringing the language and skill sets needed to a customer project. While a company may struggle with setting up operations in a different country, the outsourcer may already have operations and available staff there. Because of their multiple sites in many different countries, many outsourcers can boast of dozens of language capabilities.

Public Relations

As the economy shifted in the early years of the 21st Century, many companies had to scale back operations and lay off staff. Some of these layoffs caused a public relations "black eye" for some companies. By using an outsourcer, there is less bad press and internal heartache when a call center has to cut back staffing or close.

Outsourcing Drawbacks

While the benefits are many, there are also some drawbacks to outsourcing calls. The primary downside to outsourcing is the loss of control over the staff and perhaps customer information. While many outsourcers provide more functional access to customer information than what an internal call center might have because of its possible CRM expertise, sometimes access to this information is difficult.

Another disadvantage may be the lack of commitment to the end customer. While most outsourcers are focused on providing excellent service, agents are typically held to a set of acceptable standards and behaviors and have no reason to go above and beyond the call of duty to serve a customer, while an internal employee in an in-house center may recognize the value of doing so.

There may also be a lack of incentive for efficiency on the outsourcer's part. Since the outsourcer is paid for the calls it handles, it may have no incentive to provide customers with better numbers to call to get problems solved or questions answered, such as directing calls to a specialized internal group or directing customers to self-service alternatives.

Selection Criteria

The following criteria are crucial to the success of an outsourcing relationship. Ranging from technology to philosophy, these areas should be explored before making the decision to outsource and with whom to do business. Before beginning any outsourcing relationship, a company should clearly define objectives and expectations, conduct a thorough analysis, keep an open mind, and look to build a fair, win-win relationship with a chosen provider.

Technical Expertise

The first item in the checklist should be to ensure that the proposed outsourcer has sufficient technical capacity. This capacity should include the capability to offer quality voice and data connections, database management, and provision of needed services such as IVR or web-based services. It is important to consider not just current needs, but expected future requirements as well.

Part of the value of outsourcing is being able to rely on another company to supply state-of-the-art technology as well as the expertise to apply the technology in a way that makes sense for each business partner. Companies should ensure the vendor under consideration has the proper business contingency planning and security measures in place so customer data is protected and can be provided to the company (or another outsourcer) in the event of an emergency.

Industry Sector Experience

It may be critical to some highly specialized businesses that the outsourcer be experienced in that particular business area. Specialized knowledge and even certification (such as in the case of software certification for a technical help desk outsourcer) may be desirable or even required in order to do business. Those outsourcers that specialize in a certain sector may have a quicker ramp-up time as well as lower handle times, and customers may be better served than if a generalist outsourcer takes the calls.

Access Channel Experience

A business may wish to have the outsourcer handle calls today, but add email transactions or web chats at a later date. It is important that the outsourcer have capabilities in a multi-channel environment if that is to be a requirement in the near future. While some organizations have their phone calls handled by one outsourcer, and e-mails by another, the efficiencies and cost-savings associated with locating both types of contacts within one outsourcer should not be overlooked.

Financial Stability

In today's volatile economic market, it is important to assess the financial stability of any potential outsourcing partner. Symptoms of financial stress include declining service, staff turnover, delays in meeting project deadlines, and slow payment of bills. Since many outsourcing contracts represent long-term partnerships, the prudent buyer will investigate the financial situation of all potential partners to make sure the company will be able to deliver for the long term.

Management Team

The outsourcer and its management team that will be responsible for account management should be a good match for the client company's corporate culture and style. It is important that the outsourcer's team blend with the internal team and that management styles do not clash. It is also critical to know whether the management staff will be dedicated to one account only or spread over several accounts.

Frontline Staff

The frontline agents should also be a match to the client's corporate culture and style. It is important to take the time to investigate the specific team that will be handling calls and whether or not they will be dedicated to the account or shared with other projects. Dedicated teams have advantages, but are more expensive since economies of scale are lost. Shared teams are less expensive, but their depth of understanding of the client's customers, procedures, and business philosophies may be limited. Sometimes a dedicated core team supplemented by a pool of shared agents strikes an effective balance between the two alternatives.

Reporting Capabilities

Each business must determine what data will be needed from the caller transactions, including customer information, call statistics, and general performance information. Defining these reports and the process to create them is often one of the toughest challenges of the outsourcing relationship.

Monitoring Capabilities

Every outsourcing relationship should be outlined in writing to provide the client with the assurance that its customers are being well-treated. It is important to define various measures of service delivery and quality that provide an overall picture of customer service and performance. Most outsourcers provide a mechanism by which the client can monitor calls to ensure the call-handling process is going as planned from a procedural and quality perspective.

Customer Satisfaction Measurement

Customer satisfaction measurement is a continuation of the monitoring philosophy and process. Each business needs to know if the products and services being provided are meeting customer needs and what satisfaction levels are with each. A mechanism for customer feedback through the outsourcer as well as direct to the business is essential for making business decisions to ensure high levels of customer satisfaction.

Outsourcing Summary

There are many reasons to consider outsourcing as a staffing alternative for call centers today. Outsourcing has become a popular industry process and there are very few companies today that fail to consider it as a strategic option. It has gone beyond just being a cost-savings measure for many companies and has become a way for some businesses to accomplish customer contact strategies they would otherwise be unable to achieve without an outsourcing partner. The key question in evaluating whether this staffing strategy makes sense is to ask whether the outsourcing company can handle the customer contacts "better" than they can be handled through various means of in-house staffing alternatives.

In-House Staffing

Should a business decide to handle contacts with its own employees, the traditional model is to hire and train agents to work in the company's call center(s). Building and staffing one's own call center involves finding a site (to be discussed in Chapter 6), putting in place the appropriate call center systems and technology (to be discussed in Chapter 7), and recruiting, hiring, and managing the call center employees.

The primary operational activity regarding running one's own call center has to do with forecasting and scheduling the call center workforce. Getting the right number of people in place at the right times to handle the contact workload is the most critical function of call center management, given that up to three-fourths of call center operating costs are related to staffing. A systematic approach to forecasting workload, calculating staff requirements, and creating staff schedules must be in place in order for the call center to reach service goals and operate efficiently.

This in-house staffing plan affects every other function of the call center as well:

Facilities management. A site will be needed to house the call center and its employees. A systematic site selection process is used to find a site for a new call center or perhaps for a relocation or expansion of call center services. Ongoing effort is required to design and maintain an effective workplace, including attention to engineering concepts such as lighting, climate, and noise, as well as human factor components such as ergonomics.

Human resources administration. Recruiting and hiring will typically be done as a joint effort by the call center and the human resources department. A detailed job task analysis is performed by the call center personnel, who work with HR personnel to recruit qualified candidates, screen and interview, and then manage compensation and personnel issues.

Technology management. Deciding to staff for internal handling of contacts has implications on technology decisions as well. Provisioning of voice and data telecommunications services must be done, along with selection and implementation of automatic call distribution (ACD) equipment and other related technologies. This equipment may require a significant capital investment and ongoing maintenance costs and effort.

Quality management. A customer satisfaction assessment process will need to be put in place that regularly assesses retention and satisfaction. Quality monitoring procedures and technologies must be implemented with call center managers and supervisors held directly responsible for performance and satisfaction.

Reporting and Communications. A system of metrics must be put in place to regularly measure and report on performance, both of the individual agent and the call center as a whole. And call center personnel must develop a strategy for assimilating and distributing business intelligence throughout the organization.

Financial Management. Call center management will be responsible for creating and adhering to capital and operating budgets. And particularly if the call center is a revenue-generating entity, generating profit and loss statements will be a critical function of ongoing operations.

Risk Management. When running an in-house call center, the business must continually assess various risks to the call center operation and evaluate their impact on service and profitability. Contingency plans must be developed that include reviews of facilities, staffing, call center systems, telecommunications networks, information systems, and access channels to prevent problems from occurring as well as recovery plans should a disaster happen.

All these elements are key to planning and operating an in-house call center assuming that call center employees will be hired by the company and physically work on site.

Telecommuting

Another option to consider in setting up a call center operation is to hire employees to handle customer contacts but to have part or all of these employees work from a distant site rather than in the call center.

The practice of telecommuting for office workers is growing rapidly. The International Telework Association and Council (ITAC), based in Washington, DC, forecasts that over 30 million workers will telecommute by the end of 2004, and the numbers are growing rapidly. This growth is occurring across all sectors of business – business and legal services, health care, banking and finance, and others. The call center with its "knowledge worker" population is one of the professions best positioned to take advantage of this work option.

The technology exists today to allow agents to log in from home or any other remote site and receive calls in the same way as if they were sitting in the call center. They can be part of an ACD agent group and receive calls just like the other agents in the group, and data can be sent to their screen at home just like what they would see in the center. The technology also provides for management functions so that the remote agents' statistics are tracked and reported just like the in-house agents. Supervisors can also monitor and record their calls on a real-time or scheduled basis.

There are many advantages to a telecommuting or remote agent arrangement, as discussed below.

Schedule Flexibility

The main advantage of using remote workers as all or part of the call center workforce is the flexibility gained in scheduling. It is very difficult to cover the peaks and valleys of calls throughout the day with traditional staff. The call center may have a two-hour peak of calls in the morning and another in the afternoon. While the call center can't expect someone to come into the center and work a split shift to handle those periods, it may be reasonable to expect a person working from home to do so.

Covering night and weekend hours may also be easier to accomplish with telecommuters. Many people do not like to commute to work at night when crime and traffic risks go up. These same people may be willing to work those hours if they can do so from the comfort of their own home.

Real Estate Savings

Another primary benefit of telecommuting is the space savings accomplished by not needing to house the agent in the physical call center. Assuming that an agent occupies 50 square feet of call center space and the lease cost of this space is $20 per square foot per month, the savings per agent would be $1,000 per month or $12,000 per year. And this is just the cost of the space alone. Add to that the one-time and ongoing costs of building and maintaining workstations, furniture, lunchrooms, conference spaces, and other amenities, along with the cost of additional utilities, and that cost could easily double.

Expanded Labor Pool

Another strong reason to consider the utilization of a remote workforce is the potential to attract additional labor sources. This expanded labor pool may include those that are highly qualified workers, but are handicapped or physically challenged and unable to commute daily into the business site. Another potential source of workers may be those that are homebound caregivers, such as the growing population of baby-boomers now caring for their elderly parents.

A telecommuting option may also simply bring in a bigger pool of qualified candidates attracted to the prospect of working at home and avoiding the commuting hassles of getting to their job every day. As a matter of fact, companies not only find their candidate pool increasing, but also find that people are willing to work for less money if telecommuting is an option. In addition to the avoiding the travel time of a long commute, employees can save money on transportation costs, food costs, and a working wardrobe. These are all significant benefits to employees.

Staff Retention

Businesses generally find that their teleworking employees have a much higher job satisfaction and retention rates than traditional in-house employees. In addition to the "hard dollar" employee benefits listed above, the additional time found in their day is a big factor in overall satisfaction and quality of life.

Another retention benefit is the fact that trained employees can also be retained even if they move to another city or area of the country. Many call centers lose valuable employees when a spouse's job takes them to a new place. With remote agent capabilities, the high-quality agent can remain employed, avoiding recruiting, hiring, and training costs for new staff, not to mention the retention of valuable skills and knowledge.

Increased Productivity

Many trials of telecommuting workers versus traditional office workers suggest that telecommuters are more productive. The main reason for this higher productivity may be the fact that there are fewer interruptions to distract the employee. Their comfort and increased satisfaction from working at home may also be a contributing factor to the better productivity.

Disaster Recovery

All sorts of disasters and emergencies can happen that disable normal call center functions and having a pool of remote workers can assist the call center in carrying out its work. A flu epidemic or icy roads may prevent staff from coming into the center, but work can still be carried out in remote sites. A flood or power outage at the site can damage workstations, but assuming connectivity is still possible to the main switch, agents at home can continue to process calls.

Environmental Impact

Having fewer people driving into the call center every day can certainly reduce auto emissions and pollution. This isn't just a nice benefit, but may help some companies comply with legal regulations. The federal Clean Air Act requires companies with more than one-hundred employees in high-pollution areas to design and implement programs to reduce air pollution. Setting up a telecommuting program is one option for complying with this rule.

Telecommuting Disadvantages

Telecommuting is not for everyone however, and there are also some downsides to this staffing alternative. The major obstacle preventing many companies from doing telecommuting is the issue of equipping the agent to work at home. While the voice part of the technology is easy to accomplish and phone calls can be seamlessly made and answered, the bigger stumbling block has to do with the delivery of the data portion of the call.

Delivery of the data portion of the call to the agent's desktop at home requires equipping the agent with the proper equipment and sufficient bandwidth to enable the customer interactions. There is also concern about the delivery of private or confidential information to an agent's home where friends and family members may have access to it.

Social concerns should also be taken into consideration. Those team members that work from home may not feel as much of the team as their on-site counterparts. And it may be more difficult to keep at-home agents "in the loop" of office communications and new procedures. Many companies address this gap by having the employee come into the office at least one day a week to work.

Finally, many employees are not good candidates for telecommuting. Some may lack the experience or discipline to work without supervision. Others long for the camaraderie of being in a social workplace. It is important to define up front what the selection criteria will be and make sure a process is in place to continually monitor and coach the distant workers to ensure they effectively contribute to the goals and objectives of the center and of the overall business.

Contract Staffing

Another option for call center staffing is to have staff on site, but to let an outside agency provide the staff. This scenario, sometimes referred to as "in-sourcing," involves the use of a staffing agency to recruit, screen, hire, train, and supervise agents. The contract staffing agency may perform the recruiting, hiring, and training activities at their site, or may reside at the call center site.

The call center typically pays more for a contract staff person, since the staffing rate includes an "overhead" charge for the contract agency, but the added cost comes with many benefits, as outlined below.

Staffing Expertise

Despite the slightly higher wage rates, many call centers choose to staff through an "in-sourcer" or contract staffing agency. These agencies have a core competency of recruiting and hiring staff, so they may perhaps do a better job of it than internal call center management might do. These agencies are familiar with labor pools in various communities and most have links to various state or community vocational training programs. They are experts at helping the call center define job requirements, and then finding suitable candidates, doing careful screening to ensure a good match for the job.

Many companies use contract staffing agencies to get a new call center up and running. Once the staff is in place, the agency can train call center personnel on how to recruit and hire additional employees and then turn all the staffing tasks to call center management.

Flexibility

Another benefit of "in-sourcing" is the flexibility of procuring exactly the number and type of staff required. The call center can simply inform the contract staffing agency of how many of each type of position it needs to fill and for how long, and the agency can fill the vacancies. This flexibility is particularly useful for what might be a short-term campaign where staff will not be needed for a long period of time.

Trial Staffing

Many contract agencies have a contract with the call center where the center can hire temporary staff to be permanent company employees. This arrangement lets the call center "try before buy" in terms of adding permanent staff to the payroll. Likewise, if there is a problem with any contract employee, the call center simply has to inform the agency and does not have to go through disciplinary and severance procedures that are likely required with company employees. There are also benefits to the workers, who have an opportunity to try out the job tasks and the employer before making the commitment to take a permanent position.

Contract Staffing Disadvantages

One of the advantages of contract staffing is also one of the major disadvantages. Since the agents work for the staffing agency and not the company, the call center has less control over them than if they were company employees. And since most of the positions are temporary, the staff may decide to leave if they find other more permanent positions elsewhere, making staff turnover a bigger problem than with regular employees.

Organizational Design

Defining Structure

The success of any call center is dependent far more upon its personnel than its technology or processes. Organizational structure is important to any business, but it is particularly critical to a call center operation since the work is so labor-intensive. The same schools of thought that apply to a developing an organizational structure for the company overall apply on a smaller scale to the call center.

The three most basic types of organizational designs are functional, divisional, and matrix organizations. Functional structures, where workers are organized by what they actually do, are typically used when organizations are small, geographically centralized, and provide only a few types of services. As an organization grows, it may be difficult to coordinate processes and decision-making in a functional organization and the organization typically moves to a more divisional structure. Divisional structures are often used by large organizations that may be geographically dispersed and that offer a wide range of products or services. In a divisional structure, lateral relations are used to address communications and problems across divisions. As more coordination becomes necessary across divisions or groups, more of a matrix structure may be required to provide sufficient integration.

These types of organizational structures apply to call centers as well. Smaller organizations may organize their call center by function with one agent group responding to sales calls, while another processes mail orders, and another providing technical support, all perhaps located in the same physical location. As the organization grows, it may expand to multiple call centers, with one division handling sales calls and another doing support, or perhaps dividing responsibilities by the region in which the customer resides.

There are also various types of hierarchical structures to be considered. The three most common types are bureaucratic, flat, and team structures. In a bureaucratic design, structured layers of management exist with an upward career progression as skill levels develop. In a flat design, management is more decentralized with more decision-making authority placed in the hands of the workers. Employees tend to be more generalists in a flatter work environment with the bureaucratic environment creating more specialists. In a team environment, workers are generally more self-managed with group accountability and success based on team results. Call centers fall into each of these categories, with perhaps the team structure being the most common.

Driving Forces

In addition to the basic reasons to have one of these organizational types versus another, it is important to consider the external forces that drive the structure of the call center. These driving forces are:

> *Globalization.* Call center organizations are becoming more global in nature. The reduced cost and improved quality of communications have made geography transparent. Organizations are looking for ways to reduce costs, search for unsaturated labor markets, and exploit regional expertise and resources.

> *Diversity.* The population is changing, meaning an organization's customer mix is becoming more diverse and therefore the workforce to meet customer demands must become more diverse as well. This expanding, culturally diverse workforce is a source of both innovation and conflict and the call center must shift its organizational structure to meet the challenges and reap the benefits of a diverse workforce.

> *Flexibility.* With increased competition for qualified call center employees, organizations are finding the need to be more flexible in workplace issues. With employees being given greater autonomy and encouragement for initiative, call centers must re-think processes and structures to support these new employee relationships.

In order to adapt to business and cultural demands and meet these various needs, organizations are being forced to adopt a new paradigm in terms of organizational structure. Smart call centers recognize the need to be more flexible and adaptable to the demands and expectations of stakeholders that include customers, employees, management, and shareholders. In an effort to adapt, many call center organizations have abandoned traditional "top down" hierarchical structures in favor of more flexible, fluid structures. This flexibility usually involves a higher degree of self-regulation and active participation in the day-to-day operation of the business. This flexibility is typically achieved through the use of a team structure, and most call centers have adapted a team environment to at least some degree.

Single-Site versus Multi-Site Organizations

Managing a single-site call center is challenging enough, but many companies require more than one call center to be effective. Multiple sites may be required due to the sheer size of the operation, since many believe that the maximum effective size of one site is between 300 and 500 seats. It may be that the company operates in a wide geographic area and wants a local presence in these areas along with the benefits of multiple time zones, larger recruiting pool, and disaster recovery potential. Whatever the reason, the challenges of organizing an effective multi-site call center operation are all of the single-site issues and some unique additional ones.

One of the biggest challenges will be the division of labor and responsibility among the sites and personnel. Decisions about whether to have specialists in certain support disciplines such as quality monitoring and workforce management are generally a function of the size of the workload in a single site. But in multiple sites, there are issues of local interaction with the people at each site to be considered along with the economies of scale of centralization. There is no "right answer" to the organization plan that will work best in every situation as there are trade-offs with each choice. To a large extent, the design chosen simply reflects the management style of the people in charge at that time.

For many multi-site operations, centralization of some or all administrative and control functions makes sense. Tasks such as training, forecasting workload, handling quality control, and dealing with technologies take high levels of expertise, and it takes fewer of these experts if they are all in one place. This central team can provide support services to each of the sites effectively. However, there can be some political problems if the central team is all co-located with one of the operating call centers. The other sites may perceive a bias on the part of the central team, if for no other reason than they can more easily talk to each other and may be friends. The experts may also have been pulled from the ranks of the local operating center, further reinforcing that perception of bias. The centralized team will need to travel to the individual sites from time to time to ensure that they are meeting the needs of the whole organization.

To maximize local control and ensure high levels of interaction with the local staff, a decentralized organization structure may make sense. For example, the scheduling of staff may be done differently in two sites, with half-hour lunches in one and hour lunches in the other, more part-time used in one, and so on. A scheduler who is local with the staff understands the unique issues of these personnel and can work to find the best balance between company/customer needs and agent needs. However, the total number of staff handling the scheduling function for all sites is likely to be more than if the work is done centrally. Some training functions such as those needed by agents can be handled locally due to the high volume of this activity, but management training might more effectively be handled on a centralized basis with traveling trainers.

Roles and Responsibilities

Frontline Staff

A team structure in the call center typically begins with a functional team of anywhere from ten to twenty frontline agents, with a typical team size being twelve to fifteen. The span of control is determined by the complexity of the work, and the demands placed upon the supervisor. These frontline agents are generally responsible for call/contact handling and associated work tasks. The official job title of these employees varies widely by company: customer service representative (CSR), telephone service representative (TSR), customer associate, customer advocate, etc. For purposes of this book, the term "agent" will be used to define this frontline employee.

Frontline Supervisors

Each group or team of agents reports to a supervisor responsible for that team. The supervisor is generally responsible for the performance of the members of the team and duties will include performance coaching, training, monitoring calls, schedule administration, reporting, workload coordination, and perhaps assisting with difficult or escalated calls. Some call centers utilize a "team lead" position as an intermediate step between agent and supervisor. This lead position will likely handle calls as well as assist with supervisory duties such as training, coaching, and providing call support. This effectively expands the size of agent team that can be handled by one supervisor.

The supervisors typically report to a call center manager whose role is to direct the day-to-day operations of the center. These operational duties might include service level management, system and database management, technology management, and budgetary planning.

Operational Support Roles

Workforce Planner/Manager. This person(s) may report directly to the call center manager or may be at the same level as the call center manager reporting into a Director level position. This position is responsible for forecasting workload, determining staff requirements, creating workforce schedules, and managing daily staffing levels to maintain service levels.

Quality Specialist/Manager. This person may report directly to the call center manager or may be at a management level reporting into the Director position. This position is responsible for defining performance guidelines, setting up monitoring/recording procedures, evaluating performance, and reporting performance results. This position may work with agents directly or may report performance results to supervisors who will perform necessary coaching. In smaller call centers, this position may not exist and its duties would be performed by the supervisor or lead agent.

Training Specialist/Manager. Larger call centers will have staff devoted to employee training and development. This position may report into the call center manager or director, or may report to a human resource manager/director. In smaller centers, the supervisor or manager may be responsible for performing required training activities.

Telecom/Technology Specialist/Manager. This person may report to the call center manager or be at a management level reporting into a director position. This person is generally responsible for overseeing all the technical systems, networks, and other products or services related to the call center operation. This position will have duties for acquisition, implementation, and maintenance of these various systems including significant interaction with technology vendors. In smaller centers, the call center manager may assume some or all of this responsibility.

Client Services Manager. Another position exists in an outsourced call center that is responsible for the interaction with a company for which the outsourcer is providing call center services. This position will have duties of workload and staff planning, performance reporting, problem tracking, contract management, and business development.

Call Center Management

Some call centers, especially those with fewer than 100–200 frontline positions, may only have one level of call center management. This position may have responsibility for many of the support roles outlined above as well as being the direct manager of the supervisory staff.

In larger call centers, there is likely a higher-level position into which the call center manager and other technical and support positions report. This person may have over-all responsibility for meeting customer satisfaction objectives, budget and profitability goals, facility planning, system and equipment selection, workforce policies, workload planning, and coordination. This additional layer of management is most often found in larger call centers or ones with multiple divisions or sites.

In terms of a profession, call center management is one of the most promising careers of the new century. Call center management is a legitimate, bona fide profession. It has its own specialized vocabulary, technology, and required knowledge. There are numerous professional associations devoted to the practice of call center management, as well as many trade publications and conferences. And, as of 2002, professional certification is also available and becoming more widely recognized.

Summary

The first and most critical step in developing a call center operation is to decide how it will be staffed. Since about three-fourths of call center costs are related to labor costs, this decision is fundamental to the operation of the business. How a business chooses to get people in place to handle its customer interactions will have an impact on every other function within the center. Organizing those personnel into the most effective operating structure will require job task analysis, and decisions must be made on how specialized or generalized the roles will be to ensure all tasks are covered and the staff are assigned the appropriate authority to go with each responsibility.

CHAPTER 5:
HUMAN RESOURCE ADMINISTRATION

Introduction

Once the decision has been made to hire personnel to staff the center (rather than outsourcing), a recruiting and hiring plan must be developed. To get the right people into place requires an effective plan to attract those people, hire them for the right positions, pay them a competitive wage, and train them to be effective on the job. Managing the human resources element of the call center is critical to overall success as this is truly a "people business."

Defining the Job

Developing a call center staffing plan to meet the call center's business goals and vision is a process that involves analyzing the skills required to support the product or service the center provides, and implementing a strategy to recruit, hire, train, and retain staff based on the defined needs. A comprehensive staffing plan begins with a needs assessment, job task analysis, and creation of job descriptions and hiring profiles. Next, a staffing budget is created that includes costs associated with advertising, recruiting/hiring, training, and compensation. Then the process to actively recruit and hire staff begins.

Needs Assessment

Successful call centers allocate adequate time at the beginning of the hiring process to develop a clear understanding of their staffing needs. A needs assessment provides a baseline from which to evaluate the call center's current situation as it relates to where the call center needs to be in the future. It should take into consideration the short-term and long-term staffing requirements for positions to be staffed and what staffing resources are currently available. An effective needs assessment will provide the call center with a clear picture of the types of people and the skills that are needed to accomplish its work.

The needs assessment can be used to identify and target performance issues for current employees and identify if there are ways to avoid these issues during the hiring process. The needs assessment also includes analyzing the current staffing schedules, including the mix of full-time versus part-time staff, to determine possible staffing alternatives (including outsourcing as a potential solution). Another component of the assessment is to investigate current industry trends to forecast future skills and competencies required to remain competitive.

The needs assessment may also identify opportunities for employees to move up in the organization, and procedures that would be required to fill open positions. This step should also examine a succession plan for key employees to move into leadership roles. In centers where there are employees who are eligible for retirement, the needs assessment should track when they are eligible, and who will replace them.

Job Task Analysis

After the needs analysis for the call center has been completed, a job analysis for each call center staffing position will be created utilizing much of the data gathered during the needs assessment process. A job analysis is a process that identifies and determines job duties and requirements and the relative importance of these duties for a given position. It is defined as a process of analyzing the nature or content of a position in order to determine the corresponding job qualifications.

A job analysis generally looks at what the employee needs to accomplish, the activities or behaviors required to perform the job, equipment the employee uses to perform the job, the work environment in which the job is performed, and the job specifications needed to perform the minimum requirements of the position.

Part of the job task analysis will be to define the competencies needed to perform the job. Competencies provide a broad definition of what is meant by a knowledge or skill, and identify the skills and attributes needed to perform the job at mastery level. Defining these competencies is important for two reasons. First, a comprehensive definition of required competencies ensures the call center will get the right staff for the job in the first place. Second, these competencies, along with the behaviors that demonstrate whether or not the person in the position is performing up to expectations or not, are a key component of the performance appraisal process.

A final product of the job task analysis will be detailed job descriptions. These job descriptions add focus to recruitment and selection processes. They can also form the basis of an advertising campaign, be helpful in evaluating whether a full-time or part-time employee is required, and can play a part in evaluating whether a candidate meets or exceeds the guidelines required for each position. Finally, well-written job descriptions can help justify pay decisions, promotions, and disciplinary actions after the employee is hired. Job descriptions should be considered as works in progress since they should be altered in response to the changes that occur in the workplace. Once the job descriptions are finalized, copies should be given to each employee along with a signature form to return to indicate awareness of job expectations.

Recruiting and Hiring

Recruiting reliable, skilled, and qualified employees is a critical function for the call center operation. Advancements in technology and changing customer requirements have placed enormous pressure on the call center to acquire employees who can meet these demanding performance challenges. To meet these challenges, call center management must create a comprehensive recruiting plan to attract qualified candidates. The recruiting plan will identify the methods to be used to attract candidates, the process for screening candidates, and the interview process. The recruiting process should be the job of everyone involved in the call center operation. The recruiting team should include the traditional recruiting staff from human resources and those close to the position being filled, including current employees, supervisors, and call center management staff.

Labor Pools

To determine where to focus recruiting efforts, labor pools are divided into internal and external sources. Internal sources include utilizing promotions and transfers between departments to fill open job requisitions. Internal recruiting helps to cut recruitment costs, and the ramp-up time should be lower since the candidate is already familiar with company policy. Internal recruiting often provides a career path for a potential candidate who would otherwise not have any career advancement opportunities. Finally, internal recruiting helps to keep morale and motivation levels high when employees observe a company "hiring from within."

Just as there are advantages for recruiting from within, the disadvantages include the ripple effect (employee leaves one position which opens up another position in the company to be filled) and the possibility that employees who don't get the job become resentful and leave the company. With internal recruiting, there is no opportunity for outside objectivity and often, the call center may be required to pay a higher salary for the internal candidate than those recruited outside the company.

External recruitment provides an opportunity to introduce new ideas and perspectives into the company. Potential sources of external labor include employee referral, temporary staffing agencies or contractors, college internships, professional associations, public employment services or outplacement programs, retirement agencies, and stay-at-home caregivers. The drawback to using an external recruiting program is that the company may be sending a negative message to the current employees by limiting internal career path opportunities. External recruitment may also increase the cost of recruiting and increase the recruiting cycle to find qualified candidates.

Some of the most popular ways to locate qualified staff outside the company include job fairs, college recruitment, Internet postings, government job placement programs, employee referral programs, and outside recruiters.

Advertising Methods

Once the decision has been made regarding internal or external recruiting, or a combination of both, the recruiting process moves to the marketing stage to advertise open positions. The goal of creating a advertising campaign to attract new staff is to "get the word out" and an important decision will be where and how to advertise open positions.

A successful marketing strategy combines a variety of advertising strategies including:

- Print ads
- Radio and television ads
- Billboards
- Handbills and flyers
- Sporting events
- Local community organizations
- Professional associations

Screening and Interviewing

Once the position has been advertised and the company begins to receive responses, the next step in the process typically begins with the human resources (HR) department and ends in the call center. Once the advertising is complete, and the company has applications to consider, the HR department will generally assist the center to "weed out" unqualified candidates and determine those that best meet the job criteria. The screening process should allow the organization to rank the order of qualified applicants while eliminating those that do not meet the center's minimum requirements.

There are many components that can be included in the initial screening process. The call center may hold an open house to allow candidates to take a look around and perhaps weed themselves out if they don't like the environment or working conditions. The first step in the screening process may be an introductory telephone call, in which the screener can gauge the candidate's voice and overall telephone skills. This telephone screening is essential since it most closely reflects the applicant's ability to communicate over the telephone. Many call centers miss this opportunity by focusing on a written application as the first screening gate, but the smart recruiting team will focus on either live calls or at least a voice mailbox to weed out unsuitable candidates before taking time with a resume/application review.

Screening for potential success in the call center can also be done using an automated IVR process or via an interactive web tool. These web-based and IVR-based tools often use branching technologies to take the candidates down a path of questions that vary depending on the answers given as they go along. Reporting on the results is provided so that the most viable candidates are moved to the next step in the process and those who appear to be a poor match to the center's requirements can be screened out or given lower priority. The IVR format will limit the answers to yes/no or some numeric entry, but more current models using speech recognition can solicit more free-form answers.

To ensure a good fit to the job and the working conditions in a call center, more and more organizations are using performance-based testing. Initial aptitude testing might screen for basic skills that a candidate should possess as well as more advanced capabilities. If agents must be proficient on computers and problem solving, testing these basic skills can help the center to not only identify the right candidates, but also determine which training classes are appropriate for each person. Typically, these kinds of tests can be made available through the Internet or installed on the company's servers for use at the premises.

In addition to aptitude testing, personality profiles are often used in selecting personnel as well. These measure such traits as results-oriented drive, motivation to learn, and sales strengths and weaknesses. There are also psychometric instruments that can be matched to the call center's requirements (including questions about character traits, communications style, stress management, and dealing with conflict), competency tests, behavioral-based interview questions, and tests for cultural fit. These tools can be administered in person or via the web.

As part of the screening and assessment phase, some call centers provide a means for a candidate to "test drive" the call center job through simulation testing. Simulation is used to set up a situation for the prospective agent to work through scenarios that replicate the type of work that the agent will be asked to perform on the job. The idea is not to see how much product knowledge the candidate has, but to see how well the person handles the flow and pressure of the job including focus on customer service, handling anger, solving problems, building relationships, and navigating through the computer and telephone system. The simulation may have the candidate hear caller contact information such as name, address, and phone number and then enter the data as quickly and accurately as possible. Or the candidate may be presented with several sample comments from a customer and asked to select appropriate contextual responses.

Once candidates have passed the initial screening process, the next step is to schedule a face-to-face interview. A structured interview is a formal process with questions that focus on the job responsibilities and competencies. In addition to the telephone interview discussed earlier, interviews are also conducted in person using face-to-face conversation with a single interviewer or a panel of interviewers. Regardless of the type of interview selected, it is critical that the interview tools and process be designed thoughtfully and carefully to ensure the hiring process is effective and to be legally sound. It is important to conduct the interview in a way that puts both parties at ease since this is when initial impressions are formed. To ensure the interview proceeds smoothly, an interview guide should be created for each position.

Since the majority of the interview is based on a question and answer procedure, it is important to remember that asking the wrong questions can result in a poor choice of employees and can be legally troublesome as well. In preparing for the interview process, interview questions should be carefully created to ensure they are related to the job analysis and description, that they probe for job-related skills, and that all interview information is related to job requirements. Any question not related directly to the job may be unlawful if the information obtained is used in a discriminatory manner.

One of the key factors in creating an effective interview guide is to employ the concept of behavior-based interviewing. The purpose of behavior-based interview questions is to determine whether or not the applicant has the knowledge, skills, and attributes necessary to do the job at hand. With the assumption that past actions are the most accurate predictor of future actions, asking a candidate about past behaviors in a particular circumstance will help the interviewer ascertain if the applicant has the ability and motivation to perform certain roles and tasks.

Selection and Hiring

The final part of process is to evaluate the candidates and make a decision on who will be offered a job. All the components of the screening process should be considered, including the applicants' skills and scores on proficiency tests, education level and knowledge, relevant experience, attributes and traits assessed through personality inventories, and motivational fit for the job.

Upon making a decision on the candidates to whom to offer a position, the final step in the selection process is then to check references and background information of those candidates. The goal of this final step is to inquire how the candidate worked and related to supervisors and colleagues, ask questions about the candidate's temperament and attitude, and to probe into the circumstances of the candidate's departure. Assuming that all information checks out satisfactorily, then the final step is to make the offer.

A formal process should be in place to extend an employment offer. The timing of the offer should be immediately following the decision to hire so the candidate isn't lost to another job opening. In making the offer, it's important to sell the candidate on all the benefits of the job, taking care to communicate what might be viewed as a downside to the job as well. In pointing out the latter, it's critical to confirm the candidate understands the company's monitoring policies, performance measurement, and schedule expectations so there are no surprises and resulting turnover several weeks or months into the job. Most job offers are typically made in writing, and should include a description of the position, the rate of pay, starting date, schedule hours, and performance expectations.

Compensation Planning

An important part of creating a call center staffing plan is compensation planning. A compensation plan includes wages, benefits, and any incentives a company may provide to an employee.

There are two legislative acts that affect wages for the call center staff. The first is the Fair Labor Standards Act (FLSA), regulated by the Department of Labor. This act sets the basic minimum wage and overtime pay standards. The second act is the Family and Medical Leave Act (FMLA) which provides for up to 12 weeks of unpaid leave for certain medical and family situations for either the employee or a an eligible employee's immediate family.

Compensation Elements

A call center compensation plan includes the base pay (wages), benefits, and other incentives paid to employees. The compensation philosophy for the call center includes deciding whether to make the base pay competitive with the going rates for other call centers in the area, deciding how to define the pay-scale structure, and deciding what additional benefits or incentives need to be included as part of the compensation plan. Budgetary restraints and the availability of the workforce are factors that also impact the compensation plan, as well as deciding how to compensate employees based on productivity, seniority, and merit.

Most call centers utilize a "pay grade" for each call center position. This pay grade is created by using a low, middle, and high range for each position. The goal is to create an equitable and effective system for setting pay levels based on the jobs that contribute directly as well as indirectly support the call center's mission. The more essential the job is to the mission of the center, the higher its pay range is likely to be.

Further classification of employees divides them into full-time and part-time employees. Full-time employees generally work a full week (37 to 40 hours). Employers are required to pay payroll taxes as required by law and withhold applicable local, state, and federal taxes. Part-time employees generally work less than a full week (20 to 30 hours). Employers are required to pay the same taxes as full-time employees, but on a pro-rated scale. For temporary workers, contract employees, contractors, or outsourcing agencies, the company is not responsible for paying payroll taxes nor benefits since they are not considered employees of the company.

The Equal Pay Act mandates that the same pay must be given to employees for doing the same job -- in terms of skills, effort, working conditions, and responsibilities-- regardless of the employee's gender. The Act does allow employees to receive different pay for the same position based on experience and education, seniority, and productivity.

Incentives

Incentives are considered special rewards that the employer offers employees in addition to their base pay and benefits. These incentives may include sign-on bonuses, stock options, profit sharing, training and education, longevity bonuses, paid family leave, and so on.

To attract and retain desirable employees, many call centers today offer perks such as a fitness center, on-site day care, dry cleaning and valet services, on-site banking, free parking and postal services, to name a few.

The labor market is becoming more competitive and is forcing call centers to develop aggressive recruiting campaigns and creative strategies for compensation, benefits, and work schedules. Each of these factors impact the call center's ability to attract and retain the highest qualified candidates from the availabile talent pool.

To attract the top performers in the tight labor market, the call center needs to offer a benefits package that is more than just competitive. There needs to be a focus on what appeals to today's workforce. Competitive benefits packages may offer:

- Learning environment – The opportunity to learn new skills has become important as employees are looking to learn as much as they can. The best approach to career security is knowledge.

- Performance compensation – Many employees are motivated by rewards for good performance. While some companies offer stock options as rewards, the recent economic downturn has made this incentive less attractive than in previous years. Today, the company's ability to provide profit sharing is a more favorable option.

- Customized benefits – Employees are interested in a cafeteria plan approach for benefits that are not only generous, but highly flexible.

Compensation benchmarks exist that tell the call center recruiting team what the market is willing to pay for certain skill sets. Many companies set their wages based at least partially on reports of competitive market rates reflected in benchmark job studies. Other companies tend to pay employees at the median grade or slightly below it. Compensation information may be found at www.workforce.com, www.hr.com, and www.bls.com. For salary benchmarking, www.salary.com is one source for comparing "grades" of call center representatives.

Training and Development

One crucial component of managing workforce performance is to analyze the training requirements of the call center staff and implement a comprehensive training and development plan. The goal is to develop a training program to increase job satisfaction, improve performance, and maximize each employee's potential.

Training and development have long been recognized as key areas in motivating employees. In these changing times, training and re-training call center staff is a crucial element in an organization's ability to attract, retain, and maximize the performance of its employees. Through staff development programs, employees are provided with opportunities to enhance their current knowledge, skills, and to learn new applications.

The call center management team needs to help senior management understand that to remain competitive in today's evolving call center environment, it's not so much what employees know, but the knowledge and skills they can acquire that will help them to cope with the increasing demands and pressures of the marketplace. Training is a critical component in a company's business strategy in that it should not only take the employees somewhere, but allow the company to go further more easily.

The types of training programs found in the call center as part of the staff development training plan include the new-hire orientation program, the initial training, any ongoing or advanced programs, plus career development.

Orientation

A new agent orientation program should be designed to provide an orientation to the organization, the work environment/work group, the industry, and to the company. The major goal of the new agent orientation program is to make the agent feel welcome and to expedite the agent's integration into the call center team. The program should also be designed to engage the agent from the beginning and to create a positive impression of the call center.

Most call centers focus initial training efforts on the company's products and services. In addition, various types of "soft skills" training may be delivered. For example, a course on problem-solving techniques is excellent for agents who require analytical skills. General customer service training programs would include such topics as conversation control, tips for handling an angry caller, and telephone etiquette. For agents who are in a sales role, topics such as assertive selling might also be included.

As new agents are introduced to the call center, the call center training program needs to spend adequate time discussing the use of the ACD telephone set (or soft phone) since it is crucial for the call center management team to retrieve accurate statistics from the ACD system. If agents do not utilize ACD features correctly, the statistics will be skewed.

One "missing link" in most new agent training programs is a basic frame of reference about the overall operations of the center. The agents need to know how call center performance is measured and why, how overall call center goals translate to individual goals and how performance will be monitored and measured, how staffing levels are determined and what the impact is of just one person being out of place, what technologies are at work to deliver a call to the desktop, and any other useful information that will orient the agent to the call center work environment.

Ongoing Training

Training for the agent shouldn't stop after the new hire orientation and initial training period is completed. Training is an ongoing evolutionary process. The goal of the ongoing agent training program is to provide training for the skills necessary to perform the job, plus training for the skills necessary to enhance performance standards. As a way to gauge their success, a 30-, 60-, and 90-day checklist can be created.

During the first three to six months, the period is classified as "reality." This is the time when the agent has discovered how things really work and has a clear grasp on the job at hand. The next six to nine months is a period of "open exchange." This is the time when the agent has gained skills and can work productively most of the time. Agents also begin to offer suggestions on how their performance can be improved or possible improvements to policies or procedures. The time from nine to twelve months is a period of more productivity. During this time, the agent has been trained to be a productive team member, peers and supervisors expect full participation from the agent, and the agent is rarely referred to as a "new agent."

Since the most logical step for agents to follow is to move into a team lead or supervisory role, it is important to discuss the benefits of having a such a career path in place. A supervisory career path reinforces knowledge, develops skills, and promotes the personal and professional growth essential to the continuous improvement of the call center and for management succession planning. In most call centers, there is a high percentage of supervisors who "came up through the ranks" from agent positions. Most of these team leads or supervisors were promoted to that role because they were excellent agents, they had great customer service skills, and/or were considered the experts in their workgroup or team.

The best way to find the right candidates is no different than the procedure to find new agents. Potential team lead or supervisor candidates should be interviewed for the position. They also should take part in situational role plays and problem solving tests. Another tool that can provide valuable feedback is the use of a 360-degree instrument. With a 360-degree tool, the goal is to gather feedback from subordinates, peers, superiors, and self-evaluation to determine the strengths and weaknesses of the potential candidate.

The role of the team lead or supervisor is to monitor agents and to provide coaching, guidance, and motivation. Additional responsibilities include resource allocation and management, work assignments, agent measurement and evaluation, and to handle escalated customer calls. Other characteristics include an understanding of the organizational structure, processes, and systems, knowledge of the legal aspects of management, administrative and record-keeping skills, the ability to manage individuals and teams, the ability to give and receive feedback, and the ability to manage performance. The supervisor training program should include training related to call center specifics such as customer relationships, people management, and operations management. Customer relationship knowledge includes understanding how to maximize customer relationships, understanding the lifetime customer value, telephone best practices, and email best practices. People management includes knowledge of organizational structure and teams, recruiting, screening, hiring, training and assessment, staff retention, setting performance standards, measuring and analyzing performance, and motivation techniques. Operations management includes knowledge of ACD routing and reports, call center metrics, call center technologies and networks, forecasting and scheduling, staffing alternatives, staffing calculations, and real-time service management.

Additional supervisory topics include general coaching techniques such as monitoring and calibration, coaching and motivation, performance counseling, and performance appraisals. Finally, the supervisory program should include management and leadership topics such as organizational structure, project planning and management, budgets and finance, negotiation, problem solving, team performance, time management, progressive discipline, documentation, diversity, legal issues in the workplace, and effective communications.

Legal Issues

With the increasing number of new workforce regulations and legislation, it is crucial for call center managers and supervisors to be familiar with the wide range of employment and labor laws and how they impact recruiting, hiring, and compensation decisions. Both the call center manager and supervisors should maintain frequent contact with the human resource department and legal counsel and become familiar with the legalities that impact conduct related to the recruiting, screening, and hiring process. It is essential that all call center personnel involved in the hiring and interviewing process become familiar with and be held responsible for adherence to the following regulations.

ADA

Title I and Title V of the Americans with Disabilities Act of 1990 (ADA) – The ADA prohibits employment discrimination against qualified individuals with disabilities in the private sector and in state and local governments. The ADA prohibits discrimination on the basis of disability in all employment practices. It is necessary to understand several important ADA definitions to know whom the law protects and what constitutes illegal discrimination.

- An individual with a disability under the ADA is a person who has a physical or mental impairment that substantially limits one or more major life activities, has a record of the impairment, or is regarded as having the impairment. Major life activities are activities that an average person can perform with little or no difficulty such as walking, seeing, hearing, speaking, learning, and working.

- A qualified employee or applicant with a disability is someone who satisfies skill, experience, education, and other job-related requirements of the position held or desired, and who, with reasonable accommodation, can perform the essential functions of that position.

- Reasonable accommodation may include, but is not limited to, making existing facilities used by employees readily accessible to and usable by persons with disabilities; job restructuring; modification of work schedules; providing additional unpaid leave; reassignment to a vacant position; acquiring or modifying equipment or devices; adjusting or modifying examinations, training materials, or policies; and providing qualified readers or interpreters. Reasonable accommodation may be necessary to apply for a job, to perform job functions, or to enjoy the benefits and privileges of employment that are enjoyed by people without disabilities. An employer is not required to lower production standards to make an accommodation.

- An employer is required to make a reasonable accommodation to a qualified individual with a disability unless doing so would impose an undue hardship on the operation of the business. Undue hardship means an action that requires significant difficulty or expense when considered in relation to factors such as a business size, financial resources, and the nature and structure of its operation.

- Employees and applicants currently engaging in the illegal use of drugs are not protected by the ADA when an employer acts on the basis of such use. Tests for illegal use of drugs are not considered medical examinations and, therefore, are not subject to the ADA's restrictions on medical examinations. Employers may hold individuals who are illegally using drugs and individuals with alcoholism to the same standards of performance as other employees.

ADEA

Age Discrimination in Employment Act of 1967 (ADEA) – This act protects individuals who are 40 years of age or older. The ADEA broad ban against age discrimination specifically includes provisions related to the following items.

- Statements or specifications in job notices or advertisements of age preference and limitations are prohibited. An age limit may only be specified in the rare circumstance where age has been proven to be a bona fide occupational qualification (BFOQ).

- Discrimination on the basis of age by apprenticeship programs, including joint labor-management apprenticeship programs, is prohibited.

- Benefits to older employees cannot be denied. An employer may reduce benefits based on age only if the cost of providing the reduced benefits to older workers is the same as the cost of providing benefits to younger workers.

EEOC

Equal Employment Opportunity Commission (EEOC) – This organization is an independent federal agency that promotes equal opportunity in employment through administrative and judicial enforcement of the federal civil rights laws and through education and technical assistance. To comply with the EEOC, the call center must do the following.

• Post federal and state EEOC notices.

• File an annual form (depending on the size of the company and nature of business) that communicates to the EEOC the demographics of the workforce as it breaks down into specific job categories.

• Keep a copy of all documents (related to job applications, payroll records, discharges, and so on) in the event the company is ever involved with a discrimination suit. Records should be maintained for a period of three years and should include hiring practices, total hires within a particular job classification, and the percentage of minority and female applicants hired.

EPA

Equal Pay Act of 1963 (EPA) – This act protects men and women who perform substantially equal work from sex-based wage discrimination. The Equal Pay Act (EPA) prohibits discrimination on the basis of sex in the payment of wages or benefits, where men and women perform work of similar skill, effort, and responsibility for the same employer under similar working conditions.

• Employers may not reduce wages of either sex to equalize pay between men and women.

• A violation of the EPA may occur where a different wage was/is paid to a person who worked in the same job before or after an employee of the opposite sex.

• A violation may also occur where a labor union causes the employer to violate the law.

FCRA

The Fair Credit Reporting Act (FCRA) – This act is enforced by the Federal Trade Commission. The FCRA is designed to promote accuracy and ensure the privacy of the information used in consumer reports provided by Consumer Reporting Agencies (CRAs). A CRA may not supply information about candidates to prospective employers without the candidate's permission.

Summary

There are many human resource issues to consider in today's call center, including those concerning recruitment, hiring, training, and ongoing personnel administration.

Recruiting reliable, skilled, and qualified employees is a critical function for the call center operation. Advancements in technology and changing customer requirements have placed enormous pressure on the call center to acquire employees who can meet today's performance challenges. To meet these challenges, the call center must create a comprehensive recruiting plan to attract qualified candidates. The recruiting plan will identify the methods to be used to attract candidates, interview and screen individuals, and select the best job candidates.

Training and development of call center staff is critical to their effective assimilation into the workforce as well as maximizing performance in the long run. Careful consideration must be given to the initial orientation process as well as ongoing training and development needs.

Many different labor laws affect the recruitment, screening, hiring, and compensation process. It is critical that today's call center management team be familiar with these laws and guidelines, both to ensure an effective hiring process as well as to protect the call center and the company from legal action.

CHAPTER 6: WORKPLACE DESIGN

Introduction

Once a business has decided to operate its own call center rather than outsource to another company, one of the most critical decisions an organization will make about its call center operation is where to locate. One might even make the analogy of comparing call center site selection with that of choosing a spouse. Although it is possible to change later, that change may be overwhelmingly expensive and terribly unpleasant.

Selecting a home for a call center site is a decision that has grown more complicated with time. Ten years ago, there were relatively few areas of the country that could support the specific needs of a call center and therefore, businesses located their call center operations in the big cities that could provide them with the sophisticated telecommunications infrastructure and labor market they required.

Today, however, businesses can locate a call center almost anywhere. With the widespread availability of labor, development of high-speed digital communications networks in most cities and towns, a soft real-estate market, and advanced call center technologies that make distributed operations a reality, businesses are faced with a mind-numbing array of choices for where to locate their call center operation.

It's important to note here that the call center site selection process is not just for businesses starting a call center or opening an additional call center site. Call center site selection and evaluation is a process that all businesses should consider, since relocation of an existing center has the potential to reduce costs and provide strategic advantages over remaining in an existing site.

Selecting a Site

An example of the cost benefits of relocating an existing 300-person center from an existing location in a major metropolitan area to a new site in a smaller town is illustrated below:

	Existing Site	Alternative Site
Labor Costs		
Number of agents	300	300
Wage & benefits rate	$ 20.40	$ 16.25
Avg annual wage rate	$ 42,432	$ 33,800
Annual labor cost	$ 12,729,600	$ 10,140,000
Labor Savings		**$ 2,589,400**
Turnover Costs		
Estimated turnover rate	25%	20%
Recruiting & training costs/person	$ 2,500	$ 2,000
Annual turnover costs	$ 187,500	$ 120,000
Turnover Savings		**$ 67,500**
Facility Costs		
Square footage	25,000 sq ft	25,000 sq ft
Lease cost per square foot	$ 40	$25
Annual lease costs	$ 1,000,000	$ 625,000
Facility Savings		**$ 375,000**
Economic Incentives		
Training incentive @ $1000/person		$ 300,000
New equipment/technology grant		$ 200,000
Total Incentives		**$ 500,000**
Total Savings and Incentives		**$ 3,531,900**
Relocation Expenses:		
Relocation package		$ 100,000
Severance package		$ 400,000
Recruiting and training		$ 500,000
Moving costs		$ 400,000
New furniture		$ 200,000
Infrastructure modifications		$ 200,000
Total Relocation Costs		**$ 1,800,000**
Net Relocation Savings		**$ 1,731,900**

In this example, the biggest reduction in cost is in labor with over $2.6 million in savings. There are additional savings in terms of potential reduction in turnover and facilities costs in a comparable site in a smaller town with lower occupancy lease rates. In addition, several economic incentives are available to bring total potential savings to over $3.5 million. These savings are offset by the costs that might be incurred in the move, including but not limited to relocation and severance costs for the staff, recruiting and training costs at the new site, costs to move and purchase new furniture and equipment, and changes to be made to the telecommunications and IT infrastructure. But overall, even with these additional expenses, the savings would be $1,731,900 for the first year alone, with additional labor savings to be realized year after year.

Another reason to consider a call center site review and potential relocation in addition to better labor costs has to do with the chance to "start fresh" with the staffing plan. In a new site, creating new profiles for personnel may provide a better basis for recruiting staff that better fit job requirements that have evolved over time. And a new set of schedules may be better able to match the workforce to the workload than schedules "owned" by existing staff that are now less effective from a service and cost perspective. The center must consider the loss of expertise that will result from relocation and new personnel, so the pure cost of training is not the complete picture. Regardless of size, type of center, or existing location, every business should periodically review all the components of its call center operating costs to determine if there are economic benefits to locating its call center elsewhere.

Selection Factors

An organization should use a systematic approach in evaluating the optimal site in which to locate its call center operation. Deciding where to locate the call center will be a process driven by these main business factors:

- Labor
- Community
- Incentives
- Real estate

Labor

The old adage about the three main factors to success in business being "location, location, location" has a different answer when applied to the call center. Given that three-fourths of call center costs are related to staffing, the main factors in selecting a call center site are "labor, labor, labor." Staffing is the main call center resource and therefore weighs in first as the most crucial decision factor about where to locate.

In terms of labor availability, businesses typically look for areas with high unemployment as the major labor factor. But in a call center site selection, organizations must look beyond just employment rates to evaluate the growth of the worker population and availability of specialized skills. And a less obvious factor to consider is the "underemployment" rate – a factor that describes people who have jobs, but are looking for a better position and therefore should be considered in the available labor market.

A critical factor to consider is the labor saturation rate in an area, specifically as it relates to call center jobs. Even if unemployment is high, the area may be already highly saturated with call center jobs meaning little to no availability of the specific labor force needed.

This labor saturation rate is calculated by dividing the number of call center jobs in the area by the number of people in the workforce. For example, if there are 25 call centers in a city with approximately 100 positions in each (2,500 call center jobs) in a city with a total worker population of 125,000 workers, the labor saturation rate would be 2 percent.

Organizations will find that a labor saturation rate of less than 2% will typically yield good results in hiring as well as retention, while rates above 4–5 % will make staffing difficult, as outlined below:

Saturation Rate	Saturation Level	Staffing Indicator
1%	low	excellent potential
2%	mid-range	some competition
3%	above average	average competition
4%	high	competition and turnover
5%	very high	difficult to recruit and retain staff

As organizations move into areas with higher labor saturation rates, the local job market becomes increasingly competitive in terms of attracting and retaining quality staff. More resources will have to be devoted to advertising and recruiting beyond the simple classified ad and word-of-mouth approach, including such promotions as billboards, radio and television advertising, job fairs, and other community activities.

Another contributing factor to labor availability is the type of position and turnover rates typically associated with that type of work. For example, the labor pool for minimally trained workers to do outbound telemarketing or simple order taking may be quite large. Keep in mind, however, that there is much more turnover in some positions than others, so the labor pool may need to be quite a bit larger to support these types of functions. A higher paying technical support position may require higher education levels and therefore have a smaller pool from which to draw. But because of the higher pay and specialized work, turnover may be lower.

Companies should also consider the availability of educational programs in the area that may be available and perhaps funded by government programs. Examples include "Welfare to Work" programs and "Workforce Investment Act" programs. The Workforce Investment Act of 1998 provides the framework for a unique national workforce preparation and employment system designed to meet both the needs of the nation's businesses and the needs of job seekers and those who want to further their careers. Training and employment programs are designed and managed at the local level where the needs of businesses and individuals are best understood.

Labor Sectors

Based upon the specific requirements for the job, many call centers look for sites with access to special labor sectors. Three of these sectors include military spouses, students, and senior workers.

Military Communities

Cities and towns located near an active or soon-to-be-closed military base are good candidates for call center sites. The labor force may include the spouses of current military staff who require a second household income. In addition, there may be a large number of former service personnel there who have settled in the area after active duty, and these disciplined workers are ideal for the structured environment of the call center. Many of these ex-service personnel also have excellent technical training that can be another benefit to the call center.

The military base itself may even be considered as the call center site if it is downsizing or being closed completely. There are typically large, single-story buildings on most bases with excellent telecommunications infrastructure and ample parking. There is also generally plenty of low- to medium-income housing in the nearby area.

Student Communities

Due to the peaks and valleys generally experienced in call center workload, a flexible workforce is needed. Part-time workers are especially effective in helping to match the workforce to the arriving workload. Many businesses find that college students serve as an excellent part-time, well-trained workforce for the call center. They are particularly useful in filling the evening and weekend shifts that the regular workforce may find distasteful. While it is sometimes problematic to work around students' class schedules, many call centers find the effort pays off with an above-average education and high energy level. Some students may view the call center position as a "foot in the door" for other positions in the business once they receive their degree.

Senior Communities

More and more call centers are employing seniors and retirees for either full-time or part-time work. While more computer training may be required than for their younger counterparts, this additional investment is typically worth the effort in terms of having a dependable workforce with fewer incidences of absenteeism, turnover, and performance problems. Businesses are beginning to seek out this worker population in areas of active retirees such as Florida and Arizona in particular.

Community Factors

One of the factors to be considered in determining what region of the country in which to locate is time zone. If the organization has one or more existing call centers, then locating an additional site in another time zone may be beneficial to enable "follow the sun" routing of customer calls. For example, if a call center already exists on the East Coast, locating a second center on the Pacific Coast would enable calls to be handled during regular business hours in the new location that otherwise would require staffing from 5:00pm to 8:00pm at a perhaps higher shift differential in the first site.

Another regional factor to consider is the potential for natural disasters for the area. While no place on earth is completely safe from disasters, it is to be expected that ice and snow storms may cripple Canada and the Northeast United States at times, tornadoes are a probability throughout the Midwest and Southeast states in the spring and summer months, earthquakes plaque the western states, and hurricanes are to be expected along the Gulf Coast from time to time. It should be noted, however, that while certain types of weather-related problems are more common in some places than others, natural disasters can happen anywhere and this should probably be one of the least important factors in the site selection process. Certainly, the risk of not having enough available labor poses a far greater threat to call center operations than Mother Nature.

There are many different factors to consider in choosing a state in which to locate a call center. There can be very large differences from state to state in corporate income tax and property tax rates. Likewise, individual income tax rates vary widely from state to state. Businesses should also consider the stability of the tax rate and the overall fiscal condition of state revenues in deciding to locate a business in a given state. The general work climate of a state must be considered as well. Union organizations are more prevalent in some states, while others have right-to-work laws that make them an attractive home for new business. There is also a wide variance among state unemployment insurance rates and workers' compensation insurance rates and regulations.

There are many factors to consider in evaluating one city versus another. Some of these considerations include:

Telecommunications Infrastructure

One consideration in narrowing choices has to do with the telecommunications infrastructure that exists in a particular city. This consideration alone was a main driving factor just ten years ago as certain cities touted their cutting edge telecommunications capabilities while others were not sophisticated or reliable enough to house a mission-critical call center operation. This gap has narrowed in recent years however, and nearly all first-tier and second-tier cities have ample telecommunications capabilities to serve the typical needs of a call center.

Utilities

Another factor distinguishing one city from another is the cost and reliability of the utility system. Especially for inbound call centers that are at the mercy of the incoming calls from customers, even a short power outage can be extremely damaging to the business. In selecting a site, it is important not just to consider utility costs in the overall cost comparisons, but also to look at electrical power availability and reliability. Many areas of the country experience voltage problems due to insufficient power availability, especially in high-growth areas that have aging generating and transmission capacity.

Accessibility

Ease of access is another decision factor in site selection. A business may wish to consider the various modes of transportation available to go to and from the city of choice. If the call center is to be located in a city other than the corporate headquarters or other call center cities, then company employees may have a need to travel back and forth to the site. Companies should determine what type of airport facilities are available for private flights as well as commercial ones. And even if commercial flights are available, if the city is dominated by one airline, reduced competition may make flight costs to and from the city excessively high.

Cost of Living

Businesses will want to evaluate the cost of living in a city being considered as a potential site since this factor may drive labor rates for existing residents as well as be a determining factor for relocation to the area.

Quality of Life

Quality of life issues may also be an important factor in drawing employees to the area, as well as being a predictor of the demographic of the existing labor force. Factors that are generally associated with quality of life include cost of living, continuing education opportunities, air quality, climate, crime rate, housing market, quality of public schools, sports or arts entertainment options, and so on. There are many "quality of life" indexes available such as www.neighborhoodscout.com, www.bestplaces.net, and www.findyourspot.com. It is important to keep in mind that quality of life components are different for everyone and factors for each demographic group should be considered. For example, a college student may consider access to social activities and entertainment options to be the top factors in determining an optimal job site, while a single mother may consider daycare options in the area a more critical factor.

Public Transportation

Since transportation is an issue for many employees, the availability and quality of public transportation may be a key factor in the decision process. Businesses should look at the availability, routes, rates, and quality of the public transportation system within a city, including subway systems, train systems, bus routes, and commuter services. Businesses may also wish to get a commitment from local transportation officials to add additional routes or stops to coincide with the specific call center site selected if not already on a major route.

International Options

Another alternative that has increased in popularity over the last three to five years has been locating call center operations in other countries.

Canada

Many U.S.-based companies have call centers located in Canada. These organizations enjoy the same time-zone coverage, a highly educated workforce, and a wide variety of language skills compared to call centers located in the States. Wage rates are also very attractive due to a favorable exchange rate, as well as a lower "real wage" rate for comparable skill levels. And long-distance telecommunications costs have dropped dramatically over the past few years, making Canada a much more attractive option for many call centers. Many areas in Canada have aggressively built sophisticated telecommunications infrastructures and developed comprehensive training programs to encourage businesses to locate their call center operations there. Specifically, the provinces of Alberta and New Brunswick have launched strong efforts to attract call center business to their regions.

Europe

Many American organizations opened up call center operations in Europe in the late 1990s. Northern England was the first area for growth, followed soon by Ireland. The Netherlands has also grown substantially as a call center location for American as well as European-based companies due to the central Europe location and the multitude of languages spoken by much of the population there. Germany is also gaining popularity as a call center site with many companies opening call center operations there in the late 1990s and the early part of this century.

Asia Pacific

One of the most popular spots for internal as well as outsourced call center operations in the first few years of the 2000 decade has been in the Asia-Pacific region. India and the Philippines in particular are leading choices as they supply an English-speaking workforce at very low labor rates.

The growth in India has been astounding, from virtually no call centers in 2000 to an anticipated one million agent positions by 2008. Some of the reasons for this astounding growth are:

- India produces two million college graduates annually.

- Unemployment among Indian college graduates is as high as 20%.

- Customer service positions are viewed as careers, not just stepping-stone jobs.

- India's English speaking population is second only in size to the U.S.

- Annual turnover is 18% compared to the current U.S. rate of 42%.

While there is some concern about dialect in these international centers, voice coaches are being utilized heavily to assist the Indian agents in sounding more like Americans. These centers are also becoming more popular for processing other types of contacts, such as email and web chat, where dialect is not an issue.

Caribbean

Another wave of international expansion has been in the Caribbean as off-shore operations have begun to gain momentum in Barbados, Belize, the Dominican Republic, and Jamaica. These sites are becoming more popular due to their lower costs of labor and multi-lingual talents.

There has recently been some political and business backlash to offshore outsourcing. Some businesses have found that their customers were not able to understand the agents in the foreign centers and that the politics of shipping jobs offshore was harming their images. The result has been a stronger focus on selecting quality providers and ensuring cultural training and voice coaching, rather than choosing the lowest cost provider to save the most money.

Some U.S. state governments have put legislation into effect that prohibits the state government call centers from utilizing offshore workers, even if it means paying more for the services within their state. While the offshore provision of back-office tasks such as computer programming continues to grow unabated, phone call handling is a different issue. Time will tell whether this is a passing concern or a quality issue that largely derails the offshore successes of the last few years.

As organizations plan a more global strategy, the same factors that are important in choosing a domestic location should be applied to these sites, too. Companies should look for language capabilities, along with the necessary capabilities to route calls to the person with the required language skill, attractive fully-loaded labor costs, adequate telecommunications and information systems architecture, and government incentives. In addition, companies should carefully evaluate the political stability of the region under consideration and determine the risk associated with having a mission-critical part of the business on foreign soil.

Economic Incentives

Competition for new business to an area is keen, and organizations will be presented with all sorts of attractive options and incentives for locating their call center(s) in a particular city or region. These state and local incentives come in many forms, with tax credits, building assistance, utility subsidies, and training programs being the most commonly provided alternatives.

Tax-based incentives are a popular method of attracting and retaining businesses. Credits, deductions, exemptions, and abatements against the various taxes are offered to qualifying businesses. Credits result in a dollar-for-dollar reduction of tax liability, while deductions are taken from gross income in calculating taxable income. Exemptions and abatements are generally applied against sales and use and property taxes. While income tax credits are created at the state level, sales and use and property tax exemptions and abatements may be applied at the county, municipality, or other local level.

Tax credits are a common incentive offered to new businesses in order to attract them to an area. Almost all locations offer tax incentives of some sort. Each community's taxing and incentive scheme will attract different types of companies based on criteria such as size, type of labor required, capital outlay, business type, ancillary businesses attracted, profitability, online presence, environmental impact, and so on. The key is to determine which tax incentives make the most sense and represent the most savings to the organization.

Another type of incentive program that should not be overlooked is the type of program that encourages businesses to locate in the downtown urban renewal areas in major cities. Businesses locating in these "business renewal blocks," "renaissance zones," "enterprise communities," or "empowerment zones" are often eligible for significant grant money and/or tax incentives for bringing in new business to these impoverished areas. There may be added benefits of locating in these areas as well, in terms of suitable space to convert at a low price.

Real Estate

Another factor that impacts the selection of one city over another has to do with specific real estate options in each city. Real estate decision factors include the availability and functionality of a specific site or facility, location costs, and other site factors.

Facility

A major factor in selecting a call center site is the availability, function, and price of real estate. With a downturn in the economy, many organizations have consolidated operations, downsized, or moved their call centers offshore. The result is increased availability of "plug and play" facilities available at bargain prices. Many of these "plug and play" centers come equipped with all the necessities of a call center operation, sometimes even including the furniture and workstations. These fully equipped centers can be an attractive real estate option.

Another real estate option consists of existing business space that has previously served another function and is now vacated and available as an empty shell. Common examples include grocery stores, movie theatres, warehouses or other unused office space. In terms of price and occupancy speed, this type of space represents the second best alternative if the building can indeed be retrofitted to serve as call center space.

A final option is "build to suit" for call center operations. With plenty of budget dollars to spend, this is the ideal solution as it ensures the workplace is designed around the call center's needs. It is, however, the most expensive of the three options, although these costs may be offset in many areas by local or regional construction subsidies and incentives in order to attract a company's business to the area. Choosing the build-to-suit option also takes the longest amount of lead time to be ready for occupancy, with most centers taking 10-12 months to build from scratch.

Real Estate Costs

One of the most important factors to be considered in evaluating real estate costs is the tradeoff between purchasing a property versus leasing. Net present value calculations (discussed in Chapter 3 of this book) should be performed to look at implications of purchase versus short-term and long-term lease options.

In reviewing purchase of existing property or costs to retrofit an existing building, it is important to take into consideration the potential new construction or refurbishing incentives that may be available from the state or local governments to encourage new business in the area. Another real estate cost to be considered is the potential resale value of the property if the business decides to close or relocate the call center in the future. This resale value is sometimes referred to as "residual value" and should be considered in the valuation of property for the long-term financial impact.

Other Site Factors

There are many other factors to consider in the evaluation of real estate options for the call center site. Some of these other factors include availability and proximity of public transportation, availability of affordable housing in the area, major highway access, visibility of site, parking, and security concerns.

Public Transportation

Public transportation was mentioned earlier as a factor in taking a city into consideration as a call center site. This evaluation of public transportation needs to be made all the way to a specific site level, as a city may have public transportation options but none in the area of the chosen site. It should be determined whether bus or train routes are plentiful in potential employee housing areas, and whether or not routes cover the proposed call center site.

Housing Availability

More than one call center has located in a new affluent business and residential area, only to discover that its potential employees cannot afford to live nearby. It should be determined whether there is housing availability within a reasonable commuting distance of the call center (under 30 minutes and ideally under 20 minutes).

Highway Access and Visibility

The call center site should be located near a major highway system or several major secondary roads to ensure ease of access to the center. Visibility is a factor often not considered, but can be an important one, particularly for recruiting purposes. High visibility along well-traveled routes can be an asset during recruiting with signage and banners easily displayed.

Security and Parking

Two additional concerns in evaluating the feasibility of a site include security and parking. As many call centers employ multiple shifts of workers, safety and security during nights and weekends must be addressed. Also, an overlap in shifts can increase the need for parking facilities beyond a normal business office environment. The density of parking requirements for a call center far exceed the normal office building specification, so be sure to consider the number of individual workstations per floor and check the total space for cars, especially where public transportation is minimal. Some call centers have had to provide valet parking at the site to allow the cars to be stacked three deep in the available space.

Site Selection Steps

Site evaluation and selection is a systematic process. The following steps should be followed in the systematic approach to selecting a call center site:

Step 1 – Assemble a team.

Ideally a project team should be formed that includes individuals from varying locations and positions within the company who have a practical and strategic understanding of company objectives. This site selection team typically includes representatives from human resources, IT/telecommunications, accounting/finance, facilities/engineering, legal, and senior management.

If an organization is looking for a site to house fewer than fifty employees, then the call center site selection may be a relatively simple process. But if the size goes much above these numbers, the site and property choices become much more complex, and the specialized expertise will either have to be developed in-house or brought in by outside experts. Many firms specialize in site selection with some narrowing their focus of their business to concentrate on the specific requirements and factors associated with locating call center operations.

Site selection consultants can add tremendous value in providing advice on how to structure the selection process. While the team may consist of all the appropriate departments, it is likely that the group has never conducted a site search before. A consultant can help provide structure for the process and improve the team's effectiveness at reaching a decision. A consultant can provide an extra hand in any particular stage of the project if team members become sidetracked with other business issues so the program can stay on track. An outside specialist can be invaluable in providing a necessary neutral perspective to help the team focus on business issues, perform time-consuming research, and assist in identifying and narrowing down options. And a major reason to use a selection consultant is to provide an unbiased third-party opinion during the final selection process.

Other partners not to be overlooked in the site selection process are the economic development agencies (EDAs) that can assist with providing local resources and information related to opening a new business in the area. These agencies are tasked with bringing new business to their communities and are therefore anxious to work with organizations that may bring high-tech, white-collar jobs to the area. These agencies can provide information that may be difficult or time-consuming to obtain otherwise, such as contact information for other call centers in the region, local wage rates, turnover rates, and government incentive packages for the area.

Step 2 – Define and prioritize requirements.

It is critical at the beginning of the process to define requirements for each of the factors outlined previously. For example, outline labor requirements in terms of knowledge and technical/language skills, as well as desirable experience. Labor requirements should also outline the specific job tasks, as well as shifts and hours of operation. Prioritize requirements in terms of the tradeoffs between costs and the ideal workforce and site. This list of requirements should consist of a "must have" set of requirements as well as a "nice to have" list.

Step 3 – Select qualified sites.

Narrow the search to a "short list" of sites that meet business qualifications in terms of "must have" criteria for labor, community, real estate, and other management considerations. The sites on this list will then be further evaluated in terms of final decision criteria.

Step 4 – Evaluate sites with detailed selection criteria.

Evaluate final sites based on weighted selection criteria. Consider additional selection criteria (such as transportation, growth of workforce, tax incentives, training programs, etc.) and weight them in order of their importance to the decision and then score each site based on this criteria.

Step 5 – Visit final candidates.

It is important to visit the final candidate sites in person before making a decision. Members of the team should interview local personnel and partners to confirm information about each site and make a final decision.

Facility Design Concepts

Once a site has been selected, the next step in creating a functional workplace is designing the facility itself. Thoughtful consideration of a workplace design has the potential to have a lasting impact on call center performance and success. There are essentially two components of a workplace design: the exterior or type of building and design of the interior or call center workspace.

Building Options

It is important to understand first what the basic requirements are for call center space and how they differ from a regular office environment. While like back office environments in some respects, call centers typically have a higher density than other parts of the business. It is common for call centers to have as many as seven persons or agent workstations per 1,000 square feet of space. This 7:1 ratio can be compared to a 4:1 ratio for general administration or marketing tasks.

A preferable design for a call center is to have the operation on a single floor. This allows a more functional layout where supervisors and managers can better see the operation. For all centers that perform several different functions such as technical support, outbound sales, and customer service, a multi-story building can be suitable.

There are five different types of buildings in which a business can locate a call center:

- Vacated call center
- Conversion space
- Conventional multi-story building
- Developer's "spec" building
- Custom-designed building

If speed of occupancy is a consideration, then the options above are listed in order of fastest to slowest occupancy. If an organization's needs are compatible with the conditions in a vacated call center, occupancy can occur right away. Construction of a new build-to-suit space takes the most time.

Vacated Call Center

Call centers open and close for a variety of reasons. Some may vacate space due to a merger or acquisition, an increase or decrease in client base, or a relocation for a host of other reasons. As a result, there are vacated call centers in a large number of cities and some of these can be a very cost-effective and quick way to get a new operation up and running. The biggest advantages of moving into a vacated call center are speed of move-in and cost. Many are capable of being occupied immediately with few renovations necessary. Sometimes the previous tenant will even make available the ACD equipment and workstations, which can further cut down on occupancy time and costs. If taking advantage of pre-existing equipment, a thorough needs assessment should be performed to determine what additions, changes, or upgrades may be needed for the equipment to function as needed for the new call center operation.

Conversion Space

Vacated "big box" space may be a good solution for some centers. Wide-open spaces left by previous factories or warehouses are good examples, along with the somewhat smaller but also functional vacated grocery, discount store, or movie theatre space. These "big box" renovations are popular for adaptation to call center use. Some of these buildings may require only minor modifications to retrofit due to their high ceilings and large structural bay size. Others however will require a significant investment in heating, ventilation, power, and lighting.

Advantages of previous retail space include ample parking, which is another consideration for call center use since the density of staff in a call center space is much higher than a typical office environment. Most people in the area will know where they are (the old WalMart building or the Bijou Movie Theatre versus one of a hundred buildings in an office park complex). And these sites are typically near many amenities like child-care facilities, shopping, restaurants, as well as major public transportation routes.

Factory and warehouse conversions typically don't provide the easy access and nearby amenities of the vacated retail space but they have a number of benefits of their own. Most are plain and faceless and can be adapted easily to adopt the corporate look. They also tend to have robust power and telephone connections. And many EDAs will offer incentives for businesses to refurbish these types of buildings so they don't become eyesores in the community, so costs can be very attractive.

Conventional Office Space

Conventional, multi-story office buildings are generally not as good of a location due to "tenant compatibility" issues and the mechanical and electrical system capacity necessary for call center operations. For example, most buildings have air conditioning capacity of 350-sq.ft/ton, while call centers may require 250-sq ft/ton because of the technology and the high density of workers. These buildings also may not have the voice and data communications infrastructure required for the intense levels of communications in a call center operation. Additional power quantity may also be required, along with expanding lighting requirements. This type of space is likely to be more suitable for a smaller call center operation (under 100 seats) than a larger one. Sometimes the cost to renovate such space makes this type of space a poor alternative.

Developer Spec Building

Many developers are now building spec office buildings that are adaptable to call center use. Some understand better than others the unique requirements of building to house a call center operation and there are several architectural and engineering firms now specializing in new call center construction.

Custom Designed Building

Many companies are finding that the best alternative is to design and build a new, custom-designed building built specifically to house their unique call center business. While this option generally takes the longest, there are an increasing number of specialty project teams of developers, architects, engineers, and contractors that specialize in "fast track" call center delivery.

Workplace Design

Once the type of building has been decided, the next task at hand is to design the interior space and workstations. Considerable research has been done on the relationship between human performance and workplace design that indicates how an effective interior and workstation design can have measurable results on performance. This is particularly true within the call center due to their high-density, high-stress, and technically complex work environment.

Configuration and Space

To determine how much floor space is needed, one rule of thumb used in call center planning is to allocate between 100 and 150 square feet for each call center employee. This estimate takes into account the actual workstation space requirements of each employee as well as common space such as walkways, conference and break rooms, training rooms, support position workspace, and supervisory and management offices. The actual space associated with the agent workstation varies widely from one call center to another depending upon the function of the call center and available, affordable space. Some agent workstations are as small as 25-30 square feet, while others are as large as 100 square feet or more. Typically, agents with pure order taking or other simple responsibilities will require less space and 40–50 square feet may suffice. As their responsibilities grow, so might their workspace. And agents working in a technical support desk operation where manuals and other resources are needed may need 70–80 square feet as a minimum.

One of the factors to be considered in the setup of the call center is its position in relation to other departments and public areas. It should be determined which other departments in the company are likely to have the most interaction with the call center and what their physical space relationship should be. If the call center is linked closely to the fulfillment area, product development, or another department, careful attention should be given to ease of access to these departments if contact is typically done in person rather than electronically.

The call center should also consider what other supporting space will be needed within the call center area itself. For example, some call centers have training rooms within the call center space, while others utilize corporate training rooms that may be nearby or in another area of the building. The call center should also consider how many conference rooms are needed, as well as the number and location of copy rooms and/or filing areas. And of course, access to break rooms, restroom facilities, and cafeteria should be carefully planned to minimize the time spent traveling back and forth to these facilities.

The other space configuration has to do with the physical configuration of the agent workstations. A cluster arrangement (also called pinwheel, hub-and-spoke, and pod arrangement) is made up of four to eight work areas facing a middle core. This arrangement is most beneficial when many workstations need to be accommodated in limited space. Cluster arrangements can save anywhere from 10–25% of call center floor space and make it easier to walk around and through the call center. The drawback to the cluster workstation is limited workspace for the agent and lack of privacy.

The rectilinear or panel workstation is a good choice for call centers that require more workspace for the agent. These modular units can accommodate additional storage cabinets as well as a larger desktop area. They typically have more flexibility in panel heights between workstations as well as individual desk heights and their modular design provides the most flexibility as workstations and groups need to be moved or rearranged. And recent design enhancements have added curved and zig-zag arrangements to the standard rectangular rows to make them more aesthetically pleasing.

The free-standing workstation is less common in call center facilities. These single workstations can be configured in any way the call center desires. They are popular with staff as more personalized arrangements, but are typically more expensive and take up more space than either the cluster or rectilinear products.

Some of the most important considerations when evaluating workstations include ease of installation and reconfiguration, ease of equipment connection that minimizes impact on desk space, and the capabilities of a local dealer for ongoing support and assistance.

Lighting

One of the health problems associated with call center work is related to visual problems and eyestrain caused by lighting that does not respond to the unique requirements of video display terminals (VDTs). Call center environments require two separate, but complementary lighting systems, including uniform ambient lighting for VDTs and task lighting for other paperwork at the desktop.

According to architectural studies, the light needed for comfortable viewing at a computer terminal is about half the level needed for hard copy reading and writing. So separate task lighting for any work off the computer will be required. The best ambient lighting system to satisfy VDT design criteria is indirect lighting. Indirect lighting not only eliminates glare, but also produces a comfortable, calming level of lighting throughout the space. Task lighting, either fixed or movable, can be designed for specific work surfaces where hard copy work occurs. Task lighting should be designed with the objective of keeping the "contrast ratio" between the various work surfaces as low as possible. Otherwise, excessive eye movement between tasks will cause eyestrain. There are also studies that suggest "full spectrum" lighting has a significant impact on mood. While more expensive than standard fluorescent bulbs, it can have a payback in lower absenteeism and high job satisfaction levels.

Acoustics

Many call centers have an open office environment that facilitates ease and speed of implementation, flexibility of moves, and visibility of the call center floor. But this open workspace can be a problem for the call center staff in terms of noise from many different sources – co-workers on calls, nearby conversations, and noise from computers, printers, ventilation systems, and so on.

It is important in call center design to determine the level of privacy required for typical customer transactions as well as supervisory and managerial functions and to plan the call center acoustics carefully to accomplish these privacy levels. In a typical call center where privacy is needed, the average distance between agents is 12 to 13 feet. Acoustic privacy can be accomplished by a configuration of carpeting, partial height screens, and highly absorptive ceilings and walls. This privacy can be further enhanced by a technology called noise masking, where sound is provided by a specially designed random noise generator and a series of speakers installed throughout the ceiling structure in the call center and surrounding space. Such noise-masking systems have been shown to cut distracting noise by more than half.

Flooring and Cabling

Flooring and cabling design in a call center is critical because it affects power supply, heating and cooling, voice and data lines, and ventilation. The flooring design will also affect the call center's overall appearance and the flexibility to change workstation layout in the future.

There are two primary ways of accomplishing cabling in the call center. The first is to run telecommunications and HVAC cabling through ducts in the ceiling and then drop the wires down to the call center in columns or poles. The other approach is to have two levels of flooring and run the cabling between the two. This raised-access flooring houses cabling underneath walkway areas to connect to workstations. In a raised access floor environment, the access area houses modular cabling and environmental air running underneath the floor. Advantages of this flooring include enhanced flexibility for moves and changes, better air quality, higher comfort and control, and potential environmental tax incentives. The raised access floors are more expensive, but the panels can be removed if the call center relocates. They are therefore an asset like furniture and can be depreciated which helps to offset the higher cost of this solution.

Monitors

Not just aesthetically pleasing, flat panel monitors have been proven to result in overall lower costs if considered holistically in terms of space used in the high-density call center workplace. They are becoming increasingly affordable and provide a high-tech look to the center. These flat panel monitors can shrink workstation size by 10 to 20 percent in some cases, are more energy efficient, and require less wiring than traditional cathode ray terminals (CRTs).

Further space can be saved at the desktop if split-PCs are used. In a split-PC environment, the central processing unit (CPU) resides in a computer room, connected to the keyboard and monitor that resides at the desktop. The benefits of a split-PC arrangement are less wiring and installation cost. They reduce air conditioning requirements on the call center floor from the CPUs and wiring, and consolidate the cooling needs into a centrally-located computer room. Also, when upgrades are needed, the IT staff can perform the upgrades in one room instead of going workstation to workstation. Viruses and maintenance problems are likewise minimized by preventing the agents from loading extraneous software onto the machines. Another benefit is the reduction in vandalism and theft by having the computing units behind the secured doors of a computer room. The drawback is that agents cannot access the systems to load a diskette or CD if this capability is needed.

Call Center Ergonomics

Ergonomics is defined as the relationship between a worker and his/her work environment. It's the science of fitting the job to the worker. And while some may view ergonomics as a passing phase, it is actually an important issue that is gaining more attention in the workplace and in the legislature.

According to the Bureau of Labor and Statistics, in 1981 there were 23,000 cases of job related injuries caused by "repeat traumas" or "repetitive motion injuries" such as carpel tunnel syndrome. In the past twenty years, that number has increased to over 350,000 per year – a 1400% increase. This huge increase is due to increased computer usage in the workplace and the call center environment specifically.

The Occupational Safety and Health Administration (OSHA) estimates that employers in the United States today spend over $120 billion in direct and indirect costs related to poor ergonomics. It is estimated that an average carpel tunnel syndrome case (the most common ergonomic related injury) requiring surgery costs about $35,000. And approximately one-third of repetitive motion injuries reported are from call center employees.

There are many costs directly attributable to poor ergonomics. Some of these costs include higher insurance premiums, medical treatments, (therapy, medication, surgery), OSHA fines, legal fees, claims, administrative costs, and workers' compensation benefits. In addition, there are also several non-quantifiable, indirect costs associated with poor ergonomics. They include higher employee turnover, higher absenteeism and associated labor costs, production loss, personnel replacement, lost benefits, and more.

Designing a call center to prevent and minimize computer-related injuries should be a primary concern of any business. Good ergonomics is simply good economics. The cost of even a single injury claim can far exceed the price of ergonomic enhancements for an entire call center, so an early proactive stance to prevent work-related injuries can save substantial dollars by preventing even a single occurrence. In addition to viewing ergonomics as a cost-preventive measure, companies should also view the positive side of an ergonomically correct workplace. There are many studies that show positive benefits of good ergonomics.

According to interior design studies, the components of an ergonomically sound workplace include an adjustable chair, adjustable keyboard, wrist rest, adjustable monitor, headsets, and other items such as footrests, glare screens, and document holders. All these assist in supporting good ergonomics and can pay for themselves many times over in terms of comfort and productivity.

It is important to remember that just purchasing the ergonomically correct equipment does not guarantee benefits. It is important to train the staff how to use the equipment properly and how to practice ergonomically correct work behaviors on an ongoing basis.

Workplace Assessments

While many call centers regularly assess their technology and tools to ensure their effectiveness in maximizing staff productivity, less attention is given to the effectiveness of the workplace design. Studies indicate that, on average, most call center environments have not undergone any significant workplace design and review in the past five years. Most call centers report that even though the work has changed, the workplace has not changed to adapt to it.

Regular workplace assessments are recommended to ensure productivity is being maximized through the integration of people with the tools and the environment in which they work. These assessments are techniques for looking at specific facilities issues to determine the environmental impact on a variety of organizational and personnel performance factors. This information will indicate whether or not the facility is working as intended in the building program. These evaluations can also be used to help make policy and planning decisions, assist in the appraisal of furniture standards and products, and to determine the level of employee satisfaction with the physical environment. The data can provide insight into employee attitudes, values, and behaviors. Spatial characteristics that are relevant to attracting and retaining personnel can also be uncovered.

It is recommended that a workplace assessment of a call center workspace be undertaken at least every other year. Areas to be evaluated include:

• Ambient climate – noise, lighting, thermal conditions

• Spatial characteristics – workplace and workstations

• Physical consequences – injuries and stress

• Ergonomic workplace – empowering people and productivity

The purpose of this evaluation is to assess, in quantitative and qualitative terms, precisely how each aspect of the facility is performing, as well as how it is perceived to be impacting the work tasks, job performance, job satisfaction, and environmental satisfaction of the occupants. A workplace assessment should also include an analysis of building support services, communications pathways, conference and communal areas, distractions and interruptions, furniture and workstation suitability, security, and safety.

Parallel with these areas of investigation, surveys should incorporate issues of job performance, quality of work, group dynamics, compensation, supervision, and stress management, so a correlation can be drawn between these work climate issues and the physical environment.

Finally, these workplace assessments should regularly take place to ensure that all workplace related regulations are being met. The two regulations most closely associated with the workplace are Occupational Safety and Health Administration (OSHA) regulations and the Americans with Disabilities Act (ADA) regulations.

Summary

Selection of the optimal call center site is critical to the success of the operation. There are many choices of city and building types to consider, and many incentives from governments and local community development organizations that can impact the financial picture. Once the site has been selected, careful consideration of space layout, furnishings, lighting, and ergonomics are next. Initial workplace design and ongoing audits are essential to assess regulatory compliance as well as to ensure that call center employees are reaching their potential in terms of both productivity and satisfaction.

CHAPTER 7: TECHNOLOGY MANAGEMENT

Introduction

The modern call center invests more in technology per employee than most other departments within a company. These technologies are used to receive and generate inbound and outbound calls and faxes, process emails and web contacts, and manage the center overall.

This chapter will define the more common call center technologies and the roles they play. Examples of end-to-end handling of contacts are used to demonstrate the interaction of the systems involved in the process throughout the customer interaction. These examples are built on the telephone network and technologies available in North America, but are very similar throughout the world.

For most call centers, the bulk of the interactions are over the telephone. While other types of interactions such as email and web chat are making their way into the mix, the volume of these is still low compared to telephone contacts. The pressing need for human interaction for most contacts demands that most of this contact be done over the phone or in person.

There are efficiencies to be gained for the company in moving calls to lower cost interaction methods such as integrated voice response (IVR) or web-based interactions like emails, but not all customers are willing or able to use these tools. Self-service also reduces the company's chance to form a relationship with the customer and develop the up-sell or cross-sell opportunity, potentially resulting in reduced net revenues even while it saves expenses. So selecting and utilizing the right technologies is a key component to call center success.

The Telephone Network

Calls generally start by a customer dialing a company's telephone number and being placed into the telephone network often referred to as the Public Switched Telephone Network or PSTN. When the call reaches the call center site, it is generally received in a private switching system at the site. These switching systems distribute the calls, queue them as needed, and provide announcements and reports for management. A wide variety of peripheral equipment can be added to enhance the interaction, to automate routine processes, and to give management the information needed to improve performance.

More contacts are moving to the web, and this chapter also explores the way that an email or web chat can be delivered to the center, too. While calls are not going away anytime soon, the volume of web-based transactions is growing and centers must be prepared to handle these demands.

The telephone call generated by a caller to the call center can be handled in three primary ways. The call can be a:

- Local call where the caller and company are in the same town or calling area where 7-digit dialing is appropriate

- Long-distance call where the caller pays for the call and dials the 10-digit number of the company

- Toll-free long distance call where the caller dials a special 10-digit number and the receiving company pays for the call

When the call is a local call, the entire transmission is handled by the local telephone service provider (such as BellSouth, GTE, Verizon, etc.). This local exchange company is referred to as the LEC. When it is a long-distance call paid for by the caller, the call travels over facilities of the caller's long-distance provider (such as AT&T, MCI, Sprint, etc.) These long-distance carriers are referred to as the InterExchange Carriers or IXCs. In the case where callers are dialing a toll-free number, it is free to them, but the cost is paid by the receiving call center instead. The IXC designated by the receiving call center handles these calls.

Toll-Free Services

One of the most commonly used network services in call centers is toll-free service. Toll-free is a bit of a misnomer because someone is paying for the call. The caller is dialing a special number that means they will not pay, but the receiving company will be charged. This is sometimes referred to as 800-Service because the area code for toll-free calls was 800 for many years. However, since all of the 800 number choices have been depleted, more area codes have been designated for toll-free calling, including 877, 866, and others. This special numbering plan makes it easy for the public to know when they are dialing a call they will pay for or not, and easy for the LEC switch to recognize a call that is to be handed off based on receiver preference of carrier rather than caller preference.

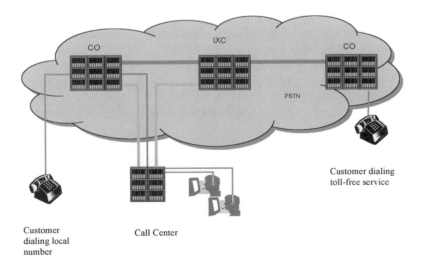

Customer
dialing local
number

Call Center

Customer dialing
toll-free service

The diagram shows the call from the customer on the right dialing an 800 number and passing through the network to the receiving call center. The Number Portability Database is a central file that is administered by a third-party that contains all of the toll-free numbers and the carriers that should be used to route the call. The LEC Central Office (CO) queries this database when an 800 number call is dialed to determine which of the IXCs should receive the call for transport. As the call is passed from the IXC to the receiving LEC, the 800 number will be translated into the local phone number of the center. The caller on the left in the diagram is dialing a local telephone number to reach the call center and is handled entirely within the LEC.

Many features have been developed for toll-free service customers. These include providing the receiving party with information on the dialed number (Dialed Number Identification Service or DNIS) or dialing number (Automatic Number Identification or ANI), the allocation of calls among multiple sites, routing based on time-of-day or day-of-week, and even network-based menus and voice response technologies. More sophisticated network-based intelligent routing technologies have also been added to utilize customer data from the company database, as well as other complex rules to route calls to certain sites or representatives. All of these features are selected and paid for by the receiving company.

Internet Services

No discussion of the routing of contacts to the center would be complete without a mention of the Internet or the web. The Internet has grown to immense proportions and continues at an exponential rate. Nearly every major enterprise has a web site on the World Wide Web today, and many individuals do, too. It has provided another whole method of communications and call centers are embracing this new media to survive.

The network of the Internet is similar to the telephone network in that there are local providers and interconnecting carriers. The local providers are referred to as Internet Service Providers (ISPs). They provide the link between a single computer, Local Area Network (LAN), or Wide Area Network (WAN) and the rest of the Internet. This is the media over which emails are sent and web chats are handled. The process parallels the telephone network in some ways and is quite different in others. Connection to the ISP by a single computer can be done via a dial-up modem transmission that is essentially a phone call, or via a dedicated circuit.

Voice over Internet Protocol (VoIP) is developing at a steady rate and allows voice calls to be integrated with data transmissions over the Internet. This is done by converting the transmission of the voice from its initial analog form into a digital form that follows the Internet Protocol.

Automatic Call Distribution (ACD)

The primary on-site telephone switching technology used by call centers is called the automatic call distributor or ACD. Once the call has traveled through the network to reach the call center's site, the ACD is the system that typically is the point of entry. The role of the ACD is to receive the call, connect it to an agent in the center, provide queuing and announcements when agents are not available, and provide management reports.

One of the most critical roles of the ACD is to distribute the workload equally to a group of people. This ensures that the callers wait the shortest time possible and a fair workload is distributed to the frontline employees.

The ACD capability can be provided in a four different ways. All have all of the basic components shown in the diagram below.

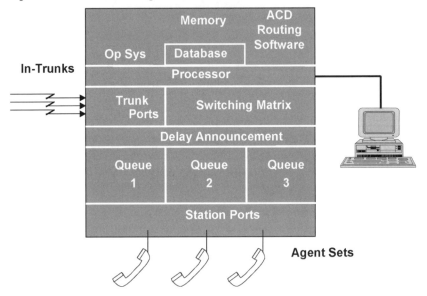

PBX-Based ACD

A private branch exchange (PBX) is the basic telephone switching system used to serve companies with more than approximately 30 telephones. (Small companies can be served by a key system that is less sophisticated and less expensive than a PBX.) Rather than every person in the company having a direct connection to the public telephone network, the PBX serves as a concentrator and supports intra-office connections. It allows calls into the system via a switchboard position where an operator answers the main telephone number, or directly to specific extension telephones via a local service offering called direct inward dialing or DID. Outbound calling is generally accessed by dialing the digit "9" first (and generally a second dial tone is heard) to connect the phone to a pool of outgoing circuits connected to the public network. Calls from one phone to another are handled by dialing just the extension number, which can be anything from 3 to 7 digits depending upon the size of the system.

This basic telephone system does not typically include the special software and hardware needed to provide the ACD functions of queuing, announcements, and reporting. This package can be added to the PBX as an upgrade and may be provided in various levels of functionality for different prices. Typical suppliers of PBX technology in North America include Avaya, Nortel, Siemens, Mitel, NEC, and a host of smaller providers.

Central Office ACD

It is possible to rent local switching services from the local telephone company rather than having a hardware platform on-site such as the PBX described above. In this case, the LEC partitions its local central office technology and assigns a segment and group of telephone numbers for a company's private use. In many places this service is called Centrex, although each LEC may have a unique marketing name in their area. With Centrex, the incoming call from the public network is connected from the public portion of the Central Office (CO) to the private portion served by the Centrex without leaving the building. At that point, the call is essentially processed in the same way as the PBX would do. Operator services, direct extension calling, pooled outbound circuits, and intra-company dialing work the same way, but the activities take place in the system at the CO instead of on-site. The connection between the CO building and the company's premise is a large quantity of connections that connect each telephone at the site directly to the CO. So a call between two phones a few feet apart will travel all the way to the telephone company CO and back again.

ACD capabilities can be offered as a feature of the Centrex in much the same way that they are with the PBX. A special software/hardware package is acquired for the Centrex that adds the queuing, reporting, etc. This is also rented rather than purchased in most cases. Some LECs also offer on-premise ACD systems that interconnect with the Centrex system, but these are essentially stand-alone ACDs as described below.

Stand-Alone ACD

The stand-alone ACD is really a specialized version of the PBX. It is a switching system that has been built specifically for the call center application. It can still provide basic dial tone, pooling of circuits, etc, but it focuses its capabilities on those needed in the call center over basic telephony needed by most office workers. These include the sophisticated call routing, queuing, announcements, reporting, and interface to a myriad of other systems that will be discussed later in this section.

The telephone set options for the system are designed for the call center agent with alphanumeric displays and headset jacks, and with buttons and features to minimize call-handling time. These sophisticated telephones are very useful in the call center, but typically too expensive for other applications. The power of the processing system and the capacity for traffic throughput on a stand-alone ACD is often greater than a PBX with the same number of phone stations. The intense needs of the call center are much higher per station than a typical phone system is built to serve.

It is not uncommon to see both the PBX and stand-alone ACD co-exist in a single company. The PBX may serve the basic telephony needs of the office workers and the ACD serves the call center. The two are generally tied together with circuits that allow calls to be transferred to support intra-company communications.

Server-Based ACD

With the functions of a telephone system and ACD largely driven by computers and software, a new kind of offering has developed in recent years. This is ACD software that largely resides on a standard data server rather than on proprietary hardware, as is typically the case with the PBX and stand-alone ACD. Some of these are taking advantage of the emergence of the VoIP capabilities on the Internet to connect widely dispersed personnel who may work at home or in offices around the country and globe.

Some of the PBX-based ACD offerings are now provided via an attached server function rather than housed in the same hardware platform as the PBX. This allows this functionality to be off-loaded from the processors handling basic telephony and concentrated in a system sized to meet the specific call center's needs.

One of the things that differentiate these offerings from those mentioned above is that the server can also house fully integrated capabilities for voice response, quality monitoring, workforce management, and a variety of other functions. Since integration of these devices from multiple manufacturers can often be difficult and expensive, accessing these functions in a single system offering can be quite attractive. While each type of system may not be "best of class," the aggregate whole will generally meet the needs of many customers, and possibly at a lower cost than buying each of the systems separately and tying them together.

Features and Functions

The basic features of the ACD are designed to automatically answer calls and place them in the order defined by the programmed rules, distribute the calls to the staff, and provide reports to manage the operation. Generally, that means the first call in is the first call handled and workload is distributed equally among the staff.

The advent of skill-based routing (SBR) has changed that basic assumption for some centers. SBR assumes that calls will be sorted into specific types based on the needs of the caller and then matched up to the staff in the center who can best handle them. Calls can be queued for more than one group of staff who can handle the calls and agents can be logged into more than one queue allowing them to handle several call types.

Various priorities can also be set. One priority setting ranks callers against other callers and is used to ensure priority callers receive special service. When agent skills are given different priorities, the result is that if several calls are in queue when the agent becomes idle, the next call handled by that agent will be the one with the highest ranking for that agent, generally the one they handle best.

When all agents are busy, the ACD places the call into a queue. Generally, a recorded announcement is played that tells callers their call has been placed in queue, and more sophisticated systems can include a prediction of how long each caller may wait in the queue. While the caller is in the queue, there is generally music or some kind of continuous message, interrupted at pre-set intervals with additional announcements about the queue state.

A wide variety of features are also available to help the agent process the call. These include such things as an alpha-numeric displays that tell the agent what greeting is appropriate for a particular call, buttons that allow the agent to enter different work states that are recorded in the reporting tools, codes that can be dialed to indicate what the caller requested, and buttons to summon a supervisor for assistance on a difficult call.

Supervisory features allow the supervisor to silently monitor both sides of a call so that neither party knows the call is being observed. This capability is used to monitor the quality of the work in the center and aid in identifying training needs.

Reporting Packages

There are two primary types of reporting capabilities available with the ACD. One provides historical data and the other real-time snapshots. The historical data can provide information on call handling, agent performance, volumes, and services levels over the last half-hour, day, shift, week, or longer. There are hundreds of standard reports offered by the vendors and customized reports can be provided, generally with an export of the data to a software package designed for customizing reports such as Crystal Reports.

The real-time data is generally provided on a color-coded computer screen and allows "corner of the eye" management. Supervisors can monitor how long an agent has been on a call or in a work status, what the speed of answer is, how long callers are waiting in queue, and a wealth of other data that helps them keep their finger on the pulse of the center.

In addition to the standard reporting packages that come with the ACD from the manufacturer, there are also third-party reporting tools. These include wall-display boards and TV monitors that provide the current queue status, service level information, and other customized messages for all in the center to see. These can keep the staff and supervisors informed and serve as a quick communications tool when updated information needs to be passed to everyone quickly. Other tools can also provide the same kind of data on a line on the agent's monitor.

Multi-Site Options

There are many companies who have call center operations in more than one site. They can serve these dispersed operations in a number of ways. These options are separate ACDs with no connection, separate ACDs in a network, or dispersed hardware of a single ACD.

When the call centers do something totally different, such as answering sales calls in one and technical support calls in another, separate ACDs can be a reasonable option. When the teams share a workload of calls, then networking becomes a good solution. Networking options vary from quite rudimentary to highly sophisticated depending on the management style and operational needs of the company. Linking multiple ACDs can also be done with third-party supplied systems managing the interflow. These systems are particularly useful if the ACDs to be networked are not all from the same manufacturer and the third-party system acts as an interpreter of the proprietary languages each uses.

In some cases, the hardware of a single ACD system can be separated to serve the multiple sites. The dispersed hardware is linked together with a proprietary network protocol that emulates the wiring inside the cabinets of equipment, just stretched out over long distances. This allows the entire company to have a single system image with easy call transfers, centralized reporting, and easier administration than multiple systems.

ACD Trends

Call centers are growing and changing very fast. New features and technologies are announced almost daily. Some of the trends over the last couple of years are fully digitized operations and integration of VoIP technologies to allow full utilization of the Internet.

Integration of the ACD with a variety of other technologies in the call center continues to expand. The ACD can be linked to a quality monitoring system to allow access to tap into the agent phone for recording the conversation. A workforce management system looks to the ACD for both real-time and historical data to update forecasting and performance data. Email management systems connect to the ACD to distribute work on a blended basis to the agents. Time clocks are linked to the ACD so when an agent logs into the ACD for work, it updates the time clock for payroll purposes. Learning management systems use the ACD to manage the agent's work state when a session of e-learning is pushed to the agent during idle periods. And the list keeps growing. Any linkage that saves data entry, coordinates functions, and aids operations should be considered. These technologies are discussed in more detail later in this chapter.

ACD systems are increasingly integrating peripheral functions that can also be purchased as separate systems from specialty suppliers. This makes the interactions between these systems easier to set up and manage, but may compromise some of the most sophisticated capabilities. These integrations include such capabilities as voice response, quality recording, workforce management, and management of web interactions.

Computer Telephony Integration (CTI)

Linking the computer in the PBX or ACD with another computer is called computer telephony integration or CTI. It is generally used to coordinate the functions of the telephone system with another data system. This can be as simple as a look-up of the calling party's phone number in a directory and displaying that name. In some cases, the whole routing and handling of the call can be altered because of data that was found about the caller.

The "screen pop" application is one that brings up a screen of information for call center agents when they answer calls. The process allows the ACD to capture information about the caller, pass it to an external computer (typically where the customer files are held) to look up the caller's account, and then presents both the call to the agent's phone and "populates" the caller's account information on the agent's monitor at the same time. This can shorten the call handling time by as much as 15 or 20 seconds per call.

The information that identifies the caller can come from a variety of sources. One common source is the network data that identifies the phone number where the call originates. This is called ANI or Automatic Number Identification. This data is passed from the 800-service carrier to the ACD as the call is presented for answering.

While this screen pop is the most common application, it is only the beginning of the possibilities. Calls can be transferred between agents and the data screens will transfer with the call. Coordinated voice/data transfer can work between sites in addition to within the same ACD.

When the external computer finds data that suggests abnormal handling, it must send a message back to the ACD to handle the call differently. This can be an instruction to prioritize, reroute to a different agent group, or play a special announcement, as examples. The external computer cannot control the call directly, but through its instructions to the ACD, it can determine what steps are next for the caller.

Voice Processing

Voice processing is an umbrella term that takes in a number of capabilities and systems. These include voice mail/messaging, automated attendant, information mailboxes/announcements, voice response systems, speech recognition, and text-to-speech. All of these involve the recording, storage, and/or manipulation of voice inputs.

One of the primary applications is voice mail. In addition, recorded menu systems and automated attendant systems allow simple choices such as "Press 1 for Sales," allowing the call to be routed to the correct department without the aid of an operator. Interactive voice response (IVR) systems allow a caller to interact with a computer database to do functions such as checking a bank account balance without the aid of a human. Each of these applications has the potential to enhance communications and to reduce the cost of such communication.

The drawback of all voice processing systems is the loss of human-to-human interaction. Machines are impersonal and poorly designed system scripts confuse and frustrate callers. Most people will tell you they hate talking to the machines so common in business today. Thoughtful design and constant vigilance in managing the systems is the key to success, but too few companies make the effort, resulting in applications that frustrate communications rather than facilitate it.

Automated Dialers

Placing single outgoing telephone calls is commonplace in most call centers, even those that are primarily dedicated to inbound call handling. Callbacks on follow-up requests, contact with other departments for research, and a myriad of other requirements can generate these calls. But there are some centers that have many outbound calls to make for telemarketing, surveys, debt collection, and other purposes. Where there is a large quantity of calls to make, an automated dialer may be appropriate. A list of numbers to be called is loaded into the dialer's database and the system generates the calls without human assistance.

There are many different types of dialers and they can operate in a variety of modes. One dialing mode is preview dialing, which is primarily used in situations where the agent must prepare for each call separately, such as a debt collections application. The dialer locates the next number in sequence, pulls up the account information and presents it to the agent's desktop. When the agent has all the information and is ready for the call, the agent presses a button that tells the dialer to dial the call. If there is a live answer, the call is completed as planned. If no one answers or there is a busy signal, the dialer will disconnect the call and place that number back into the database for another try later. If an answering machine is reached, the dialer can either disconnect or the agent can leave a message. In either case, the called number will generally be put into the database for another try. The primary benefit of this technology is list management since little time is saved in the actually dialing process for the agent.

In a progressive or predictive mode, the dialer also has a list of numbers to call, but the calls are essentially all alike so that an agent does not need to prepare separately prior to each call. These might be telemarketing calls in which the same sales pitch is given to everyone on the list. In this case, the dialer will place the calls without an agent on the line. If a busy signal or no answer is reached, the call will be disconnected and the number stored for another try later. If the call reaches a live person, the dialer will look for an idle agent in the center to connect to the call, hopefully instantaneously. If the call reaches an answering machine, it can be programmed to disconnect or to connect an agent to leave a message as appropriate. The predictive dialer works on a sophisticated mathematical algorithm that dials at a speed that will maximize utilization of the agents without dialing too fast so that answered calls find no agent available. The benefit of this kind of dialer is clearly in the automation of the dialing process as well as the list management. The improvement in productivity can be as much as 300% with the use of such systems since the agents are only involved in calls that successfully reach the called party.

The drawback of predictive dialers is that they can dial too fast, resulting in calls that reach a live answer, but there is no agent in the center to take the call. Customers find it highly annoying to have the phone ring, answer it, and have only silence greet them. The level of sophistication of the algorithm and detection of live versus machine answer can separate good dialers from poor, and justifies the widespread pricing that accompanies them. With the restrictions in the Telephone Consumer Protection Act, this detection and handling of live answers versus machine answers becomes critical to compliance with the law.

Dialers can be stand-alone systems that need only connection to the public telephone network to operate. The dialer can also be sold as a software package for an ACD or host computer that relies on other devices for most or all of the hardware components. But integration of the dialer with the telephone network is often done in call centers by linking the dialer to the ACD as if it were an agent telephone.

EMail and Web Technologies

Email has become a major communications tool over the last few years. Agents use email to communicate with one another, with supervisors, and sometimes with people outside the company. But the primary issue for call centers is the management of incoming emails from customers and prospects. Management of the emails themselves is a function of automatic receipt, placement into a queue, distribution to agents, and tracking progress for reporting. Emails to a central mailbox that will be handled by a group of individuals must be managed differently from those individual emails that are received by a single person. With a group of people sharing responsibility for responding, it is important to ensure handling in the desired order, distribution of work in a fair manner, and information to manage the process.

In a sense, the email management system is like an ACD for another kind of contact. The receipt of the email is often acknowledged by an automated message sent within a few minutes telling the sender when a full reply is likely. The message callers see is like the announcement that a caller hears when going into queue on the ACD. Emails are held in a centralized queue much like the queues in an ACD, and may be sorted by type based on the reference line or other content, just like the ACD has different queues for different skill requirements. The emails are distributed to the agents for processing (or may wait for the agent to manually take them out of queue) on a basis that reflects the center's desires for equitable workload, skills match, prioritization of some requests, etc., and that also replicates the ACD. Reporting is provided, although this is somewhat different, primarily due to the longer response time that is acceptable for emails (hours rather than seconds typically). The reports need to identify such things as emails that have been partially worked by an agent who may have called in sick today. The supervisor may need to pull those back from assignment to that agent and reassign them to another agent if the response is to meet the deadline, for example.

One popular feature of email management systems is the automated reply. When an email is received, the system immediately sends out a canned reply that acknowledges receipt and lets the sender know the anticipated response time. This is reassuring to the sender. Since the response time the sender anticipated and the actual time that the company is likely to respond may be quite different, this automated acknowledgement can prevent another email or call from the sender.

More sophisticated email management systems can also have an element of artificial intelligence that looks for key words and phrases in the email and selects probable replies. These probable replies are then sent to the agent with the original email for approval and editing. This can increase productivity when the system selects the right choices, but can be risky if the agents are not carefully reading both inquiry and response to ensure that there is a good match.

Another tool that can be part of the system is the "call me" button on the web site. Customers click on that button when they want someone at the company to call them, filling in time and telephone number. This sends a message to the company to schedule the outbound call. This can be highly automated with a dialer function to schedule and make the calls, or may simply send an email to the company for follow-up manually.

Web chats are a cross between the real-time interaction of a phone call and the delayed response technology of the email. If a customer has a technical problem with a product, for example, the customer can go to the web site to find answers. But if the answer does not seem to be on the web site, the customer enters a web chat session with an agent by clicking on the option in the web page. A message is sent to the call center that a customer is in queue and as soon as an idle agent is available that agent will open an interactive session with the customer. Questions and answers go back and forth until the customer is satisfied and ends the chat session.

The benefits of the interactive web chat to customers include having a near real-time conversation with an agent who can answer their questions. It does not have the inherent delays associated with emails in which the reply may come in a few hours and the risk that the reply will be incomplete or generate another question and another round of emails. It may not be quite as fast as the phone call, but a written record of the instructions in the reply can be a valuable result over a verbal interchange that is not recorded for the customer.

For the call center, the web chat can typically be handled at a lower cost than a call. Part of that savings is in the cost of the toll-free call minutes that is replaced by an Internet exchange. Another savings may be in the cost of the labor to accomplish the tasks. While the customer is typing in his question, time would be wasted for the agent just waiting for that to happen, so it is common for web chat agents to handle more than one transaction at the same time. However, if the agent is busy with another customer when the text comes in, there may be a longer than normal delay for the agent to reply which can annoy the customer. There are some who suggest that an agent can handle five transactions or more simultaneously, but the response time and quality may suffer. The overlapping nature of this kind of work also minimizes the opportunity for the agent to ever get a rest between transactions like they sometimes have between calls.

Desktop Tools

Once the contact has reached the inbound call center, tools are needed for the agent to process the requests and perform the necessary tasks. These include the desktop applications on the computer, imaging systems, and video interaction tools. On a broader scale, the workflow management and knowledge management systems offer tools that may handle certain tasks or offer solutions to the customer's requests on an automated basis.

The applications and programs available to call center agents from their computers are generally referred to as desktop tools. These can include company-specific applications such as a program developed in-house to handle orders for the company's products. In addition, there may be a host of commercially available programs that are used such as word processing, spreadsheets, and directory services. While some companies still have mainframe computer applications that are accessed via dumb terminals (or terminal emulation programs), most call centers today use personal computers for the agents.

The company-specific applications generally provide the customer information files with the data about each customer's accounts, purchases, balance, address, phone, email address, and any other data that is needed. An insurance company might have files that include the specific type of coverage the person has, their claims history, and physician that the patient is assigned to for primary care, for example. A catalog operation may have an inventory management system that tracks the status of items in the warehouse so that agents can tell customers when an order might be shipped. While these applications may be generally available programs made for the industry, they may be modified for the specific company, or be written entirely by in-house programmers. Each industry and company has unique needs and there are a host of vendors available to provide industry-specific programs.

Some call centers utilize scripts to assist the agent in handling calls. The text of the script displays on the agent's screen for guidance, and depending on the customer's response (which the agent enters into the computer), the script will branch to the appropriate response and/or next question. This kind of scripting minimizes training for new hires so they can take calls before they have memorized every possible choice and what to do next. For example, volunteers handling a survey for a non-profit organization would find this kind of tool helpful in ensuring that they get all the right information. The skilled agent can paraphrase the script and even disable it when fully competent.

It is becoming more common to see the functions of the telephone integrated into the computer screen for the agent. The agent can answer a call, place it on hold, transfer and disconnect by clicking the mouse or possibly touching the screen. The ACD work states such as after-call work can be entered on the screen too. In fact, nearly anything that can typically be done from the agent's telephone can be integrated into a button or display on the telephony interface. This integrated telephone set allows agents to remove the telephone from their desks and have only one system to interact with to do all of the normal functions. The headset is plugged into the PC for audio. One issue that should be noted with these integrated telephony functions is that in the event of power failure disabling the PC, the agent will also lose phone service. While an ACD might have a battery backup that would keep phones operational, now the PC must also have an alternative power source.

Where letters and numbers are not sufficient to support communications, pictures may be required. These images can be supported in several ways. Facsimile systems and image scanning are the most common tools. Storage techniques are important for these systems as well, so that specific images can be accessed as needed. Image scanning systems work in much the same way as a copier or facsimile machine by taking a picture of the item and storing it as a digital file. For example, doctors might send claims in to an insurance company on written forms. The paper copy arrives at the insurance company and can be stored in the client's files, but often the insurance company would prefer to have this file stored electronically rather than on paper. These claims documents can be scanned by the imaging system and then the files stored electronically. This allows agents to easily pull up a picture of the form on their computer screens without having to find the paper copy, which may be stored hundreds of miles away at the company headquarters. While the data on the claim form may be entered either automatically or manually into the standard claims system, referring to the actual form may be needed to check for data entry errors, look for proper signatures, etc.

Another popular use of imaging is in catalog operations. While the agents could have paper copies of the company's catalogs at their desktops, it is also possible to convert the entire file to images that can be digitally stored and accessed. Perhaps the company sells parts for camper awning systems and a customer calls in looking for a repair item. The agent can key in the brand and model of the awning and see a picture of all of the parts that might be needed. Using this image, the customer and agent can explore the options and find just the right piece when neither of them may know exactly what it is called or the part number.

Workflow Management

The work done in a call center is often part of a chain of tasks that must be accomplished to complete the customer's request. This chain may require the aid of other departments, outside resources, and multiple steps. It can be frustrating to the call center agent to have to hand off the task to some other group without knowing if it ever got done. Then when the customer calls back and says "What happened to my request? I haven't heard anything," there is little the agent can do to track it down. These interdepartmental handoffs are problematic and a significant number of them do not succeed in getting everything done in the right order and on time. This is the problem a workflow management system is designed to address.

Think about a car loan at the bank as an example of a process that can be aided by a workflow system. The process starts with the customer calling the bank's call center, stating that he is thinking about buying a specific new car and would like to arrange for a loan. The agent asks the customer for the necessary information to fill out the loan application, but the customer doesn't have one item that is needed such as the account number of an investment held by his broker that will be used to guarantee the loan. So the agent makes a note in the file that that item is missing and that the customer will call back. The workflow management system now takes over and places the item in a queue, waiting a pre-set period for the customer to call back. If no entry is made in the file within the period set, then the workflow system sends a message back to the call center to make an outbound call to the customer to track it down. Once all of the loan information has been filled in, the agent releases the application and the workflow system may start a series of tasks. One would be to generate an automated inquiry from a credit reporting bureau and append the report to the file, all without human interaction. Once that information is completed, the file may then be routed to a loan officer for review and approval. It is placed in a queue for that group to handle. When the loan has been approved, the system will send a message to the call center to notify the customer that the loan is approved and to arrange for him to visit a branch office to turn in the title and sign the paper work. The customer selects a convenient branch and the agent releases the loan identifying the appropriate branch. The system then sends the print messages to the printer at the branch along with a message that indicates who the customer is and that the branch needs to collect the car title for collateral. When the customer walks in the branch, the employee accesses the file, prints the forms for signature (if they were not printed ahead of time), and completes the loan process with the customer. The system then sends a message to deposit the money in the customer's account, and generates a message to the call center to follow up with the customer in a couple of weeks. When the time comes, a message pops up in the agent's work queue to make the outbound call to complete the satisfaction survey.

Knowledge Management

One of the most valuable assets an organization has is the knowledge of its employees. But capturing the knowledge and making it available to everyone who needs it is very difficult. Knowledge management systems are designed to fit this need because they are essentially data storage and retrieval systems. They organize the data in such a way that it can easily be searched to find the answer to questions.

Technical support help desks are heavy users of knowledge management systems. For example, perhaps a customer calls and wants to know if the computer system he has is compatible with a specific printer. The agent would type the computer model and the printer name into the search window, and the knowledge management system would find all the data on the specified model and then search for the printer type. When the information has been located, the data about compatibility, known issues, where to go to download the appropriate printer drivers, etc., will be displayed for the agent so that she can answer the customer's question. So even though this agent may never have heard of the printer, the information that was stored by someone else is there to solve the problem.

It is important to note that while these tools can improve service in highly complex environments, they require a great deal of maintenance. Each time a new issue or problem is identified, or the company makes a new product, all of the relevant data must be entered into the system so that those who need it can access it. In many organizations, this updating process requires that the most experienced agents or others test the solution to ensure its accuracy before it can be entered in the system. This prevents erroneous or incomplete data from being entered and proliferating. The initial data entry to set up the system is generally a huge task, but the ongoing maintenance is essential to ensure that the system stays up-to-date and as effective as possible.

Workforce Management

Workforce management is the process of ensuring that the right number of staff is in place to answer the calls within an acceptable service goal. This process requires that a reasonably accurate forecast be developed as to how many contacts are expected by half-hour and how long it takes to handle each one. With the forecast of workload done, the next task is to determine the number of staff required to meet the service goal. Then the schedules are developed that match the staff to the workload. Tracking the actual performance each day against the plan helps management determine if adjustments are necessary and what they should be. All these steps are automated in a workforce management system.

Forecasting is based on history and the system must have historical data on contact arrivals and handling times to establish the patterns and expectations. There is a data link between the workforce management system and the ACD reporting system that provides data on a half-hourly basis. This data is stored in the workforce management system and called up when a new forecast is done. For example, some workforce management systems require the user to select several historical weeks to use as a pattern for the upcoming week being forecast. Special patterns may be stored to represent repeated events such as weeks with holidays, marketing campaigns, billing cycles, or whatever events drive the specific center's workload.

In addition to the basic functions performed by a workforce management system, a range of optional functions can be added to manage real-time agent adherence to schedules, plan and manage non-phone contacts such as email, and administer vacation time. The workforce management system is often linked to other systems in the center that benefit from a scheduling component, such as a quality monitoring or e-learning system.

Quality Monitoring/Recording

Nearly every ACD is equipped with the capability to support silent monitoring of calls by a supervisor. This allows the supervisor to access a call currently in progress, listening to both sides of the conversation between the caller and agent without either of them knowing the supervisor is observing. The drawback of this approach is that it requires the supervisor (or quality control manager) to access these conversations in real-time. If there are few calls in progress, the supervisor can waste a fair amount of time waiting for a call to come to the specific agent targeted. And during the busy times, the supervisor may be needed on the floor to assist agents. While centers typically set a goal of listening to several calls per agent per month, when silent monitoring in real time is the only option, the goal is often missed.

Automated recording of the calls is the role of the quality monitoring system. While some organizations record every call for business purposes, most do not. The quality monitoring system typically is set to record randomly, sampling each agent at different times of day and days of week throughout the period to ensure a fair sampling. Alternatively, the system may also record the agent's data screens during the calls so that the supervisor can see exactly what the agents saw on the screen and what keystrokes they entered as they processed the calls.

With a recording, the supervisors can review the calls whenever they have time. Recordings can be accessed from outside the center by phone in some cases, and the data portions accessed through the Internet, so the supervisors can even do it from home. One of the additional benefits is that the supervisor and agent can listen to the recording together in a coaching session. With the system recording on a regular basis, there is little risk of missing the goal of monitoring the number of calls needed to ensure quality control. But supervisors must still find the time to listen to the calls and score them based on the criteria that is pre-set for this purpose.

Learning Management System

The advent of e-learning has changed the face of employee training. While classroom instruction is essential for many kinds of training, self-paced training via the computer can be an effective tool for disseminating information and knowledge. Learning management systems (LMS) are designed to serve as repositories of these self-paced modules and to provide scheduling and tracking of all educational modules that employees have completed. In addition, a LMS for call centers may include the capability to "push" a module of e-learning to an agent's desktop at a scheduled time, or to allow the agent to access it on demand. Knowledge tests can be included in the content to ensure that the student has completed the course with the appropriate learning, or is directed back to those modules that need more review.

Some of the LMS tools include the functions that support the development of e-learning programs in addition to storing and managing the processes. The system provides the basic layout and page advance functions, allowing the instructional designer to develop the text and graphics within the basic framework. The systems can be used to deliver a "tip of the day" or small amounts of information that do not need all of the functions found in a full course. The common length of a learning module is about fifteen minutes, with multiple modules linked together to create a full course. This allows a module to be completed by an agent in a reasonable period that can be scheduled off the phones during a shift. Games and interactive instructional tools are common and needed to maintain the student's interest in the programs, but the quality of the actual course materials vary widely. The recent emergence of technical standards should make it easier to transport a program written for one platform to another, but much of the existing material is somewhat limited in terms of platform portability.

CRM Technologies

Some of the systems and tools in the center are designed to assist personnel in managing the relationship with the customer. For example, a technical support help desk needs to track the trouble request it receives in order to solve individual customer problems, but also to identify trends of technical issues that need to be addressed. Sales people need to track the multiple steps of interaction with a prospect to maximize the potential to close the sale. Nearly every company wants to know more about its customers including their demographics, interests, hobbies, product likes and dislikes, etc., so it can better target marketing efforts and improve customer retention. These functions are performed by the systems described below, but nearly every product vendor suggests that their system supports Customer Relationship Management (CRM) requirements if it affects interactions in any way, so it is difficult to sort out what is really CRM and what is marketing hype.

Contact Management Systems

Whether the contact being tracked is a trouble ticket reported to a help desk, a sales lead, or a customer interaction requesting some service, a contact management system can assist. This type of system tracks interactions by customer but also provides the databases and analytical tools to look for trends and sort by demographics. For example, if a customer reports a technical problem with his product, a trouble ticket number may be assigned to the report and all of the relevant data about the request and the solution are recorded in the system (via data entry by the agent typically). If the customer calls in later with the same problem telling the agent that the suggested solution did not work, using the ticket number and customer ID, the agent can find the record of the prior interaction. This allows the agent to see what has already been tried unsuccessfully so that she can suggest something else, or transfer the caller to the higher skilled agents.

A sales person wants to track interactions with a prospect including when he called, to whom he talked, and what was promised for the next step. The system can be flagged to notify the sales person when the next step is scheduled so that it is not forgotten. Management can review the pipeline of sales prospects and the interactions to make better informed decisions about what the sales forecast should be and which sales people may need some coaching on their techniques or level of activity.

In a call center, the contact management system provides a record of all the prior interactions with the customer whether they took place by phone, email, IVR, or in person in the branch or store. The customers find they do not have to tell their whole history to the agent, and the agent can see what has been done or promised by others. As the agent converses with the caller, a variety of personal information may be revealed such as hobbies, interests, grandchildren, etc. This information can be recorded in the system for later analysis by marketing. For example, the bank might be planning a campaign to promote boat loans and targeting all of the customers who are noted to have an interest in water sports can make this offering more effective. Another analysis might reveal customers who prefer to do business via the web rather than by phone and these can be targeted via email rather than through telemarketing.

Data Warehousing

Analysis of customer data requires a central storehouse of all of the information a company has on its customers. This data is often housed in departmental systems that do not communicate or share information because they were designed to handle very specific and separate processes. Data warehouse systems are essentially central repositories of all of this data in databases that can be effectively searched, sorted, and analyzed.

There are major challenges in implementing these central repositories, not the least of which is getting the departments to deposit their data. Most organizations have provided incentives and competitive pressures between departments so that each wants to "own" the customer relationship and keep the others out. Breaking down this barrier takes a directive from the top of the organization and a great deal of patience. It may even require a change in the compensation plan to change the rewards from competitive product or departmental goals to those that focus on the entire relationship with the enterprise.

The next challenge is scrubbing the data so that Jack Jones, J. Jones, John R. Jones and J. R. Jones are all united into one record if they are in fact the same person. Addresses and other information conflicts must be reconciled as some systems may have been updated while others have not been changed over time. Little of this scrubbing can be done on an automated basis, requiring a massive effort by the implementation team. And with new data coming in all the time, the process never really ends.

The technical requirements of data warehousing are huge storage capacity and the processing power to access and sort the data, and a network that is robust enough to support the high levels of interaction with the system anticipated by the centralization process. This places a significant load on the IT department that can slow these implementations.

When all the data has been centralized and scrubbed, the analytical tools (sometimes referred to as data mining) can sort and summarize the information in a variety of ways that support market segmentation, sales initiatives, customer retention strategies, etc. The key capabilities of these systems are to quantify the value of the customer interaction, set thresholds that trigger rules and events for automation, and help qualify customer information. Many of the analytical tools available are designed to meet the needs of a specific industry. This simplifies the implementation and shortens the time it takes to get valuable management information out of the data. There are a number of general analytical tools that can be configured to meet nearly any company's needs, but they take more time and knowledge of what is desired at the outset to be successful.

Web Assistance Tools

It is well known that a significant percentage of items placed in electronic shopping carts on the web are abandoned. Many customers become confused on the web site and would be delighted to be able to access live assistance. These are the issues addressed by web collaboration tools.

A simple form of tool these too is a "call me" button on the web site. The customer who selects that button enters a telephone number to call, a time to call, and a brief description of the question on the web page that pops up. That generates a message to the call center to make an outbound call to the customer at the time designated, and it can be managed by a dialer or manually.

A more sophisticated version of this tool is the "help me" button on the web site. When the customer selects that button, a message is sent to the call center immediately and a response is generated while the customer is still on the system. This could take the form of a web chat in which a message box pops up on the customer's computer with typed messages from the agent and a place for the customer to type in responses in real-time. It could also take the form of a phone call from the agent to the customer. If the customer has a second phone line so both call and web session can be handled, the call could be separate. But for the client with only one line, the voice portion can be handled via Voice over Internet Protocol (VoIP).

Web collaboration makes it possible for both the agent and the customer to be on the web site together with the agent pushing pages to the customer and directing the interaction. This makes it easy for the agent to ensure that customers can find just what they are looking for and train them on how to better utilize the site in the future.

Summary

The following diagram provides an overview of the technologies discussed above and the connections among them. Some are connected together via the ACD, while others use the LAN as the primary connection. It is a highly complex and interdependent eco-structure in which all of the parts must function reliably to ensure the center can achieve its mission.

Today's Contact Center

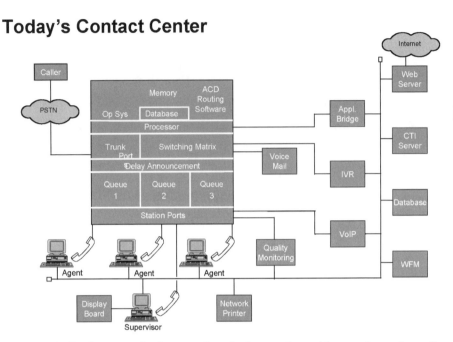

The vast bulk of communications are by telephone today, with some incoming calls generated by the customer and some outgoing, generated by the center. Other technologies such as fax have been around for years, while newer forms such as email, web chat and video interactions are growing in popularity.

Once the contact is connected, then a variety of technologies can aid the routing to an appropriately skilled agent and assist management in ensuring that the agent has the right information available to handle whatever the contact may bring. And ultimately, management must be able to view and report on the activities so that the more effective results can be achieved. All of these tools link together into a comprehensive eco-system in the modern call center.

CHAPTER 8: MANAGING VENDOR RELATIONSHIPS

Introduction

Making the decision to acquire a technology, system, or service can be a career-enhancing process or one fraught with risk and challenges. The solution must fit the call center's needs, so a business case analysis is an absolute first step. Once a decision has been made to acquire from an outside vendor, then a thorough and objective selection process will ensure the best solution, for the best price, provided by the most qualified vendor. A systematic contract negotiation process will pay significant dividends over the life of the relationship. As the project is planned and implemented, and as the ongoing relationship is managed, it's important to work closely with the vendor to make the capabilities come to fruition in the call center.

This chapter outlines the process of needs assessment, business case analysis, vendor selection, contract negotiation, and ongoing relationship management.

Needs Assessment

The call center manager may be required to acquire technology and services to start a new center, but also on an ongoing basis to meet new requirements. This acquisition process may be orchestrated by the company's purchasing department (often referred to as supply chain management) or may be the sole responsibility of call center management.

The first step in the acquisition process is to perform a thorough review of the current needs of the center, the capabilities of the existing systems, and any gaps that may exist. It is common for the needs to potentially be satisfied with existing systems, so new technologies are not always needed. Most system capabilities are not used because the employees within the center and even in the telecom and IT departments do not know what their systems are capable of doing. Those employees trained when the system was first acquired may have moved on to new positions, providing only a portion of their knowledge to their replacements. A discussion with the vendors can be helpful but nothing is as effective as personally reviewing the documentation. However, where the identified gaps cannot be filled with the capabilities of existing systems or services, acquisition of new ones may be required.

The needs assessment should include observations of the ways the employees actually use the system, not just how supervisors and managers think the systems are used. There are often significant differences that can derail a project's return on investment. For example, a health care company decided to implement a contact management system to gain control of the patients who called repeatedly seeking approval of a procedure that was not included in the benefit plan. Management had instructed agents to make an entry in the existing customer information system on every call and believed that was happening. In fact, simple calls that just requested information of a general nature were rarely documented and the customer's file was often not even opened. The return on investment (ROI) for the contact management system was based on the call handling time not changing, but as the system was implemented, the handling time increased by over 30 seconds per call. This is because the new system required the agents to make an entry in a customer file on every call before it would allow the agent to take another call. The ROI projected for the contact management system vanished even though the number of calls dropped significantly, and in fact the system resulted in significantly increased costs as the additional time on every call was accommodated. A simple process of observing agents actually doing the work prior to the project justification would have revealed the reality in time to prevent the erroneous assumption in the ROI calculation.

The needs analysis must be documented in sufficient detail to support a request for proposal that will separate the vendors from one another and allow the center to make a good choice of the best system to meet the defined needs. Those capabilities that are essential and those that are just "nice to have" should be clearly identified against the gaps defined in the needs analysis.

Business Case

A business case is an analysis, evaluation, and presentation of data to support a specific business need and its proposed solution. A business case is developed to demonstrate that a project is economically sound, will be well managed, and will benefit the enterprise. The basis of the business case is the problem, not the solution. With a clear definition of the problem to be solved and the value of solving it, analysis of all reasonable options for the solution including both financial and non-financial considerations, the best solution should be a result of the business case. It is reasonable that some business case efforts will result in a recommendation to maintain the status quo since no acceptable solution could be found.

There are important reasons for creating a business case. These include:

- Justification of the need to bring an idea to fruition
- Verification or substantiation of the needs of the business
- Identification of solutions that increase revenue or profitability
- Process to validate or eliminate an idea
- Communication of the objectives to others
- Coordination of implementation activities
- Basis to measure actual versus expected results
- A vehicle for achieving buy-in

Steps of the Business Case

The steps of developing a business case are outlined below, with each step illustrated with a call center example of the process.

Step 1 - Define objectives

The objectives of the business case should be stated and the resources required to develop the business case should be identified. This is the time for the business case owner to obtain approval from senior management to continue developing the business case and spend the company's resources to do the necessary research and analysis to determine the full nature of the problem, explore the potential solutions, and make a recommendation. The process may require personnel in other departments to assist, spend time within the call center, and contribute other material resources, so it is important that the senior manager agree that it is worthwhile to do the business case. If there is no capital budget money available, it may not matter how compelling the business case is, so it is good to know that before the effort is expended. But it is also important to remember that the only resources being requested at this point are those needed to complete the study and the business case itself, not the final solution.

Approval to go ahead with the business case should not be confused with approval to go forward with the recommended solution. That will come later if the business case recommendation itself is approved. If the call center manager does not have senior management buy-in on the definition of the problem and the willingness to make some investment in addressing it, the effort of building the business case will be a waste of the manager's time and other resources.

Call Center Scenario

The help desk manager for a software company believes there is a problem with productivity and efficiency in the call center, with first call resolution being suspected as the area in need of improvement. Customer satisfaction scores are lower than desired and turnover of agents is increasing. The supervisors are doing manual monitoring of the agents, but they say they don't have time to coach. The supervisors have indicated they think the agents could be more effective, but they don't know how to increase productivity and efficiency. The help desk manager decides to seek approval from senior management to build a business case for a solution to improve agent productivity and efficiency (the business case subject), which will ultimately affect customer and employee satisfaction/retention. Senior management reviews the help desk manager's presentation, sees the link back to enterprise objectives (to increase customer satisfaction and reduced employee turnover), and gives approval for the help desk to continue developing the business case. With this authorization, the help desk manager is now ready to identify people who can assist in the development of the business case.

Step 2 – Recruit the team

In this step, team members should be identified who represent the stakeholders, users, finance office, executive management, and other departments across the enterprise that will be required to assist with the development of the business case. Necessary skill sets should be identified and team members selected. It is common to need the assistance of someone from the finance department to analyze costs and project financial benefits, if for no other reason than to be able to say that the numbers have been reviewed and approved by that person or area. This involvement up front minimizes the detailed scrutiny of numbers by senior management when the case is presented for final approval. The same is true of legal counsel or human resources when any issues involving their expertise is involved. Facilities management, IT experts, marketing and risk management may also need to be included in the process where appropriate. It is best to involve others where possible to broaden the perspective and share the work, but it is also important to share the credit for the results among the team.

Team Member	Roles & Responsibilities
Agent with less than six months experience	Provide perspective of someone fresh from initial training and to assess current skills and reaction to any proposed solutions.
Agent with more than 1 year experience	Provide perspective of someone who has worked on the front lines for some time and her skills and reaction to any proposed solutions.
Help Desk Trainer	Assist in identifying training issues and/or opportunities in the case.
Financial Manager or Analyst	Assist in developing and validating numbers within the case.
IT/Telecom Manager	Assess the feasibility and costs of any technological solutions under consideration.
Team Leader	Provide perspective from the senior agent level and to test out skills and processes that agents might use.
Supervisors	Assist in identifying the nature of the monitoring and coaching processes, the results, and the limitations of the current environment. Provide input on any solutions that may be considered that impact the role of the supervisor.
Marketing Manager	Assist in identifying opportunities that might impact customer satisfaction and quantifying the potential results of any initiatives suggested by the case.
Human Resources Manager	Provide input from exit interviews and other HR data on the current environment and to assure that any potential solutions comply with HR practices and policies.

Step 3 – Assess current situation

The situation assessment is the step in which data is gathered, sorted, and organized. It answers the question "What is happening now?" As the investigation begins, it is important to consider if anything is "broken" or under-performing, but also to identify areas that are working well. In the situation assessment, research the business case subject or problem and the impact it is having on the total enterprise. In looking at impact, consider all of the following that apply:

• External/internal environment – Is there anything inside or outside of the company that has a potential impact on or from the problem?

- Competition – Who is the competition? What impact does the problem have on competitive position and how could solving the problem improve competitive opportunities?

- The customer – Who are the customers that are affected by the problem? Are they internal or external customers? Are the affected customers designated as "high value" customers where large relationships are at stake? Have the customers provided any input as to the impact the problem is having on them?

- Financial situation – What are the financial impacts in terms of revenue and/or costs from the problem?

- Staff – How is the staff impacted by the problem? What is the current turnover rate? Have the staff members provided any input as to the impact the problem is having on them? Has an employee satisfaction survey been conducted?

- Cross-functional areas - How are other departments affected by the problem? How do other departments contribute to the problem? What is the nature of the impacts?

A summary of the situation should be prepared that includes an understanding of the case subject and the impact on the enterprise. Again, the business case at this stage should focus on the subject or problem, not the solution. The better the problem is identified, quantified, and linked to results that impact the enterprise goals, the more likely that the rest of the case will fall into place. Be careful not to overstate the problem, but focusing on too narrow of a scope can also be detrimental to the case.

Call Center Scenario

In the software company help desk, a situation assessment is completed with the following observations:

> *a. Customer satisfaction scores are low. Results from a recent telephone survey show the majority of the customers feel the agents are pleasant, but the solutions suggested don't always solve the problem the first time.*

> *b. Supervisors are doing live service observation whenever the time permits, but there is significant inconsistency in the number of calls monitored per agent.*

> *c. Supervisors each score the calls they monitor in their own ways, as there is no approved and standard form for the call monitoring process.*

> *d. Experienced agents indicate their supervisors largely ignore them as the new hires take up all of the supervisors' time. This results in dissatisfaction since there is little reward for doing things well.*

> *e. Agents at all levels of experience indicate their frustration with not receiving timely and consistent feedback from supervisors.*

> *f. Agents indicate that they generally like the work they do and find that solving customer problems is rewarding.*

> *g. Supervisors indicate that they have little time in the day to review the results*

of the monitoring processes with the agents. They only deal with the most poorly handled calls and agents requiring disciplinary action.

h. Supervisors have had no training on how to identify and fix performance problems in their teams, and no training has been received on coaching techniques.

i. The finance department indicates that the help desk is over budget for training due to the turnover rate of 52% so far this year.

j. Wages for help desk personnel have been analyzed and are competitive within the region.

Step 4 – Prepare SWOT analysis

SWOT is an acronym for strengths, weaknesses, opportunities, and threats. It is an analytical tool used to understand a need, problem, or situation in terms of current and future environment. Given the assessment of the case subject or problem, the strengths (positive) and weaknesses (negative) should be considered current facts. Opportunities (positive) and threats (negative) are viewed as future possibilities. Weaknesses and threats must be addressed to achieve success.

Call Center Scenario

The team assembled by the call center manager prepares a SWOT analysis with the following results:

STRENGTHS (internal)	WEAKNESSES (internal)
Management's desire to do a better job	High agent turnover
Agents' desire to make customers happy	No consistent monitoring process
Agent compensation is competitive	No coaching skills
	No consistent training program

OPPORTUNITIES (external)	THREATS (external)
Improved customer retention through higher first call resolution	Customer attrition
Increased revenue stream through higher retention of customers	Employee loss to many other call centers in the area

As an option, the team may choose to evaluate each one of these items and rank them with respect to relevancy to the project and importance to the business case.

Step 5 – Define objectives

The objectives should answer, "Where are you going?" and "What do you want to happen?" The objectives should be clear after completing the SWOT analysis and should be the vision of success. Objectives should be aggressive enough to solve the problem and should include a description of the action and what the business case will address. At this point, it is important to ensure the objectives track with what senior management approved in Step 1. If the objectives do not match, the call center manager should go back to Step 1 for approval based on the new objectives.

Defining the objectives does not mean defining the solution. It simply means that the team has reached consensus on what the ideal (or at least improved) situation would look like if the problem could be solved. This is the "what" of the business case recommendation, not the "how." For example, the objective may be to reduce turnover in the call center from 40% to 30% within six months and to 20% within a year. How that will be accomplished will be defined in the next step. It is generally not possible to address every item in the SWOT analysis in a single business case, and it is best to keep the case focused on a narrow set of objectives.

It is important that the objectives identified be quantifiable and measurable wherever possible. This will set the stage for the before-and-after analysis that will be done when the project is completed to prove that it met its objectives. An objective such as "Improve customer retention" is too nebulous and generally difficult to measure. A better objective would be to "Improve cost per call by a minimum of $.15 per call within six months."

Call Center Scenario

After reviewing the SWOT analysis, the help desk manager defines the objectives of the business case as:

- *Improve the frequency and consistency of feedback on job performance to improve employee satisfaction and reduce turnover to less than 30% within one year.*

- *Improve first call resolution by at least 5% within three months.*

- *Improve customer satisfaction scores by at least one point on a 7-point scale within six months.*

Step 6 – Identify potential solutions

The objective of the business case is the "what" and the solution is the "how." In this step, the team will brainstorm all possible solutions. To investigate possible solutions, it is important to consider the solution relative to the change it may bring to the organization. People, methods, processes, training, technology, and changes to support systems should all be weighed as possible solutions. The team should be willing to change or abandon solutions as needed and weigh each solution relative to its impact on the organization. At the end of this step, the team should have narrowed the list of potential solutions to only those worth final cost/benefit analysis.

Call Center Example

The help desk project team lists the following potential solutions to the objectives identified in the previous step:

1. Design and implement a standard monitoring form and communicate to agents the items that will be monitored and why.

2. Design and implement a new-hire orientation program. Current employees will be required to attend refresher training to ensure all procedures are followed consistently.

3. Implement a training program for supervisors with a focus on consistent monitoring and effective coaching practices.

4. Purchase and implement an automated recording and monitoring system to randomly record both audio and data activities to support coaching.

5. Establish a peer review process to allow agents to monitor and score other agents and provide feedback.

6. Establish a calibration process to ensure that all supervisors (and agents who do monitoring) score calls in the same way.

Step 7 – Identify assumptions and methodology

In this step, the team will record all assumptions. Methods used to achieve the calculations and conclusions should also be defined. This may include the method used to arrive at costs or define benefits (e.g., time saving estimates). For example, the cost of an agent may include the direct salary, benefits, overhead, and administration. This assumption should be validated with both the human resources and finance departments to ensure that no errors or omissions have occurred.

Any estimate of time saved must also provide some indication whether this time can be effectively redeployed to the company's benefit. For instance, if the average handle time of a call is reduced by 20 seconds, this is likely to translate into real dollars and/or reduced head count since the ACD forces calls to the agents when they are idle. However, if a sales person saves five minutes on a drive across town to a customer appointment, the question remains as to whether these five minutes will return any real value to the company.

Call Center Scenario

The help desk project team documented the following assumptions:

- *Customer satisfaction scores are low due to poor first call resolution because agents are not trained as well as they could be, but also because they were not given sufficient feedback on how to make improvements in their performance.*

- *If a training program for the agents and the supervisors is implemented, there should be an increase in customer and agent satisfaction, which will improve customer retention and reduce agent turnover.*

- *The agent training programs can be developed internally with existing resources.*

• *A supervisory training program must be obtained from an external resource as no one in the company has been identified who has the appropriate skills to teach supervisors how to do performance management in the call center and how to coach the agents. A Request for Information (RFI) to several training companies has identified potential resources and a range of prices.*

• *There are multiple vendors who can supply automated recording systems and an RFI to the vendors identified potential suppliers and a range of prices.*

• *Three days of consulting time is required to assist in development of a standardized monitoring form and calibration of scoring with supervisors, as there is no one in the call center with these skills.*

Step 8 – Identify metrics

A metric is a standard measure used to assess performance. The team should reach consensus on the metrics to be used and identify who will do the calculations. The source of the data should be identified and also how the data will be used. It is important that the metrics selected for the business case relate to the problem and objectives identified and that they will measure the current situation and improvements that are forecast.

Sample call center metrics include customer satisfaction scores, agent satisfaction scores, speed of answer, quality of service scores, agent turnover rate, and agent productivity. For non-financial costs, it is important to identify how the conclusions were drawn, even if there is no financial value that can be assigned. The process for measuring any item that is not numerical must also be documented.

Call Center Scenario

The metrics identified by the help desk project team include the following:

• *Current customer satisfaction scores are 4.2 on a scale of 7 points. Surveys are typically done quarterly. The team projects an increase in satisfaction scores of at least one point within six months following the implementation of the proposed solutions.*

• *Current agent satisfaction scores are 5.2 on a scale of 7 points. Surveys are typically done semi-annually. The team projects an increase in satisfaction scores of at least one-half point within six months follow the implementation of the supervisor training program.*

• *Current turnover in the help desk is 52% annually. The team projects a reduction in agent turnover rate of between 10 and 15 percentage points beginning within six months following the implementation of the proposed solutions. Measurement quarterly and at the end of one year will be conducted.*

Step 9 – Quantify costs

The financial impact on the organization should include costs for the startup, implementation, and tracking. Some common financial metrics include Net Present Value

(NPV), Return on Investment (ROI), and Payback. Other supporting financial metrics include market share and profitability. (Calculation of these important financial measures is detailed in Chapter 3.)

It is critical for the business case to consider all of the costs of the proposed solution, not just the initial pricing from vendors. Such costs would include maintenance fees, training time (including time away from the job that may need to be covered by other personnel or overtime), consulting fees, telecommunications charges, IT infrastructure costs, increased call handling time, and any other charges or time loss that will be incurred. The business case should also include any projected changes in revenue such as the impact of improved customer retention, up-sell and cross-sell revenues, and direct revenues from sales. Benefits such as reduced call volumes or higher utilization of self-service over agent-handled calls should also be projected. It is best to be conservative on all numbers projecting benefits so that any surprises in the process are positive ones. If the business case does not project positive returns without exaggeration of the benefits, it is wise to be honest at this point rather than after the case fails to achieve its projections.

Call Center Scenario

Costs projected for the software company help desk project include:

- *The cost for developing the training program (consultant, train-the-trainer program, training materials). The program might include alternate delivery methodologies for the both the supervisors and agents to include not only instructor-led training, but also computer-based training (CBT) and possibly web-based training (WBT).*

- *The cost for the consultant to assist in developing the standardized monitoring forms and calibration techniques.*

- *The cost for the agents and supervisors to be "off the phone" and not available during the training and rollout.*

- *A range of costs for the automated recording system.*

- *An estimate of the financial impact of improved customer retention as a result of improved customer satisfaction.*

- *Two ROI analyses that bracket the conservative and aggressive results of the project with the automated recording system and two without the automated recording system. These are prepared by the financial analyst on the team and reviewed by the CFO for accuracy of assumptions and processes.*

Step 10 – Identify risks

During the SWOT analysis in Step 4, the risks were identified as weaknesses and threats. A risk assessment should rank the risks and present the results in rank order. Factors with a strong impact on the results, and those that are more likely to occur, deserve the most attention. Individual risks should be kept in view and should not be grouped together. Risks should be identified that need to be addressed in the project's contingency plan, implementation plan, and during tracking of the business case after implementation. Risks include not only those in the SWOT, but the risks of something going wrong in the implementation of the project itself. So a contingency plan for such an event should be part of the implementation plan.

Call Center Scenario

The software company help desk's threats and weaknesses focus on losing both customers and employees. Each of these is addressed in the business case and a contingency plan for any implementation issues has also been developed.

- *High agent turnover and loss to other call centers in the area – Improving the feedback system for agents and coaching for improved performance will increase agent satisfaction and reduce turnover. In addition, spending time with strong performers as well as weak ones will improve the likelihood that the best performers will stay with the company. However, there is also a risk that a consistent monitoring and coaching process will place poor performers under greater pressure than in the past, and turnover among these employees may see a temporary increase.*

- *Inconsistent monitoring process – Standardizing the monitoring form and calibration of scoring will resolve this issue and increase fairness of the process.*

- *Lack of coaching skills – Training of supervisors on performance management and coaching skills will address this weakness.*

- *Inconsistent training program – This weakness will be addressed with coaching skills and development of the new orientation program for agents.*

- *Customer attrition – Improving agent performance, increased first call resolution, and reducing turnover of agents will improve customer satisfaction scores, resulting in reduced customer attrition.*

- *Implementation risk of recording technology – IT involvement in the selection and negotiation of the contract will help to alleviate technology incompatibility risks. HR involvement will assist in ensuring fairness of treatment and compliance with regulations in the implementation as well. Legal advice will be sought to ensure compliance with laws on informing agents and customers about the potential recording of calls.*

Step 11 – Quantify benefits

The benefits to the call center and to the organization should be grouped as financial and non-financial. One of the capital budgeting methods mentioned earlier in this section will be chosen to quantify the analysis. Examples of non-financial benefits include goodwill or image, customer satisfaction, and employee morale. The final recommended solution for the business case is based on weighing the costs, risks, and benefits and should be evident during this stage of the business case process.

The business case should also identify how and when the benefits will be measured after the implementation. Many projects have unexpected results and these are often added benefits that no one on the project team could foresee. These should be identified after the project is completed and communicated to the team and the management who approved the project. This post-project analysis will improve the chances of approval of the next project placed before the management team, and enhance the careers of all of the team members who were part of the initial project group. However, when there are unforeseen negatives that show up after implementation, it is just as important to capture the data and identify the root causes of those variations as well. These should also be communicated with an understanding of how the new problems will be addressed. This assures management that the team is thorough and willing to be truthful about all of the impacts on this project and any future ones. Management expects there will be mistakes and unforeseen issues, but they must be made visible to avoid the same risks in the future.

Call Center Scenario

The software company help desk team has identified the greatest benefits as improved customer retention and reduced employee turnover. However, improved morale in the center among both supervisors and agents is an important benefit, as is having defensible processes in terms of performance review and management of human resources.

There is also the potential for other metrics to be impacted by the improved performance of the agents. These include shorter queue times, shorter AHT, a reduction in call volumes due to completion of more contacts in the first interaction, and greater schedule adherence by agents. Less stress for supervisors may result from having the automated monitoring system that allows them to coach their personnel effectively and be on the floor during peaks instead of doing real-time monitoring. While the business case may not want to predict specific impacts on these factors, they should all be measured on a before-and-after basis to determine if any benefits have developed. However, these metrics can also be impacted by many other factors, so it is important to try to isolate the benefits of one project from other projects and other influences.

The team chooses the ROI model to do the analysis and makes both conservative and aggressive estimates of savings and benefits resulting in two separate analyses that bracket the reasonable possibilities.

Step 12 – Develop implementation plan

The implementation plan is a blueprint for execution. It should be specific, identify key personnel, incorporate accountability, and communicate the process. While it is not reasonable to do a complete PERT chart for the project prior to it being approved, it does make sense to make estimates of the timeframe of the project, the effort required from the key personnel, and the basic milestones that will be encountered along the way. A proposed project manager should be designated or at least a couple of candidates recommended. The final selection can be made after approval to proceed.

Once the business plan is approved, the full project management process should be initiated. This will include the formal Gantt chart or PERT process.

Call Center Scenario

The business case implementation plan for the software company help desk will include:

- *Identify project management and project team.*
- *Schedule project kick-off meeting with all appropriate players.*
- *Develop request for proposal (RFP) for selection of training company and delivery method.*
- *Develop RFP for automated recording system.*
- *Select consultant to assist in form design and calibration.*
- *Select training company and recording systems.*
- *Develop customized training programs.*
- *Pilot training programs for both the agents and supervisors followed by full rollout with adjustments as needed.*
- *Develop standardized monitoring forms.*
- *Calibrate performance monitoring and scoring process.*
- *Deliver first agent coaching sessions.*
- *Collect performance metrics on a weekly basis after coaching.*
- *Perform regular customer satisfaction and employee satisfaction surveys.*
- *Collect agent turnover data at quarterly and 12-month intervals.*
- *Tally final results for project and communicate to team and management.*

Step 13 – Create a contingency plan

A contingency plan is developed to identify preventable risks and to provide the best possible recovery capability in the event that something goes wrong with the implementation plan. The value of the contingency plan is that the planning takes place before something goes wrong, therefore saving valuable time and minimizing losses.

It is not necessary at the business case stage to have all of the details of the contingency and recovery plan identified, but the risks and general concepts that will be used to address those risks need to be clearly identified. This will assure the managers approving the plan that the team has considered the possibility of things going wrong and will prepare the necessary plans to address the problems if the project is approved.

Call Center Scenario

The software company contingency plan includes implementing a pilot program for both the agents and supervisors. In using a pilot training program, adjustments can be made to incorporate necessary changes as required.

Implementation of the automated recording technology will need a more complete contingency plan addressing the technology issues, acceptance issues, and legal/HR issues.

Step 14 – Prepare presentation

The presentation should begin with an executive summary that is a persuasive narrative about the case in general. It includes the bottom-line results and actions to be taken. The executive summary appears first in the presentation, but it is the last section to be written. It should be no more than two pages in length, but concise enough to give a manager too busy to read the entire document all of the pertinent information needed for a decision.

The second section of the presentation includes the case subject statement that describes the setting for the case and establishes the reader's expectations. It defines what the case is about and includes what will happen if the business case is approved.

The third section is the situation assessment that covers the scope and boundaries of the project. The project description follows with the names and details for the team members and analysts.

The fourth section is the solution overview that includes any assumptions made plus the methods and metrics used. Using the data gathered during the development of the business case, a recap of the costs, benefits, implementation plan, risk assessment, and SWOT analysis should follow the solution overview.

Finally, the conclusion and recommendation section should be presented with a focus on more than the financial projections. If some reasonable solutions have been eliminated during the analysis, it is a good idea to mention them and the reasons for rejection here. The conclusion should identify the projected contributions and include anything that could be misinterpreted. This last section should include a formal statement of what actions should occur and why.

Appendices to the business case can supply the myriad of details that support the analysis. This allows the case document and presentation itself to be more general, but provides the details for those who are interested in them.

Once the final document has been completed, it is a good idea to have a manager who has not been involved in the process read it and provide input. If something is unclear or a conclusion is not well supported, a fresh perspective may help to identify it before the formal presentation for approval takes place.

Why Business Cases Fail

A surprising number of business cases fail to win approval. There are some common reasons why this occurs. One of the most common is lack of any history from previous business cases that address a similar problem or use a similar solution. Being first to try out some new technique or technology is not comfortable for every executive, so finding a reference to another situation will help the comfort level.

Another important issue is a data or method error in the case documentation. While this may not totally derail the efforts, it can certainly create delays while the team has to redo the calculations or find the needed data. That is why it is so important to have an outsider read the case before presenting it, and having the finance chief approve the numbers in the document as well. Watch for not only errors, but also for data that is out of date.

Another risk is that the scope of the case is defined too narrowly. Almost anything that the call center might want to do will impact other departments and these impacts need to be understood and documented clearly. Appropriate metrics for measuring these impacts need to be included, and estimates of the time these personnel will need to devote to the project give the approving managers confidence that the process has been thorough.

A final reason business cases fail is that the benefits are viewed as unrealistic, and often these are the benefits that are non-financial. In terms of the estimates of financial benefits, be sure to either be conservative or provide both conservative and aggressive potentials to bracket the possibilities. As far as the non-financial benefits, these should be quoted as additional side benefits and not as the basis for the business case. It is important to prove the value of the project with the numbers first, and then add these on as extras. Relying on the soft-dollar benefits and non-quantifiable benefits is a sure way to set the case up for rejection.

Acquisition

The acquisition process can include a variety of options. One of these would be the development of a system by employees within the company. When the company's needs are unique, there may be no vendor system available that will effectively meet the requirements. Modification of vendor systems may not be sufficient to customize to the company's needs or may be cost-prohibitive or take longer than the company is willing to wait.

When the decision is made that an outside acquisition is appropriate, there are a variety of options still available. Strategic alliances can be negotiated with potential providers. This is appropriate when there is mutual benefit in the alliance that can be exploited well beyond the value of the single system acquisition. A joint venture may be considered when the capabilities desired need to be developed and there is potential for additional sales after the development is completed. Both parties jointly develop the system the company needs, and then join in the sales of the system to others with similar needs. Occasionally, acquisition of the entire vendor organization can be appropriate. This may be a considered when the needed technology is only available from a vendor organization that is not a viable firm long term.

When the system or services are to be acquired from vendors, it is common to use the Request for Information (RFI) or Request for Proposal (RFP) processes. The RFI is a document that assists the company in exploring the options available in the marketplace without requesting a firm bid for a specific system. It can be helpful in understanding options and the tradeoffs of various options prior to the formal RFP process.

The RFP is more common than the RFI. The RFP carefully defines the company's needs and expectations. It requires a legally binding price quote and answers to questions about the offerings that can become part of a contract between the parties. This is designed to be a fair and equal process that allows all vendors to compete equally, but to also assess the differences in vendor offerings at a very detailed level.

The RFP provides the specifications of requirements and the desired capabilities that the company is trying to acquire. It ensures that all vendors will be bidding on a similar set of specifications so that bids are comparable. The RFP contains various sections with questions each vendor must answer in order to be considered for further review. Typical sections of the RFP include vendor qualifications, technical specifications of the service or technology being proposed, and a financial analysis of the proposed solution.

Call centers should employ a systematic decision process in narrowing options and making a final decision. The selection criteria are first based on the "must-haves." These are the capabilities the vendor must provide to be considered for further review. Should vendors be missing any of the "must-haves," they will be eliminated from the review cycle. For example, an RFP might specify, "the system must be capable of expanding to serve 500 agents." If it cannot, it must be eliminated from consideration.

The next step is to assign 100 points between each of the RFP selection criteria categories. The committee should agree upon how many points each category should be assigned based on its relative importance. For example, if the most important factor is the cost of the solution, more points will be assigned to the "cost" or financial category. If it is more important to make the selection of the vendor based on the capabilities of the solution, more points will be assigned to the technology section. Once the major categories have been assigned points, the "line items" in each category (those desirable characteristics, not the "must-haves") will need to be assigned a portion of the section's points, again based on the relative importance of the item. These points represent the weight that is given to each item and the total should equal 100 percent of the decision value.

A matrix is created using the "section" and "line items" points for each category. The committee should then score the vendors on a scale of 1 to 10 with 10 representing the highest score. Vendors are scored against one another with the best vendor for each criterion receiving a score of 10. Every other vendor is compared to the best for each line item. Vendors should not be compared to an "ideal" vendor but only to the actual bidders in the process, and each criterion must be considered independently from all the others. The following matrix displays a distribution of 40 points for the "technology section" of an RFP with the total points divided between each of the line items based on the importance of the item to the selection of the vendor and solution. In addition, the score for each vendor on each line item is provided and this score is then multiplied times the weight (points) to calculated the weighted score.

Sample Vendor Selection Matrix

When the weighted scores are tallied at the end of the review process, the "winner" will be the vendor with the highest score (based on a scale of 1000 possible points).

TECHNOLOGY (Weight = 45)		Vendor A		Vendor B		Vendor C	
Category	Weight	Score	Weighted Score	Score	Weighted Score	Score	Weighted Score
Proven technology	**15**	10	150	5	75	4	60
System expandability	**5**	9	45	10	50	5	25
Ease of maintenance	**5**	5	25	9	45	10	50
User operational characteristics	**5**	10	50	9	45	6	30
Redundancy and reliability	**5**	6	30	10	50	9	45
Ease of installation	**10**	9	90	7	70	10	100
Total Score			390		35		310

In the above example, the "section winner" is Vendor A since it received the highest score for the technology section. With 50% of the decision yet to be decided in the other categories, it is possible for Vendor A to lose the "bid" if that company does poorly in the other sections. The selection criteria matrix provides the call center manager with the best-balanced choice, it resolves statistical ties, and is easy to sell to senior management. This process is ideally suited to complex decisions in which there are many important factors and to bringing a committee that has widely varying perspectives to a consensus.

Contract Negotiation

Negotiating and managing contracts is a skill that is needed by every person in a management role and the call center manager is no exception. Contracts can cover many aspects of the call center world including:

- Vendor contracts for equipment or services
- Outsourcing agreements
- Employment contracts (including union agreements)
- Agreements with customers (both internal and external)

While there is likely to be some level of support from the purchasing department and/or legal counsel, neither of these teams will be intimate with the specific issues that need to be covered from a call center management perspective, so turning the entire process over to these teams may be risky. The purchasing departments in many organizations are incented to reduce the price offered in the beginning of discussions, and the purchasing agent may be willing to exchange some important terms and conditions to achieve that goal. The attorney's role is to protect the legal interests of the company, but often at the risk of a negotiation process that drags out for weeks or months, even if time is of the essence in closing the negotiation. The vendor wants to get the best price possible for the least commitment of resources. So the call center manager must balance what each stakeholder wants and stay involved in the entire process to ensure that the end result is financially reasonable, legally defensible, and operationally feasible.

The overall objective of contract negotiation is to achieve a win-win deal in which the seller can and will deliver a quality project that can be used as a reference, and make a decent profit so the vendor can stay in business and continue to support and develop the product/service for future enhancements. It is also an agreement that gives the buyer a competitive price, a reasonable delivery timeframe, appropriate measures of success for the project, and the legal framework to defend buyer rights if things go wrong. It is unrealistic to squeeze a vendor for every dime of profit in a project, and then expect them to go the extra mile in the implementation or in support after the sale. So fair play is in the best interests of all parties.

A good starting point for negotiating a complete and fair contract is to list the objectives of the contract. These will include the objectives from both the buyer's and seller's perspectives. Then each team should put a weight on each objective to indicate those things that are very important and those that are more negotiable. This will serve as a base document to begin the negotiations process and to keep each team on track when the issues become unclear. For example, meeting the installation date may be critical to allow a new site to open its doors on time, or the date may be fairly flexible since the system is replacing another to allow future enhancement. If the date is critical, an incentive or penalty may be tied to it, and intermediate milestones developed to measure progress. But if time is not critical, it may be appropriate to give up emphasis on this point to gain an advantage in another area that is more important.

The next step is to develop a list of potential risks. Identify anything that could go wrong, the likelihood of it happening, and the impact if it did. This is much like developing a contingency plan as discussed in Chapter 13. The period immediately after the vendor is selected but prior to serious contract negotiations is typically referred to as the "honeymoon period." Everyone within both teams is convinced that this is going to be a great relationship and everyone involved is a "good guy." But it is important to be aware of all the things that could go wrong so that prevention and recovery techniques can be built into the contract. Many of the prevention and recovery techniques can be stated as penalties for non-performance and/or rewards for achieving results beyond the requirements. For example, when the due date is critical, there might be a financial penalty for each day the system is late, but an added bonus for every day it is early as long as it meets acceptance criteria. Think of penalties and rewards that will get people's attention. Money is not always the best or only choice.

Incentives for exceptional performance should also be considered and outlined in the contract. Being willing to serve as a reference account, allowing the vendor to bring prospects on site, and even doing a video reference can be a huge incentive to the vendor, and it will cost little more than some time.

When it comes to the legal language within the contract, there is no substitute for engaging an attorney who is familiar with the company's needs and the unique issues of the industry involved. In general, working out the legal language is somewhat separated from working out the particulars of the "deal," but in the end all of the pieces have to fit together in a unified and enforceable document.

There will be very specific legal issues that are involved only in a particular type of contract or industry, and it is unrealistic to expect an attorney to be totally familiar with them all without guidance from the specialists. This is particularly true in the call center industry with so much specialized technology and jargon. The basic purpose of the contract is to memorialize and formally document the entire agreement between the parties, including every assumption and every promise that has been made verbally as the process has developed. The contract should be written so that a person totally unfamiliar with the project and its circumstances could ascertain from the document alone what has been agreed and how the project will proceed.

Attached to the basic contract will usually be a series of schedules or attachments. These list the specific items in the contract, all equipment components, software versions and features, and any assumed infrastructure that the call center must have in place for the system to operate. A list of the delivery dates and progress payments assigned to them might be included, along with detailed pricing for the initial and add-on components. If special training is to be developed and delivered it should be spelled out along with any job aids, or training materials that will be provided. Where system maintenance is an issue, there is generally an attachment that defines the maintenance offerings and the costs associated with them.

One of the most important parts of the document is often missing or minimal. This is the listing of acceptance criteria that will be used to determine that the contract requirements have been successfully met and the customer is satisfied. Negotiating acceptance criteria before the work begins is essential to a smooth process where everyone knows exactly what the rules are that will be applied. The acceptance criteria must be reasonable and achievable, but they must also demonstrate that the vendor has successfully delivered what was promised. The customer will also be constrained from making unreasonable demands if the rules are clear in the beginning, further reinforcing the concept that a contract should be designed to achieve a win-win situation.

Relationship Management

Once the initial contract between buyer and seller is completed, contract and relationship management begins. When the purchasing agents, attorneys, and professional contract negotiators are finished, the implementation work is turned over to the operations team. It is common for the contract and all of the custom-negotiated terms and conditions to be filed away and not shared with the people who are meant to make it happen. So the first order of business at the initial implementation team meeting is to ensure that every member of the team has a copy of the contract and knows what is required by it. The project manager should have a copy at every team meeting and refer to it to resolve any kind of dispute that arises that might be addressed in the document. It is also common for the primary goals of the project not to be communicated well to the entire team, especially if team members were selected after the vendor presentations and RFP analysis were done. So making sure everyone knows what the objectives are will also be helpful.

A detailed project plan should be the next step in the process. This plan needs to include all of the contractual dates and deliverables and define the responsibilities of each member of the team. This project plan is typically developed by the vendor and becomes another base document that the project managers refer to at every meeting. If progress is tracked regularly and problems are identified early, most difficulties can be resolved without impacting the project. However, if the milestones are weeks apart and include a host of tasks that must be done to achieve each one, tracking the progress toward that goal is difficult. Some small but critical task may jeopardize the entire project, but go unnoticed for weeks.

When things are not going well, it is common for project teams to fool themselves into thinking they can make it up somewhere else. There is a great reluctance to deliver the bad news to the senior managers, but bad news does not improve with age. The sooner a challenge can be identified and brought to the attention of those who can fix it, the better the chance that it will be resolved successfully.

As the contract nears conclusion, the acceptance testing process will commence. It is important to be rigorous in applying the agreed upon rules and ensuring that both teams sign off on the final completion. If anything remains incomplete or unsatisfactory, acceptance should not be signed without a very specific document that defines the deficiency and the date by when it will be resolved. Too many contracts end up in arbitration and/or court because there was no acceptance criteria, or the customer felt pressured to sign the acceptance when the project was not really satisfactory. And it is hard to convince the court that the job was not done correctly when the acceptance documents contain the customer's signature.

When acceptance has been completed and signed, the contract management may be turned over to an ongoing maintenance team. This team could be a completely separate group of individuals on either or both teams, so a smooth transition to daily operations should include a review of the project's objectives, the components acquired and implemented, and what is expected in the future. If there is a warranty period, the new team must understand the rules and when it expires. Where there are multiple maintenance contract options, one should be selected. Procedures for reporting and resolving problems should be detailed and reports between the parties defined in the contract, but if they have not been detailed, this is the time for that negotiation to take place.

Project Management

There is a difference between day-to-day operations and project management. Even though projects can vary in scope and content, there are two characteristics that make projects different from normal workplace activities. First, projects are unique in that every project has a different set of objectives. Since each project is unique, there is also a different starting point, mid-point, and ending point for the project. Normal workplace activities usually involve a set of repetitive tasks carried out on a regular basis. Projects are not permanent and/or ongoing.

Second, a project has a specific outcome that is tangible and observable. The outcome may be referred to as a work product or deliverable. This outcome is an observable result such as a product or service. The outcome helps to identify when the project has been completed successfully, and can also help to analyze whether or not the project has achieved what it was intended to achieve.

Large projects are often broken up into phases to provide better management control. Even though the project may have different phases, each phase will also have a tangible outcome or deliverable for that particular part of the project. When projects consist of different phases, the phases combine to create the life cycle of a project. The life cycle includes what work should be completed in each phase and who should be involved. The life cycle defines the progress from start to finish. Each project may have similar or unique phases. For example, an implementation phase and approval phase would be similar from project to project, while a feasibility study may be unique for some projects.

Step 1 – Project initiation

Initiation is the process for recognizing and approving the project and authorizing it to move forward. This first step is crucial for the success of the project. The initiation stage starts with recognizing a business need for the project. (If a formal business case has been completed, this step can be minimized.) A business need is a gap between the current status and the desired status. Next, options are identified to determine a variety of potential solutions to a business need. The project team then selects the best option to meet the business need using a set of selection criteria. The selection criteria are the factors to be considered when choosing a suitable option. These factors may include items such as schedule, time, and cost. Finally, a project charter is created authorizing the project to begin. A project charter is a clear and concise statement used to formally initiate a project.

Using the previous example for the software company help desk, assuming the business case presented to senior management was approved, this step of project management would not be required.

Step 2 – Project scope

The project scope is the total product or service the project will provide to meet a business need. The goal of creating a project scope is to provide a clear definition to everyone involved with the project of what the team is expected to deliver and what they are not expected to deliver. The outcome of the project scope will be a written document called a project scope statement. The scope statement will include the product or service provided by the project, the project objectives, and the project deliverables. The phrase "out of scope" refers to the project team providing a product or service not required by the project.

In the software company help desk example, the business case and project was approved for a) the design and implementation of a monitoring form, b) the design and implementation of a new-hire training program, and c) implementation of a training program for supervisors. Should the project team decide to send out an RFP to vendors for a quality monitoring software program, this activity would be considered "out of scope" since it refers to providing a service not required by the project.

Step 3 – Project activities

An activity is an element of work that can be carried out to create a deliverable. Each project needs an activity list. An activity list tells exactly what needs to be done to create each deliverable. The activity list is often called a work breakdown structure (WBS), which is an organized grouping of project activities that defines the total scope of the project. Each activity has an associated cost, duration, and personnel requirement to successfully complete the activity. To manage the project, a Gantt Chart is typically used. These charts show all the project activities, their tasks, their sequence, and how long each sequence will take. For more complex project, the Project Evaluation and Review Technique (PERT) process can be used. It relates every task to those that are predecessors or dependent and uses sophisticated mathematical models to assist in making necessary adjustments as the project proceeds. There are a number of software tools available today that make the Gantt and PERT processes easier to apply.

The project manager for the software company help desk may decide to use a Gantt Chart to capture the activity list for the project. The following represents a few of the activities included for the design of the new-hire orientation program:

Develop content targeted to the experience level of the trainees.

Incorporate principles of adult learning into course design.

Design exercises to simulate job tasks.

Create job-aids to supplement course material.

Step 4 – Project costs

Project costs are usually estimated using a systematic approach. The benefits of cost estimation include clearer assumptions, increased credibility, better planning, and minimized over-budgeting. There are three basic estimation strategies that could be implemented:

- Top-down – This approach compares the new project with similar completed projects with known costs. This estimation strategy is called "top-down" because costs are estimated by starting with a single overall cost figure and working down to greater levels of detail.

• Bottom-up – The "bottom-up" estimation strategy first calculates the costs of the smallest individual element of a project. To get the total cost for the project, all of the individual costs estimated are added together.

• Parametric modeling – This estimation strategy creates an estimate by applying a standard formula to known project elements. With this approach, a mathematical model is identified based on a large amount of historical data showing average costs for various project components. The project estimate is made using calculations based on these figures, with any necessary adjustments.

The best approach to estimation is to use more than one strategy to be more certain of the final project costs.

The project manager for the software company help desk decides to use the "bottom-up" estimation strategy since this was the first training program that was being designed in-house and no other projects were similar in scope.

Step 5 – Project execution

Each new project should start with a kick-off meeting to clarify project vision, goals, roles and responsibilities, procedural guidelines, deliverables, and gain both individual and team commitment before the project work begins. As the project is launched, a clear and concise communication and reporting strategy should be implemented to ensure everyone knows the status of the project for each phase through completion.

The project manager for the software company help desk invites the team members for the project to a kick-off meeting to discuss the three goals for the project. Each team member should be provided with a copy of the business case to gain background information about the project. They should also receive a copy of a draft Gantt Chart created by the project manager and the rough estimates.

Step 6 – Project management

Team leadership is essential to the success of the project by motivating the team and leading them toward project completion. One part of managing the project successfully is the ability to compare where the project is versus where the project should be. The project manager should analyze variances throughout the project, not just at the beginning or the end. The ability to adjust for variances throughout the project will help to keep the project on target.

The project manager for the software company help desk will likely send out weekly updates to the Gantt Chart as an attachment as email to all team members. Team members may be expected to attend a bi-weekly team meeting to discuss the status of each milestone and celebrate the completion of previously completed activities.

Step 7 – Project close

At the conclusion of the project, documentation should be compiled concerning project results and formally acknowledging project completion. This formal closure stops the project from continuing on endlessly, ensures the work of the project team is formally acknowledged, and that lessons learned from the project are documented for future project review. Many projects need to be handed off to the operations team to manage the new product or service on an on-going basis. This hand-off should be formally done at the end of the project to ensure that the operations team's questions and issues are addressed as they take over control.

At the conclusion of the software company help desk project, the project manager might create a folder on the company's LAN with subdirectories for each of the stages of the project. The project information should include a copy of the Gantt chart with final statistics, along with notes and project documents in electronic format. The information may also be created and sent to appropriate members of the management team who may wish to review project details.

Summary

Making the decision to acquire a technology, system, or service deserves a great deal of attention. The solution must fit the call center's needs so a thorough analysis of the needs and the business case are required first steps. Once a decision has been made to acquire from an outside vendor, then a thorough and objective bidding process will ensure that the best solution for the best price and vendor is the final selection. Attention to the contract negotiations will pay significant dividends over the life of the relationship.

CHAPTER 9: WORKFORCE MANAGEMENT

Introduction

Workforce management – the art and science of getting the "just right" number of staff in place to respond to customer contacts to meet service goals and minimize cost – is one of the most critical functions in the call center. Since more than two-thirds of operating costs are related to staff, it is critical to find the balance of achieving the speed of answer customers expect and eliminating any waste in the staffing budget caused by inefficient scheduling.

NOTE: This chapter will provide an overview of the workforce management process. For those needing a more detailed, step-by-step explanation of the process and calculations, refer to *Call Center Staffing: The Complete, Practical Guide to Workforce Management* book from The Call Center School Press.

Workforce Management Overview

Perhaps the most critical operational function in the call center is making sure enough people are on the phones to respond to callers with a minimum of delay. The process of making this happen is called workforce management. It's defined as the art and science of getting the "just right" number of staff in place every period of the day to meet service levels while minimizing cost. The goal is to have the precise number needed every single half-hour of the day long – too many and not too few.

The process of workforce management is complicated by the fact that incoming call center workload is out of the call center's control. The telephone call workload arrives whenever customers decide to place a call and for the most part, the call center is at the mercy of the arriving calls. While the call center does have control over workload in an outbound center, that work too is somewhat controlled by the customer as the center struggles to call at the best time to find the customer available and willing to take a call.

The workforce management process is both an art and a science. It's an art because it is, after all, predicting the future. And the accuracy of any staffing plan will be due in some part to judgment and experience. But it's also a science – a step-by-step mathematical process that takes past history and uses it to predict future events. A working knowledge of these specialized statistical techniques is critical for every call center manager. And those organizations that have workforce management software in place that automates the forecasting and scheduling process aren't off the hook. It's just as critical for these centers to understand these calculations as it is for someone that's doing them by hand. It's important to understand the numbers coming from the software tool to verify accuracy of results and perhaps more importantly, explain the numbers to management. So even with tools to help, learning the fundamentals of workforce management is worthwhile.

The process of workforce management is critical to the success of every call center.

Here are the basic steps of the workforce management process:

1. Gather and analyze historical data.

2. Forecast call workload.

3. Calculate staff requirements.

4. Create staff schedules.

5. Track and manage daily performance.

Data Gathering and Analysis

The first assumption behind workforce management is that past history is the best predictor of the future in most call centers, so gathering this history is the first task. The most obvious source of this information will be historical reports from the ACD - specifically the number of calls offered and handle time information by half hour.

It is critical to gather representative samples from sources that are accurate. The basis of any good staffing plan is accurate input data. Without a precise forecast of the work to be expected, the most sophisticated effort to calculate staff numbers and create intricate schedule plans is wasted effort. The old adage of "garbage in, garbage out" is especially true when applied to call center workforce management. Accurate data to feed into the forecasting process is the most important step of the process. In terms of how far back to delve into historical reports, it's ideal to have two years worth of past history if it's available and if it's relevant. Less than two years worth may suffice, but won't provide the most accurate tracking of trends and monthly/seasonal patterns that 24 months will clearly show.

In terms of what specific information to gather, the two numbers to look for by half-hour are call volume and average handle time (AHT). It's important to note that we typically assume the call volume information from the ACD accurately portrays the workload for which a center needs to staff. This assumption is valid as long as "all calls are getting in" and that none are blocked at the network level by insufficient telephone trunks. It's always a good idea to validate this assumption by requesting periodic "busy studies" from local and long distance carriers. In situations where the queue is very long and a significant number of callers abandon the queue and call back later, the number of calls may also be somewhat inflated by these multiple attempts to reach the agent.

Forecasting Workload

The next stage in the process translates the raw data into a prediction of what's coming for a future month. There are several approaches to get to this future forecast:

> **Point Estimate.** This is the simplest approach and assumes that any point in the future will match the corresponding point in the past. (i.e., the first Monday in April next year will be the same as the first Monday in April of this year). This approach has obvious shortcomings in that it does not account for any upward or downward trends in calling patterns. It's also dangerous in that the forecast can be dramatically different if the original data was atypical.

Averaging Approaches. There are a variety of methods that incorporate simple mathematical averaging, ranging from a simple average of several past numbers, to a moving average where older data is dropped out when new numbers are available. The most accurate averaging approach involves weighted averaging, where more recent events are given more weight or significance than older events. But while the weighted average approach is probably the closest to what an actual forecast would be, it still misses the upward trend that occurs in most call center data that simply can't be identified and incorporated by averaging together old numbers.

Time Series. The recommended approach for call center forecasting involves a process called time series analysis. This approach takes historical information and allows the isolation of the effects of trend (the rate of change) as well as seasonal or monthly differences. It is the approach used in most call centers and serves as the basis for most of the automated workforce management forecasting models. The basic assumption is that call volume is influenced by a variety of factors over time and that each of the factors can be isolated and used to predict the future.

The first step in a time series approach is to isolate the effect of trend. Trend is basically just the rate of change in the calls. While that trend can be upward or downward, in most call centers, trend simply means the growth rate. It is important to determine this rate as an annual trend rate as well as a month-to-month change.

Once the trend rate has been determined, the next factor to isolate is the effect of seasonality or month-to-month variances. The trend rates and seasonal patterns identified using time series analysis are then used to pinpoint specific future monthly forecasts. The time series process is the recommended approach to forecasting future workload and if done precisely, can generally create forecasts with 95% or higher forecasting accuracy.

Once monthly forecasts are in place, the next step involves breaking down the monthly forecast into a daily prediction, then further down into hourly or half-hourly numbers. To predict daily workload, day-of-week factors are calculated. Many call centers have a busier day on Monday than other days of week and it's important to know what percentage of the week's workload this day and others represent.

Once the daily forecast is in place, it's time to repeat the process for time-of-day patterns. It would be nice and easy to schedule staff if the calls came in evenly throughout the day, but since that's not reality, it's critical to know when the peaks, valleys, and average times are. To do this, gather several "clear" weeks of data and evaluate the Mondays to look at how each half-hour of the day compares to the daily total to create Monday half-hourly patterns. Then repeat for the other days of the week. The result will be 24 hourly or 48 half-hourly percentages that represent intra-day call patterns for each day of week.

The historical data and past trends have been analyzed to develop a monthly, then daily, then half-hourly forecast of workload. Keep in mind that this forecast must include not only call *volume* predictions, but should include a prediction about *aver-*

age handle time (AHT) as well. To calculate workload and predict staffing and schedule requirements later, a call center must have the total picture of workload, which is number of calls multiplied by average handle time. It is critical to represent handle time predictions accurately that reflect the time of year, day of week, and time of day, since call length may vary for a number of reasons having to do business variations as well as caller behavior.

The final step in the forecasting process is an important one. There are many factors that influence the call center's workload and the smart workforce planner will have a process in place that considers all these factors in the forecasting process.

Think about all the different areas of an organization that influence the calls the call center will receive. The most obvious one is the marketing department who has tremendous impact on work based on the sales and marketing promotions they do. Ideally there should be a formal communications process in place to hear about marketing plans well ahead of the actual event so they can be built into the forecasting assumptions.

All other areas that impact calling should be considered in the planning process as well. Will the billing department's new invoice format cause a flood of calls? How about sales forecasts from the Sales VP that could assist in planning staff based on the new customer account base a year from now? Is the fulfillment area changing the way they package and ship products that may cause an increase (or decrease!) in call volume? It's critical that the workforce planning process incorporate all these influencers of call center workload in preparing and fine-tuning the forecast. In a sense, the call center is a support organization to these other departments, so a coordinated effort of predicting and managing the workflow in the call center will serve these "client" departments well.

Calculating Staff Requirements

Once the forecast is in place, the next step is calculating staff requirements to meet service goals. With the call volume forecasts and some assumptions about average handle time, workload is calculated by multiplying the number of forecast calls for an hour by the average handle time of a call.

The workload number is then used to determine how many base staff are needed to handle the calls. The part that makes staffing for a call center different than any other kind of staffing situation is that this workload doesn't represent typical work patterns. Let's compare an incoming call center to a group of clerical workers processing mail in the same company. Between 8:00 and 9:00am, the clerical staff has 400 pieces of mail to process and each piece takes 3 minutes to handle. That's 1200 minutes or 20 hours of workload. To process 20 hours of workload, 20 staff would be needed. The reason for the 1:1 ratio is that the mail tasks represent sequential workload. In other words, the staff can process the work as back-to-back tasks and each person can accomplish one hour of work in an hour timeframe.

Applying those same numbers in a call center scenario will yield a different result. These employees are getting 400 calls and each one takes an average of three minutes to handle – 2 minutes of conversation and another minute of after-call work. The workload is again 1200 minutes or 20 hours of workload, but in this situation, the work cannot be handled with only 20 people. At 8:05, there may be 22 calls arriving, meaning all 20 agents are busy, with another 2 calls in queue. Then at 8:15, there may only be 16 calls in progress, meaning 4 staff are idle. Those 4 people won't be able to accomplish a full hour's work, simply because of the way the calls have arrived. In an incoming call center, the work doesn't arrive in a back-to-back fashion. Rather, the work arrives whenever customers decide to place calls. So we have random workload instead of sequential work. This brings us to the most important math rule of call center staffing: *You must have more staff hours in place than hours of actual work to do.*

So how many extra staff would be needed? The number of staff needed depends on the speed of answer the call center wishes to deliver. Obviously, the more staff available, the shorter the delay will be. The fewer the staff, the longer the caller will wait.

Determining what happens with a given number of resources in place to accomplish a defined amount of workload requires a mathematical model that replicates the situation at hand. There are several telephone traffic engineering models available and one of these in particular is well-suited to the world of incoming call centers. Most call centers use a model called Erlang C that takes into account the randomness of the arriving workload as well as the queuing behavior (holding for the first available rep) of the calls.

Erlang C

Let's take a look at Erlang C predictions based on the 20 hours of workload defined earlier. The table below shows what would happen with anywhere from 21 to 28 staff (Column 1) in place to handle the 20 hours of incoming call workload.

The second column shows the portion of calls that would find no agent available and go into queue and the third column shows how long those delayed callers would wait on average. So, with 24 staff in place, the Erlang C model predicts that 30% of callers would be delayed and that they would wait an average of 45 seconds in queue.

Number of Staff	Delayed Portion	Delay of Delayed Callers	Average Delay (ASA)	Service Level (in 20 sec)
21	76 %	180 sec	137 sec	32%
22	57%	90 sec	51 sec	55%
23	42%	60 sec	25 sec	70%
24	**30%**	**45 sec**	**13 sec**	**81%**
25	21%	36 sec	8 sec	88%
26	14%	30 sec	4 sec	93%
27	9%	26 sec	2 sec	96%
28	6%	23 sec	1 sec	97%

The third column represents the average delay of all calls, including the ones that are answered immediately. So, with 24 staff in place, 30% of calls would go to the queue and wait there 45 seconds, while the other 70% would be answered immediately. The average delay, or average speed of answer (ASA), is the weighted average of both these groups [(45 x .30) + (0 x .70)] = 13 seconds. It's important to understand that this ASA number is not the average queue experience for the callers. Either they wait (and do so for an average of 45 seconds), or they don't wait at all. The ASA isn't a "real life" number – it's a statistic to represent the average of the two other numbers.

The fourth column represents service level. Service level represents X% of callers that are handled in Y seconds of delay time. This table shows the percentage that is handled within a specified 20 seconds of wait time. A common call center service goal is 80% of the calls handled in 20 seconds or less. To meet this goal, 24 staff or "bodies in chairs" would be needed, yielding a service level of 81% in 20 seconds. ("Bodies in chairs" is the number of staff logged into the ACD and available to take calls and must not be confused with the number of staff scheduled or the number on the payroll, which will be discussed later in this section.)

In determining what a call center service goal should be, there's really no such thing as an "industry standard." Setting a speed of answer goal depends upon many different factors. Call centers need to consider enterprise goals and marketing strategies, competitor standards, and most importantly the expectations of customers. We often find that call center management marches toward the same service goal year after year without ever considering if the goal should be higher or lower based on the business environment or customer demands. And the same speed of answer goal for all types of calls and all customers may be inappropriate as well.

Customer expectations have certainly risen when it comes to speed of answer. More and more callers are basing their expectations and judging your service on their last, best service experience. Taking a look at a call center's ACD reports and looking at when callers begin to abandon calls will provide some idea about a "worst case" delay scenario. But setting the "best case" goal should involve getting feedback from senior management, customers, competitors, and other centers – and then evaluating cost and service trade-offs to determine the impact on cost and on service of raising or lowering the goal.

Relationship of Staffing and Service

Let's take one more look at the staffing table and review the impact on service as staff numbers change. Obviously, delay times increase as agents are subtracted, and service improves as bodies in chairs are added. But service is not affected to the same degree each way, and this is a critically important phenomenon to understand about call center staffing.

Let's say a center needs to have 24 staff in place to handle the 20 hours of telephone workload in order to meet an 80% in 20 seconds service level goal. If the staff numbers are adjusted up or down, there are two very different impacts. First, if a person or two is added, the average speed of answer (ASA) improves from 13 seconds to 8 seconds with 25 staff, and then to 4 seconds with 26 staff. The first person added yielded a 5-second improvement; with the next person gaining the center only a 4-second improvement, and a third person would result in an ASA of 2 seconds, a 2-

second improvement. Adding staff results in diminishing returns, with less and less impact as the staff numbers get higher.

Now let's look at the effect of subtracting staff from the 24 person requirement. When subtracting one, two, and three persons the ASA increases to 25 seconds, 51 seconds, and 137 seconds respectively. The first person out resulted in an increase of 12 seconds, the second in another 26-second decline, and the third in a jump of another 86 seconds! By taking staff away, service worsens and it does so dramatically at some point. There are especially big jumps as the staff number gets closer and closer to the hours of workload.

This impact on service can be viewed as both good news and bad news. The good news is that centers delivering poor service can improve it dramatically by adding just one more person. On the other hand, when service levels are mediocre to bad, one more person dropping out can send service into such a downhill slide that it's nearly impossible to recover.

Shrinkage

The numbers discussed so far are purely "bodies in chairs" numbers. These numbers assume that all agents are always available to handle call workload. But agents aren't available much of the time. And it's critical to factor in this unavailability into schedule requirements so the center ends up with enough staff to answer the phones.

In calculating staff requirements, a final adjustment needs to be made to factor in all the activities and situations that make staff "unproductive." This unproductive time is referred to as staff shrinkage and defined as any time for which employees are being paid but not available to handle calls. Include such activities as breaks, meetings, training sessions, off-phone work, and general unproductive or "where the heck are they?" time. Look at one example below of a sample call center's shrinkage amounts and their impact on staff availability.

Shrinkage Category	Sample Calculation	Annual Hours
Paid Breaks	1/2 hour/day x 5 days x 50 weeks	125 hours
Paid Time Off	8 hours x 11 days/year	88 hours
Meetings/Training	3 hours/week x 50 weeks	150 hours
Off-Phone Time	1 hour/day x 5 days x 50 weeks	250 hours
Unexplained Time	1/4 hour/day x 5 days x 50 weeks	62 hours
	TOTAL SHRINKAGE	675 hours
	Potential Hours	2080 hours
	PERCENT SHRINKAGE	**32%**

In most centers, staff shrinkage ranges from 20–35%. Account for this shrinkage factor in the staff requirement by dividing the Erlang staff requirement by the productive staff percentage (or 1 minus the shrinkage percentage). In this example, if 24 agents are needed and the shrinkage factor is 32%, then 24/.68 yields a requirement of 35 personnel in the staffing pool who could be scheduled.

Some of the people in the staffing pool will be unavailable due to planned absences such as vacations or training classes. These are generally known well ahead of time. However, some of these absences will occur at the last minute and not be known when the actual schedule for that day is developed. These include last-minute sick calls, tardies, and the unexplained time. So part of the shrinkage factor will be replaced by known absences as the plan develops while another part of the shrinkage factor will remain unknown as the day or week begins. But if the extra staff is not planned into the schedule, these last-minute absences will result in unexpectedly poor service.

Staffing Tradeoffs

There are several staffing tradeoffs that should be examined when arriving at the proper staffing level. These tradeoffs include the arrival rate of calls, economies of scale, staff occupancy, and the tradeoff with telecommunications costs.

Call Arrival Rate

As discussed earlier, calls generally arrive at call centers in a random fashion, resulting in some minutes experiencing high volumes and others low or none. And because of this random pattern, a call center will always need more staff hours in place than the actual workload hours to be accomplished.

On the other hand, if calls arrive in a smoother pattern (closer to a task-after-task paperwork environment), then the number of staff needed would be closer to the workload hours. One might expect to see outbound calling follow this pattern, especially if an automated dialer is in use. The workload (outbound calling) occurs in a back-to-back sequential pattern rather than a random one. Likewise, responding to emails typically represents sequential workload as well, assuming that there is a backlog of emails in the work queue and personnel respond to these contacts one right behind the other. In both these cases, the number of staff required is equivalent to workload hours (assuming the staff can work at 100% productivity).

On the other hand, what if the workload arrives in a peaked pattern rather than a smooth one? Let's consider the call center that is responding to calls based on television advertising. There may be no calls arriving at 11:05, but a flood of calls arrives at 11:09 after an advertisement at 11:08. And then the calls drop again at 11:15 but peak again at 11:25. This "all or nothing" pattern requires enough staff to be in place to handle peaks of calls when they arrive, and agents will be idle during the lulls, meaning more staff would be required than a typical random pattern.

Group Size and Economies of Scale

Another factor that has a major impact on staffing is the size of the center or the agent group. Centers handling larger volumes of calls will naturally be more efficient than smaller groups. This is due to the economies of scale of large groups.

As seen in the example below, doubling the call volume does not require two times the number of staff to meet the same service goal of 80% in 20 seconds. And when call volume increases eight times, only about six times the number of staff is needed. As the volume grows, the staff to workload ratio gets smaller and smaller.

The reason for these increased efficiencies and the lower staff to workload ratio is simply that with a higher volume of calls, there's a greater likelihood that when an agent is finished with a call, there's another one coming in right behind it for that person to handle. With a bigger volume, each person has the opportunity to process more calls each hour. Each person spends less time in the available state waiting on a call to arrive and with each person handling more calls, not as many agents are needed.

Calls per Hour	Workload Hours	Staff Required	Staff:Work Ratio	Staff Occupancy (workload/staff)
100	8.33	12	1.44	.69
200	16.67	21	1.26	.79
400	33.33	39	1.17	.85
800	66.67	74	1.10	.90
1600	133.33	142	1.06	.94

Staff Occupancy

So if a higher volume of calls means that each person is busier, then one might assume that bigger is always better. After all, if agents are being paid to sit and handle calls, don't call centers want them busy all the time doing just that? The answer is yes…and no. While call center management wants staff to be busy processing calls, having them too busy (in other words, no available time or "breather" between calls) isn't such a good idea either.

The measure of how busy agents are is called agent occupancy. It's the percentage of logged in time that an agent is actually busy in talk or wrap-up time. It's calculated by dividing the amount of workload by the staff hours in place. In the previous table, with 12 staff handling 8.33 hours of workload, agent occupancy is only 69%. At double the call volume with 21 staff in place, twice the workload is being handled without doubling the workforce, so each person is busier. In this case occupancy has increased to 79%.

As the volume of calls grows, increased efficiencies and economies of scale come into effect, meaning occupancy goes higher and higher. And while call centers want staff to be productive and busy, asking staff to stay occupied at a 94% rate is not realistic. Most call centers aim for the 85–90% range since occupancy rates higher than that lead to all kinds of undesirable call handling behaviors as well as a high turnover rate.

Telecommunications Tradeoffs

A final staffing tradeoff has to do with the relationship of staff to service and cost. Call centers are typically being asked to cut costs and to do more with fewer resources and the first strategy may be to cut staff. It is all too common to think of layoffs and reduction in staff as a way to respond to the call from senior management to tighten belts. But before writing up the pink slips, understand the implications of staff reductions.

Take the example of a fairly small call center with fewer than 50 agent seats. (A larger center can view these numbers as representative of a specialized agent group within the bigger call center structure.) Most days the center is meeting a service goal of 70% in 30 seconds. The snapshot below indicates the staffing picture with varying numbers of staff during a half-hour in which the center is getting 175 calls.

As seen in the table, staffing with 33 "bodies in chairs" would enable the center to meet service level fairly consistently. But the loss of one person would worsen service level from 74% to 62% (or average speed of answer from 30 seconds to 54 seconds). Eliminating another person would drop service level to 46%, and the average delay would double to 107 seconds! And reducing staffing levels by three would horribly deteriorate service level to only 24%, resulting in an average delay of 298 seconds! So those callers accustomed to waiting for only half a minute in queue would now be waiting nearly five minutes!

Number of Staff	Avg Delay (ASA)	Service Level (in 30 sec)	Staff Occupancy
30	298 sec	24%	97%
31	107 sec	46%	94%
32	54 sec	62%	91%
33	30 sec	74%	88%
34	18 sec	82%	86%
35	11 sec	88%	83%

And service isn't the only thing that suffers. With 33 staff in place to handle the call workload, agent occupancy (the measure of how busy agents are during the period of time they're logged in and available) is in a good range at 88%. Taking one body away raises occupancy levels to 91%; taking two away results in 94% occupancy; and taking three away means staff would be busy 97% of the time during the hour. In other words, there would be only 3% (108 seconds) of "breathing room" between calls. Such a high level of occupancy can't be maintained for long. The likely result will be longer handle times, longer periods spent in after-call work to "catch their breath," burnout, and turnover.

And there's another point to consider. The reduction in staff might be outweighed by the increased telephone costs associated with the longer delay times. In this example, with 33 staff in place the average delay is 30 seconds per call. Multiply that by 350 calls per hour and that's 10,500 seconds (or 175 minutes) of delay. If we apply a fully loaded telephone cost per minute of toll-free service to that usage of $.06 per minute, that's $10.50 for the queue time. If we try and staff with 30 staff, remember our average delay increases to 298 seconds of delay. Multiply that by 350 calls and that's 1738 minutes of delay, priced at $.06 for a total of $104.30 for the queue time that hour. In other words, by eliminating three staff to save money, the call center has just increased its telephone bill by $ 93.80 for that hour! And this doesn't even take into account the likelihood of a longer call while the customer complains about the long wait in the queue. Telephone charges would likely increase even further. Since telephone charges are not always included in the call center's budget, this tradeoff may not be as obvious as it should be. But a joint analysis by the IT/Telecom staff and the call center can reveal the overall impact of these staffing decisions.

This situation is even more dangerous in a revenue-producing center. If the value of a contact is $50, and agent salaries are $20 per hour, it is easy to see that putting another agent on the phone will pay for itself even if the agent only answers one call per hour that would otherwise have abandoned from the queue. Even if the value of the call is only $5, there is clearly a tradeoff in determining the staffing level that will produce the highest net bottom line. The return on appropriate staffing must be argued against budget constraints.

So, from three different perspectives, it is clear that a simple staff reduction may not save a call center any money. In fact, it may cost more in terms of poor service, reduced revenues, excessive occupancy levels, as well as increased telephone costs.

Staff Scheduling

After reviewing the factors that affect the number of staff needed to handle the contacts half-hour by half hour, the next step is figuring out how to schedule in order to get the right number of people in place at the right times. Once a "bodies in chairs" number has been determined by half-hour, the next step is to translate this staff requirement into a schedule requirement number.

Take the example where a call center is staffing for 450 calls between 10:30–11:00 am and average handle time (AHT) is 270 seconds (or 67.5 erlangs of workload). For a service objective of 70% of calls answered in 30 seconds, the center would need 72 staff to meet its service goals. So, if 72 people are needed for the peak calling time between 10:30 and 11:00, does that mean the call center would schedule 72 people to work the 8:00am–5:00pm shift?

Oh, if only it were that easy! The problem is that with a group of agents that started at 8:00am, naturally they're going to want to take a break around 10:30am. And then a few will be calling in sick today. Perhaps another group is out in a training session. And don't forget the agents that need time to do off-phone work.

This reduction in workforce is referred to as workforce shrinkage and it's important to account for this shrinkage or "overhead" when calculating how many people to schedule on certain shifts. The call center must schedule enough staff so that when the workforce shrinks, there will still be enough bodies in chairs to handle the calls.

While shrinkage is low in some centers at about 20%, it can be extremely high (over 50%) in others. It's important to measure it regularly and use a number that reflects reality. Also be aware that the shrinkage percentage changes by month, day of week, and time of day just like call volume and handle time. For example, most centers do not train on their busiest calling day, and absenteeism is generally higher on Mondays and Fridays than on Wednesdays.

To factor shrinkage into the schedule calculation, divide the base staff requirement by the productive percentage of time. Let's say call center shrinkage is 35%. In the previous staffing problem where 72 bodies in chairs are needed, the actual schedule requirement would be calculated by dividing 72 by the productive percentage of 65% (72/.65 = 111 staff). This calculation gives us the 100% number the center needs to have available to schedule for this half-hour so that when the workforce shrinks by 35% it ends up with 72 people on the phones.

The 111 staff calculated above is not the number on the payroll in many cases, since there needs to be staff for all shifts and days of the week that the center is open, but this is the number who could be scheduled for this period. When planning well into the future, such as during budget projections, the full adjustment for all shrinkage must be taken into account to ensure that there will be enough personnel available to meet all the needs. But as the week approaches for the actual work to be done, many of the absences will already be known, and only the unplanned portion of the shrinkage will need to be accommodated in the number of schedules created and assigned to the staff.

Defining Schedules

Once a schedule count has been determined for each half-hour, the next step is deciding how to define the actual schedules. This is the step where the lengths of shifts are defined, as well as the scheme of days on/off. Call centers will need to determine if mostly 8-hour x 5 day schedules will be used with each person working five consecutive days versus trying some variations such as four 10-hour days or even three 13-hour days (as one call center has surprisingly found to be a favorable combination for overnight shifts!) Think about varying the full-time definition further and try out three 10-hour days and two 5-hour days. Split the days off so they don't have to come together sometimes. There are dozens of possible schedule definitions, even within the restriction of full-time schedules.

Expanding the schedule mix further to include part-time schedules will have tremendous payback in terms of increased schedule flexibility to meet the fluctuation workload. Four-hour or six-hour schedules give a center so much more flexibility in matching the workforce to the workload that it's typically well worth the extra effort it takes to employ a part-time workforce. While part-time staff generally have higher turnover and are more expensive to train (since the same training effort is expended on more employees), it is equally important to note that sometimes the part-timers may be less expensive in terms of benefit costs, and may actually be more productive employees given their shorter exposure each day. In evaluating the many tradeoffs, the biggest one that cannot be ignored is how much better a fit of schedules to requirements a call center will have with part-time staff.

Another definition in creating work schedules is the start time interval. Some call centers have staff start "on the hour," while others have staff starting every half-hour. These start time intervals are another factor in determining the best fit of schedules to match the workload, with half-hour, or even quarter-hour start times being more effective in coverage as seen in the table below.

60-Minute Start Times	30-Minute Start Times	15-Minute Start Times
132 FTE	124 FTE	114 FTE

By staggering start times to the half-hour or quarter-hour, the call center will naturally be staggering break times and other activities throughout the day. And for centers willing to split staff into four starting intervals within the hour and use 15-minute start times, the savings can be substantial. In this example, switching from 30-minute start times (the most common call center scenario) to 15-minute intervals saves 8% total headcount while producing a consistent speed of answer to callers.

Preferences Versus Requirements

Another issue plaguing workforce schedulers is whether employee preferences should drive schedule definitions or whether the service requirement is the primary driver. In today's world of high staff turnover, many call centers are doing whatever it takes to keep their staff happy, including pick of schedules. But beware! Giving all employees their first pick of schedule can be extremely expensive in terms of both service and cost.

One call center that recently evaluated the staffing implications of preference-based versus requirements-based schedules found that 162 FTE would be required for preference-based scheduling, while only 139 FTE were actually required based on workload requirements. This call center settled on a "happy medium" of guaranteeing each agent one of their top four choices of schedules (so still meeting a preference) while getting a much better match to the actual requirements. The increased flexibility of this intermediate solution required 152 FTE and managed to meet service goals while still giving staff some say about work schedules.

Schedule Horizon

A question call centers frequently ask is "How often should a call center create schedules or go through the bidding process?" The frequency of schedule creation and bidding is mostly a function of how volatile the workload is and how difficult the bidding or assignment of schedules is. For a call center whose volume and patterns don't change all that much, creating schedules once every three to six months may be just fine. And a longer schedule horizon certainly has its advantages in terms of more stability for the staff and less work for the workforce scheduler.

On the other hand, in an environment that is changing rapidly or is affected by many outside business drivers, forecasting and scheduling need to happen more often. Some call centers will need to schedule week by week, or at least once a month. And while frequent changes are tough on the workforce and the scheduler, a more frequent forecasting and scheduling cycle will result in a better match of workforce to workload and lower costs overall.

The approach that often strikes a reasonable balance is one where a base or foundation of schedules is in place and doesn't change much weekly or even monthly. Then the variations in workload each week can be met by a flexible set of schedules that change as needed to meet caller demands. The base schedules are generally the most desirable ones, and typically belong to the more senior staff. However, more and more call centers are beginning to use performance scores as a method to assign schedules to staff, since pick of schedules is a huge motivator. Call center management may want to think about a scheme where pick of schedules is assigned based on a weighed factor of seniority, attendance, and performance to get the best of both worlds.

Managing Daily Staffing and Service

Now that the many factors that go into defining and assigning workforce schedules have been defined, the next step is managing the schedules on a daily basis and making needed adjustments. After gathering and analyzing mounds of historical information to arrive at a call forecast, calculating the number of staff needed by half-hour to meet speed of answer goals, and juggling schedules to arrive at a reasonable mix of efficiency and acceptability, the next step is making sure the plan is working.

There are three steps in the daily performance tracking process:

Step 1: Tracking and Analysis

Step 2: Communications

Step 3: Reaction

Tracking and Analysis

Tracking performance within the day means tracking the three elements that affect service: call volume, average handle time (AHT), and staffing levels.

Let's take a look at how a variation in any one of these components might affect net staffing and service. For example, what if staff adhered to schedule and the call volume forecast was right on target, but calls took 30 seconds longer than normal?

It's easy to imagine a scenario where calls simply take longer to handle than planned. Perhaps the computer system is slower than usual, or a different format for the billing statement causes an extra question per call. Or perhaps this is the week a new hire class comes on the phones and their longer handle time drives up the average from 320 seconds to 350 seconds.

Time	Call Volume	Forecast AHT	Forecast Staff	Actual Calls	Actual AHT	Required Staff	Net Staff
6:00	280	320	56	280	350	61	- 5
6:30	310	320	62	310	350	68	- 6
7:00	350	320	69	350	350	76	- 7
7:30	380	320	75	380	350	82	- 7
8:00	420	320	82	420	350	90	- 8
8:30	450	320	88	450	350	96	- 8

With this longer handle time as the only variation, staff requirements are affected significantly. In the above example, staffing at 8:00 would need to be adjusted from 82 to 90 staff in order to meet an 80% in 20 seconds service goal. If staffing is not adjusted, the service level will drop to only 6% of calls answered in 20 seconds.

Of course, things might go the opposite direction and workload could be less than forecast. Consider the effect on staffing requirements and service level if the marketing campaign doesn't go as well as expected and call volume is 10% lower than planned. This time at 8:00, only 75 staff will be needed instead of the 82 that are scheduled to work. With everyone on the phones, service level will be 98% in 20 seconds. And while that's great from a service perspective, the overstaffing represents an unnecessary expense.

Schedule Adherence

Since one of the three factors to track by half-hour is staffing, a critical piece of the daily management plan is tracking and managing schedule adherence. The call center will want to match up real-time status and work state information from the ACD against planned schedules and daily schedule exceptions to effectively track whether staff members are doing what they're supposed to be doing.

Historical information about adherence and compliance is useful, but what's really needed in an intra-day environment is real-time adherence information. This can be achieved by walking around and checking filled seats or can be done quite effectively by a workforce management system. These real-time adherence systems can take real-time status messages from the ACD and compare to an agent's work schedule for the day. Any variations that exceed user-set thresholds are reported immediately.

The Real-Time Picture

It's important to track the three components of call volume, handle time, and staffing levels throughout the day to see what the impact will be on net staffing. Tracking should start early in the day and the numbers should be watched to see if any significant patterns are developing. As soon as a trend is spotted that seems to be consistent, it's time to reforecast based on the new numbers and predict what net staffing will be as a result for the remainder of the day. If the problem is caught in time, it can be fixed before it's too late to meet service goals.

While all three numbers should be tracked against one another and used to calculate net staffing, there are single numbers of half-hourly performance that may provide a quicker look at whether or not a call center is in trouble. These measures of call center performance can indicate if all is well or about to get out of hand.

For this snapshot of performance, some call centers use a measure of the number of calls in queue. They may set a threshold so that as soon as a certain number of waiting calls exist in the queue, a reactive process occurs. Others use the age or length of the oldest call in queue and when that wait time exceeds a defined limit, a reaction is imminent. Both of these are true real-time measures and represent a snapshot in time.

The question at hand is whether these are the measures that should be used to actually direct the real-time reaction process. While these two measures are useful as warning signals, using them to initiate adjustments may be ill advised. Think instead of setting and meeting service objectives as one half-hour race rather than six five-minute sprints. While an exceedingly high number of calls in queue at any given time might be alarming, it is likely that this number may go back to normal within five or ten minutes as breaks overlap or the natural ebb and flow of random calls happens.

The call center should evaluate carefully before using these real-time measures to drive changes and adjustments.

Reaction Strategies

Once the numbers indicate that overstaffing or understaffing is happening, the next steps are to communicate the problem and initiate a reaction strategy. It is likely that the workforce planning specialist or team will be the first to know there is a problem. This group may communicate directly with staff for the necessary adjustments, or may relay the information by team or by supervisor where changes are needed. This communication may begin as soon as there are warning indicators in order to provide a "heads up" about coming changes, or may not occur until it is time to actually make the adjustments.

It's important that every call center have a reaction plan for situations that require just a little tweaking as well as major adjustments. Those in charge of workforce management should always know the options whether the call center needs to add or subtract two staff or twenty.

Selecting a strategy depends upon answers to the following questions:

- How severe is the problem?
- What is the effect on service level to customers?
- What is the cause of the problem?
- Can you fix the cause rather than react?
- How long will the problem last?
- What are the options from easiest to hardest?
- What will each adjustment cost in terms of dollars, resources, and effort?

Common staffing reaction strategies for understaffing include:

- Have supervisors or other staff take calls.
- Delay meetings or training.
- Eliminate optional call content.
- Engage other qualified staff or outsource.

Likewise, understaffing can also be addressed by making technology changes such as:

- Re-route calls to other sites or groups.
- Adjust delay announcements.
- Change ring delay settings.
- Adjust the number of incoming trunks to create busy signals.
- Invoke other technologies such as IVR or callback messaging.

As seen in an earlier example, sometimes the adjustments need to go the other way. In cases where overstaffing is apparent, the following reaction strategies might be used:

- Do impromptu training.
- Schedule team meetings.
- Catch up on paperwork.
- Make proactive outbound calls.
- Offer time off without pay.

Once the forecast is in place, staff calculations are complete, and staff schedules are assigned, there's daily work to be done in the workforce management process. Tracking the half-hourly components of call volume, handle time, and staffing levels will provide the call center with the information it needs to communicate status and make necessary changes to ensure service goals are consistently met. The key is having a systematic process in place to track the information so there's sufficient time to react to make a difference for the day.

Summary

Workforce management – the art and science of getting the "just right" number of staff in place to respond to customer contacts to meet service goals and minimize cost – is one of the most critical functions in the call center. Nothing more directly affects the service provided to customers or the bottom line of the operation. Everything hinges on developing an accurate forecast of the workload to be handled. With an accurate forecast, staffing needs can be determined, and schedules created to assign to the staff. Once the plan is in place, the focus of the intra-day management process is to ensure execution of the plan, and adjustment for unforeseen changes that may occur. The overall result should be a consistently acceptable speed of answer for callers, and a fair and reasonable workload for the staff.

CHAPTER 10: REPORTING AND COMMUNICATIONS

Introduction

Reporting on the key elements of call center performance is central to ensuring that performance meets expectations consistently. The first step is determining what to measure and why. Then the source of the information and the process of manipulating the data into meaningful reports can follow.

In addition to measuring performance, the call center plays a pivotal role in gathering and disseminating information about customers to the rest of the organization. Determining the level of information, the format, the delivery frequency, and the distribution list for various reports is also important to ensure that decision makers have the needed information in a timely and useful fashion.

Performance Measurement System

Every call center must have a system of measures in place that addresses the concerns of the customer, senior management, and the frontline staff. This section will explore what this system of measures typically looks like in a call center.

From a call center manager's perspective, there are numerous reasons to measure performance in the center. Some of these reasons are:

- Review center-wide performance.
- Analyze trends.
- Determine root cause of problems.
- Improve internal reporting and accountability.
- Ensure effective use of resources.
- Aid in goal setting.
- Support strategic planning.

For the performance measures to be effective in supporting these objectives, it's important that a systematic approach be used to ensure the right things are being measured in the first place, that measurement approaches are appropriate, and that performance results are being analyzed and reported effectively. Using a systematic approach will provide the call center management team with a tool to plan, monitor, and manage the call center.

Developing an effective performance measurement system is made up of three steps:

1. Stratgegy
2. Performance measures
3. Reporting

There are literally hundreds of items a call center can measure. But just because a measure can be obtained easily does not make it relevant, and just because something needs to be measured does not mean that measurement will be easy. The key in creating a performance measurement system is to define the most critical measures in priority order. Therefore, one of the first questions to ask is what the system needs to include in order to assess how well the center is supporting the overall mission and goals of the business as a whole. (The various ways in which the call center can support the overall goals of the organization were outlined in Chapter 2 of this book.) These goals, and therefore the objectives of the center, might be one or more of the following:

- Support the organization's "brand" by delivering high-speed service, unmatched quality, or a fun interaction.

- Generate revenue in terms of direct sales and/or up-sell opportunities.

- Contribute to customer retention by delivering effective problem resolution.

- Gather market research data to drive product development or future marketing initiatives.

Whatever the call center's primary function or role in the organization actually is should be the first indicator of what the center should measure on a regular basis. What the top few measures of performance are for one call center may not even be in the top 10 for another. The measures of performance should be ones that effectively measure the business objectives of the call center, with those objectives hopefully having been set to maximize contribution to the company's overall business objectives and bottom line.

In developing a performance measurement strategy, ask the following questions:

- What performance measures will contribute to enterprise business objectives?

- What would be useful information to other departments in the company?

- What does the customer care about most and how can it be measured?

- What does the employee care about most and how can it be measured?

Many companies today follow a "balanced scorecard" approach in setting their business objectives and performance measures. The call center should be no different. All performance measurement systems should be based on a set of objectives and measures that evaluate how well the entity is doing in a variety of areas.

One of the best-known business texts for developing a balanced scorecard approach for performance measurement is *The Balanced Scorecard* by Robert Kaplan and David Norton. The book outlines the importance of measuring performance in four distinct areas:

- Financial
- Business Processes
- Customers
- Learning and Innovation

The balanced scorecard model incorporates both financial and non-financial factor and helps to align key performance measures at all organizational levels. The balanced scorecard approach is often applied to measures of success for the business as a whole, but it can also be used to define a balanced set of measures for the call center. As call center measures are defined, they should be reviewed against the balanced scorecard framework to ensure all areas are being reviewed so that call center management has a comprehensive picture of the operation.

Another approach to developing a measurement strategy is to ask what each of the call center's "stakeholders" cares about most and shape measures around their top concerns. The three main call center stakeholders – the three groups that call center management needs to keep happy – are customers, senior management, and frontline staff. Below are the typical concerns of each of these stakeholder groups. Defining performance measures that address each of these concerns is another approach in achieving a balanced system of call center measures.

Customers	Senior Management	Frontline Staff
Accessibility	Customer Service/Retention	Working Conditions
Speed of Service	Productivity/Efficiency	Environment
Quality of Service	Revenue	Development
Resolution	Employee Satisfaction/Retention	Rewards

Call Center Performance Measures

Service Measures

There are four main categories of service measures: accessibility, speed of service, quality of service, and resolution. Each of these measures is described below:

Accessibility

The following measures address the degree to which the caller actually accesses the resource needed for the interaction:

Hours/Days of Operation. One definition of availability addresses the coverage provided by the hours and days of operation of the center. If the call center is not open 24 hours per day, 7 days per week, call centers should evaluate the number of contacts that attempt to arrive outside operating hours. Conversely, those with 24 x 7 operations should measure the percentage of calls that arrive each half-hour of each day to determine if all hours support truly makes sense for the business.

Trunk Blockage. Another crucial measure of availability has to do with accessibility during operating hours. Call centers should measure blockage and incidents of busy signals to ensure sufficient resources are available to deliver calls into the center.

Self-Service Availability and Usage. An integral part of the customer access strategy for many call centers is a self-service option. In most cases, this self-service option involves use of integrated voice response (IVR) or speech recognition system. Two important measures of self-service availability are 1) the percentage of contacts

$$\text{Blockage} = \frac{\text{Number of callers experiencing a busy signal}}{\text{Total number of calls attempted}}$$

accessing the self-service alternative in the first place, and 2) the percentage of callers who complete their interaction in the IVR without exiting for a human interaction.

The percentage of contacts that access the IVR will indicate how well the self-service option is placed and marketed, while the second completion measure will indicate how well the system is designed and scripted. Evaluating the transactions that do not complete in the IVR and noting where they exit can help pinpoint opportunities to improve menus and scripting.

Today, self-service availability must also include the Internet options. The company web site will often offer customers some or all of the same options that can be accomplished via an IVR or by talking to an agent. The usefulness of the web site and the ability of customers to access human help as required will also need to be considered.

Abandon Rate. The abandon rate refers to the percentage of calls that abandon during the queue before reaching an agent. Abandon rate is affected by many factors, including caller tolerance for delay or wait time, urgency of transaction, availability of other company contact channels, availability of competitive alternatives, and caller expectations set by other call center interactions.

Speed of Service

Service Level. The most common measure of speed of service is service level, commonly referred to as X% of calls answered in Y seconds or less. A common goal for service level is to answer 80% of calls in 20 seconds or less. Service level is measured by half- hour. Service level is typically reported as either the cumulative average for the day, or as a weighted average number based on the percentage distribution of calls.

$$\text{Abandon Rate} = \frac{\text{Number of Calls Abandoned}}{\text{Total Answered} + \text{Abandoned Calls}}$$

Average Speed of Answer (ASA). Another common way to describe queue time or delay time is average speed of answer or ASA. This statistic represents the average delay of all calls for the period, including those calls that experience no queue at all. For example, if half the calls go into queue and wait an average of 60 seconds, and the other half go to an agent immediately and wait 0 seconds, the ASA would be 30 seconds.

Quality Measures

Most of the elements that describe the quality of the call are measured by either a customer satisfaction survey or via a quality monitoring process.

Quality Monitoring Scores. "This call may be monitored to ensure quality" is a frequently heard phrase in the call center industry. There are many measures of performance in place that are used in conjunction with the quality monitoring process. Call centers typically monitor for certain behaviors that are synonymous with good service and attach a quantitative score to the demonstration of these behaviors. Performance criteria typically include such items as adherence to scripts, accurate data entry, proper telephone techniques, and perceived problem resolution.

Error/Rework Rate. Many call centers focus on the occurrence or percentage of contacts that contain errors and have to be redone. Information about errors and rework generally comes from a customer information system, or may be sampled by call monitoring.

$$\text{Rework Rate} = \frac{\text{Total errors or repeated processes}}{\text{Total number of contacts}}$$

Customer Satisfaction Scores. Of course, the ultimate indicator of performance is the actual score given by the customer on a variety of satisfaction measures. While some organizations use only a general company survey to gauge customer satisfaction, some call centers take a more proactive approach and design surveys to evaluate the call center experience exclusively. These scores are excellent indicators of the overall customer experience, especially in viewing how well the calls are handled.

Resolution

Perhaps the single most critical factor of customer satisfaction is whether or not a specific need is met or problem is resolved. Therefore, a resolution rate or resolution factor is used by many call centers as a top measure of performance.

First Call Resolution. The most common measure of resolution success is the degree to which the interaction is completed in a single call. While not always easy to measure, even with a customer information system in place, the percentage of calls completed in a single transaction correlates positively with high customer satisfaction ratings.

Transfer Rate. One of callers' pet peeves is to be transferred from one person or department to another to get a problem solved or question answered. Their irritation is multiplied many times over if they have to repeat their account information or relay the problem over and over again. It is important to measure the number of calls that transfer from the original answering source to another person to be handled. This transfer rate correlates negatively with customer satisfaction scores, and may be an indicator where training may be needed to better equip a frontline associate to handle the call completely in one transaction. But it can also indicate a badly designed call routing function that is directing callers to the wrong resources in the center.

Efficiency Measures

In addition to measures that address the service concerns, there must be measures of performance that ascertain how well the call center is being run from an efficiency standpoint. These measures are generally divided into two categories: measures that indicate how efficiently the contact is being handled and those that measure how effectively the call center is using its resources.

Contact Handling

One way to analyze the effectiveness of the contact handling process is to evaluate each of the components that make up the call to ensure each phase is taking as long as, but not longer than, necessary.

Average Handle Time (AHT). AHT is made up of talk time plus any after-call work (ACW) time. Call centers measure AHT to ensure that it is in the "normal" range, with variations significantly above or below average a cause for concern. The biggest part of AHT is generally talk time with the customer and call centers should be careful in their zeal for efficiency that they do not drive talk time too low and therefore sacrifice quality and additional business opportunities while on the phone with the customer.

One component of talk time that call centers should strive to reduce is "on-hold" time. This is the time that callers are put on hold by the agent after the call begins (not to be confused with the delay time they experience while in queue waiting for the call to begin). Since the number of occurrences of being placed on hold and the length of time on hold correlate negatively with customer satisfaction ratings, call centers should track this particular component of AHT carefully and strive to minimize it.

After-Call Work (ACW). The other component of AHT is ACW time. This time, also referred to as post-call work (PCW) or wrap-up time, is the period after conversation with the caller is complete that the agent needs to spend processing the call. This time might be devoted to keying in tracking components for a type of call, updating a customer record, etc. While completely necessary in many cases, ACW can also be abused and is needlessly high in many call centers. Since ACW removes the agent from being available to handle the next call, figures that are too high can affect a call center's staffing numbers dramatically.

Calls Per Hour. One of the most commonly tracked measures of call center performance is the number of calls handled per hour (or half-hour) by an individual agent. While it is one of the most common performance measures, it is one that is most often used incorrectly in measuring individual performance. Other than keeping their AHT in a reasonable range by not abusing hold time or ACW, call center agents have no control over the number of calls they receive or handle in a given period. There will be peaks and valleys throughout the day and the number of calls received and processed will be a function of how many calls arrive and how the call center is staffed during that period. Since agents have no direct control over this measure, it is not recommended that this number be used as a key indicator of individual performance in the center.

Those call centers that focus on calls per hour as a key performance indicator may find they are encouraging various types of undesirable behavior as frontline agents devise methods to increase their individual call counts. Some agents may rush the customer through a call, or worse, even terminate the call before it is complete in order to make arbitrary call counts for the period.

Contribution. In order to measure an individual agent's call center performance, a better measure of efficiency in handling call center workload might be a contribution percentage. A growing number of call centers use this number to look at an agent's minutes of contribution for the period (half-hour, hour, or day) compared to the contribution of others. This method is a more fair evaluation of each person's availability to handle calls and contribution to the overall call handling process. One center visited by the author measures "customer focus time" which is essentially talk time, after call work time, and time in the available state.

Staff Utilization

A critical measure of a call center's success will be how well its most expensive resource – the staff – are being utilized. Some of the measures associated with staff utilization are listed below.

Agent Occupancy. Agent occupancy is defined as workload hours divided by staff hours, or the percent of time that agents are logged in that they are actively busy processing calls (either in talk or ACW mode) compared to idle, available time. It should be noted that, like calls per hour, it is not a measure under the agents' control. Rather it is a function of staffing levels compared to the workload at hand.

While most call centers want occupancy to be high since the staff are indeed being paid to process call workload, a careful watch is needed to ensure that occupancy levels do not go too high. The ideal range for agent occupancy is in the 85–90% range. In other words, a call center should see agents busy on calls for about 50–54 minutes out of the hour they're available. Occupancy levels above 90% mean there are few opportunities for agents to "catch their breath" between calls and if there are too many periods in which occupancy exceeds this amount, agents will quickly find ways to take a break that remove them from the available, staff pool, making occupancy even higher for their peers.

Staff Shrinkage. Staff shrinkage or overhead is the amount of paid time that agents are not available to handle telephone calls. It is a factor used to inflate "bodies in chairs" staff requirements into schedule requirements. Shrinkage should be tracked and measured carefully to ensure that staff hours are not being needlessly wasted, as well as to have an accurate number to feed the scheduling process.

Net Staffing. A measure of scheduling efficiency is the net staffing that occurs each half-hour as a result of the scheduling process. A positive number indicates that staffing numbers are higher than needed for service level, resulting in over-staffing and inflated costs, while a negative number indicates understaffing and potential service problems. The net staff should be noted each half-hour with the goal being to minimize this number. An overall net for the day can be calculated that balances out the overstaffing and understaffing situations, but it is more important to note the total number of "overs" plus the total number of "unders" and work to lower that number since it represents how well the center is controlling the variability of staff utilization.

Schedule Adherence. Schedule adherence is both an individual measure of performance as well as an efficiency measure for the center as a whole. This measure can be used to measure each agent's contribution to service level. It is a measure that compares the specific actual hours worked to a person's work schedule. (not to be confused with compliance, which generally refers to the total hours worked compared to the total hours scheduled). While these numbers can be accumulated and measured on a manual basis, schedule adherence is much more easily and accurately reported in call centers with a workforce management system in place.

Profitability Measures

For many businesses, the call center adds revenue directly to the bottom line. Whether the call center's primary function is to take orders, such as in a catalog or reservations environment, or whether the function is primarily service with an occasional opportunity to sell an additional product or service, measuring how effective the call center is at revenue generation is an important performance indicator. There are two primary measures associated with revenue generation, as outlined below.

Revenue Per Call. The call center will want to evaluate revenue as it relates to call volume. Therefore, revenue per call is a standard measure that should be evaluated in a variety of forms. Call center management will want to calculate average revenue per call by individual, by team, by skill group, and by center. Revenue per call will likely be evaluated at various times of day or week, as well as compared over time to ensure stability or growth.

Up-Sell/Cross-Sell Percentage. Even if the primary function of the center is not sales, there is likely at least some opportunity for a call center to generate revenue in an up-sell or cross-sell scenario. Call centers should measure the percent of contacts in which a successful up-sell or cross-sell is made, and likewise measure by individual, team, and across the center as a whole.

In looking at the whole picture of call center profitability, the flip side of measuring revenue is to measure call center operating costs.

Cost per Call. There are many variables associated with measuring the cost of doing business in the call center. The primary cost is associated with call center staffing and sometimes the labor cost alone is used for calculating cost per call or cost per transaction. In other cases, a fully-loaded cost is used in the calculation that includes staffing, telecommunications costs, depreciation on equipment and technology, facilities, and overhead costs, etc. When evaluating cost per call, it is critical for benchmarking purposes to understand precisely what has been included in the calculation of each entity's cost to make a fair comparison between centers.

$$\text{Cost per Call} = \frac{\text{Total Cost}}{\text{Number of Calls}}$$

Retention Measures

A concern of any business is the degree to which customers and employees are being successfully retained. Both measures should certainly be on the list of key performance indicators, since employee retention is a key cost and service concern that may link directly to customer retention.

Staff Turnover. Although it's preferable to look at the positive side and think about ways to maximize employee retention, the inverse is what is typically measured in the call center. The staff turnover rate should be evaluated on an ongoing basis and should be measured not just for the overall business, but within the call center, and even more specifically by team. Since many of the factors contributing to turnover are supervisory related, it's especially important to evaluate by team or group to see where specific problems need to be addressed at a supervisory level.

The turnover rate is calculated quite simply by dividing the number of staff that leaves by the total number of employees. Call centers will probably want to calculate two different numbers here; one for internal turnover where employees leave the center but stay within the company, and external turnover where employees leave the company entirely.

Employee Satisfaction. Another measure that cannot be ignored in terms of managing a call center is the level of satisfaction of the frontline staff. Since unhappy agents translate into unhappy customers, it is critical to solicit their feedback regularly to ensure low turnover rate and ultimately customer satisfaction. Regular surveys that address compensation, workload, working conditions, rewards and incentives, and supervisory relationships play a key role in assessing and addressing employee concerns before they become unmanageable. Satisfaction data may be gathered via surveys, focus groups, or one-to-one interviews.

Outbound Measures

There are several unique measures associated with managing an outbound call center. These measures include:

Completion Rate. Completion rate measures the percentage of contacts that are "complete" by the call center's definition. A completed call may be defined only as a call that results in direct customer contact or may be designated as complete if it meets a another definition set by the user, such as a fixed number of attempts or occurrences of reaching an answering device.

Abandon Rate. The definition of an "abandoned call" for an outbound center is different than one for an inbound center. In an outbound call center environment, an abandoned call is one in which the calling party (the call center) abandons the call because an outbound agent is not available for the call at the time outbound dialer technology has connected with the called party. The dialer is typically set to maximize potential conversations, while minimizing down time on the agent's part in between calls and the numbers of abandoned calls.

Example of the Measures

Each call center should decide upon a set of key performance indicators that best reflects that call center's business focus and its contribution to the organization. Because call centers play such different roles within an organization, the "top ten" measures for one call center may be very different than another's goals and measures, as seen in the example. The table shows the top ten key performance indicators being utilized by a catalog call center and an internal help desk operation. Can you explain why the top measures of performance each has chosen are different from the other organization?

Catalog	Help Desk
1. Revenue per call	1. First call resolution rate
2. Up-sell/cross-sell percentage	2. Transfer rate
3. Abandon rate	3. Quality monitoring/accuracy
4. Sales per agent	4. Error/re-work percentage
5. Customer satisfaction scores	5. Self-service/web percentage
6. Customer retention	6. Cost per call
7. Service level	7. Service level
8. Quality monitoring/soft skills	8. Staff occupancy
9. Average handle time	9. Staff turnover
10. Agent occupancy	10. Customer satisfaction

Another factor to consider in setting performance indicators and determining what to measure is the fact that the call center often is the central repository of data for the organization. And the call center certainly talks to more customers in a week than most departments will interact with in a year. Therefore, the call center manager should also look for things to measure that would be of use to others in the organization. Data might be supplied to strengthen relationships with other departments, such as supplying campaign results to marketing or customer feedback to the product development area. As measurements for the call center are defined, it is important to look beyond the basic call center measures and look for ways to demonstrate value to the enterprise.

Another decision factor in creating a measurement system is the distinction between real-time and historical measures of performance. Real-time data provides specifics for "right now" while historical data comprises cumulative statistics over a day, week, month, or quarter. Any call center's measures of performance should be made up of both types of information. Historical reports will provide trend information for planning and indicate performance against goals over the long-term. Real-time measures will identify developments and be a useful tool in identifying adjustments needed to the operation on a short-term basis.

Performance Reporting

Once performance goals have been set and a system of measures developed, the final step in the performance measurement process is to develop a reporting mechanism. Reports inform management and employees about performance and will help identify areas for improvement or corrective action. When developing a reporting strategy, it is critical to provide information upon which decisions can be made or behaviors changed.

What Agents Should See	What Management Should See
1. Average handle time	1 Resource utilization
2. Schedule adherence	2. Service level
3. Transfer percentage	3. Cost per call
4. Quality scores	4. Revenue per call
5. Customer satisfaction scores	5. Customer satisfaction scores
6. Resolution rate	6. Quality measurements

An effective reporting strategy will provide a complete review of the current state of performance in the call center and should provide the means to identify gaps in performance, evaluate strengths and weaknesses, and suggest steps to improve call center operations. The reporting strategy should include what information will be presented, the frequency, the format, and the reporting medium. For example, agents may need to see their performance statistics daily and those might be provided via the company's intranet or an email. Other statistics such as service level may need to be communicated on a real-time basis to the center as a whole and readerboards might be used. Revenue reports might go to senior management monthly and be delivered via a paper report.

Reporting Methodologies

The call center is by its nature a hub of communications. Customer calls, emails, web chats, faxes, and correspondence are handled there. Even an internal support call center handles interactions with its internal customers in a variety of media. So it is natural that the call center will need to communicate with all of the enterprise stakeholders. Agents need feedback to understand how well their performance is meeting expectations and understand changes that need to be made. Senior managers need to know how well the call center is utilizing the company's resources and how well customer needs are being met. Other departments can greatly benefit from communications with the call center to hear the "voice of the customer," especially if these departments are insulated from direct interaction with customers.

Developing a communications plan involves building a framework that defines the purpose of each report, the recipients, the sources of data, and the metric that is to be used. Different channels of communication must also be considered to ensure that the information arrives in an efficient and effective manner. Each group of recipients needs a specific level of detail on the measures that apply to them, with the detail or summary level that makes the data useful for decision-making. There are a variety of charts and graphs that can be used for analysis of the data as well, and choosing the right format will help to make the data as relevant and useful as possible. Whether the goal is to inform agents of their performance so that a continuous improvement plan can be realized, or updates to senior management with summary trend analysis, having a clear plan for the reporting and communication effort will maximize the value of the data in managing the enterprise and minimize redundant or irrelevant reports circulating through the company.

To be effective, the reporting provided by the call center must be relevant, accurate, and timely. If the information is meant to result in a change, it needs to reach the appropriate people in time for that change to be accomplished. For example, if an agent is having a difficult time with a specific call, the supervisor must receive the information quickly if she is to assist that agent in completing the call quickly and successfully. In the case of data provided on customer product needs or complaints, the information needs to reach the product development team while there is still time to modify the next release of the product.

Trend and summary data such as reports on key performance indicators for senior management are likely to be produced less frequently than the more detailed data that is shared among the call center management team on a daily basis. The call center managers are likely to react to information that indicates a problem quickly, while senior management is less likely to press for instant changes based on report data they receive.

The level of detail in the reports must also be appropriate for the audience. The agent needs to see details on his performance, perhaps even on a single call. But this level of information would be overwhelming for a call center manager with 300 agents. So at each succeeding level of the hierarchy, the level of detail generally diminishes to be replaced by summary statistics and trend analysis. If these summaries spark interest in more information, the details can always be requested and provided for further study.

Real-Time Reporting

The primary reason to have access to real-time data is to be able to affect a needed change as quickly as possible. One such change that consumes a great deal of energy in nearly every call center is ensuring that the number of agents available to handle the workload is matched to the actual workload as it arrives. The real-time displays that are provided with the automatic call distributor (ACD) provide the supervisors and others in the call center with information that can be refreshed as frequently as every few seconds. This data will inform the staff if there are calls in queue, how long they have waited, whether there are agents available, and what work state each agent is in at that moment. Should the delay be longer than the center's goal, the supervisors can identify agents who need to be encouraged to pick up calls, or even log in themselves to handle a few calls to reduce the wait time for customers.

Many call centers use wall-mounted displays or alert boxes on the agent's screen to provide access to these real-time statistics. This allows everyone in the center to see the status of the queues and other important information. This empowers agents to take responsibility for logging in to handle calls when the queue backs up, and allows supervisors to keep an eye on the situation even when away from their desks and real-time monitoring terminals. These displays can also provide real-time information in a text message that is needed to handle the calls appropriately. For example, a cellular service provider may have a technical problem in one area and may expect calls from customers regarding dropped calls or other failures. Sending a message to all agents in the center so that these calls can be handled knowledgably and quickly can be done via a text message on the wall display or on the text message area of the agents' desktop.

Communicating Performance Results

Development of a performance communication plan requires two primary components – a framework for the communication plan and a clear understanding of the purposes that the reports are meant to serve. The reporting strategy should align each of the report elements and measurements to the enterprise goals and ultimately to the mission and vision statements. The enterprise goals are communicated from the top of the organization with breakdowns into the appropriate requirements for each business unit, department, team and individual. These goals at the call center level, team level, and individual level should be clearly reflected in the key performance indicators of the call center.

Looking at the performance reports, the analysis typically starts at the smallest unit and rolls up to the top of the organization. Individual performance reports roll up into team goals. Team results roll up into department results for the call center, which combine with other departments to make up business unit results such as those for the customer care unit or a regional unit of a multi-site operation. Ultimately, the business unit goals and results roll up to the total organization. Therefore, the alignment of the call center's measurements and reports must align with the goals as they roll up through the organization.

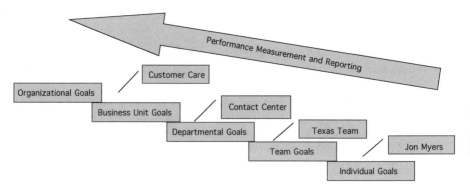

Developing a Framework

Reporting and communication should not "just happen" but follow a plan that addresses what needs to be communicated, to whom, when, and at what level of detail. Each enterprise goal that the call center can contribute to should have some reporting elements that identify how well that goal is being met. Developing a reporting framework is a useful process that organizes the effort and identifies each of the elements that must be addressed in the reports. In the example below, a model for a reporting framework is provided to serve as a basic outline to develop the reporting and communications plan.

Each of the columns is intended to assist the call center manager in developing the plan for the reports and communication processes that need to be accomplished. The explanation of the columns below includes an example using a goal for speed of answer measurement as an element of ensuring accessibility to customers.

- **Report Group and Title** – This is the name that will be given to the report so that it can be easily identified. There may be a series of reports that are grouped together to convey various elements of the same performance metric as well. An example might be "Weekly Speed of Answer Report" which could be part of a series of reports that include Daily, Weekly, Monthly Trend Analysis, and even half-hourly reports that will be needed for the different levels of the organization.

Report Group And Title:	Purpose	Info Reported Goals	Source	Recipients	Distribution Frequency	Channel Used	Report Owner

- **Purpose** – The reason that the report is provided is the purpose and this ties back to the enterprise goal. For example, the speed of answer reports are provided to measure the call center's performance against the goal of providing accessibility for customers or being "easy to reach." Other accessibility reports might include analysis of call attempts turned away after-hours, busy signals, and web site availability percentages.

- **Info Reported and Goals** – This column is used to provide the specific data fields that will be included in the report, the calculation where appropriate, and the goals that are being measured. In the case of the speed of answer goal, the report might indicate that 70% of calls are being handled within 20 seconds in 75% of the half-hours of the day. The report might illustrate how the data is calculated based on the percent of calls that are answered within 20 seconds.

- **Source** – This column provides the source of the data that will support the calculations and data elements. The source will identify the system reports or other places that the raw data will be found that support the calculations that are in the report, such as the ACD daily service level report. Some reports will require multiple data sources.

- **Recipients** – This column identifies who will receive the report and may include titles and/or specific names. It is easier to use the plan document when names are used as well as titles, but it will require more upkeep to keep the plan current as personnel change roles in the company. The speed of answer report will be broken down into several levels of data and each will be provided to a different group of recipients. For example, the call center supervisors will need the half-hourly report while the senior management will probably prefer the monthly trend analysis.

- **Distribution Frequency** – This column defines how often the report will be generated and distributed to the defined recipients. In some cases, there will need to be intermediate data provided to roll up into the specific report and that should be clearly defined with a timeframe for when the components are due in the hands of the final report developer to ensure that the composite report is completed on time.

- **Channel Used** – This column defines the way the reports will be distributed. Some may be made available on a company intranet and not actually distributed, but simply posted for the recipients to access as desired, while others will be printed and presented or provided via an email attachment. The reports on speed of answer that are distributed within the call center are likely to be posted on the wall for all to see, while the monthly reports are more likely to be e-mailed or printed and distributed since some of them will go to personnel who are not in the call center every day.

- **Report Owner** – This column defines who in the organization has responsibility for development and distribution of each report. The speed of answer report is likely to be the responsibility of the workforce management team within the call center, but a specific individual should be identified for each one to avoid confusion and missed reports. Once again, job titles and names would be helpful so that when a person changes roles, someone can easily identify the tasks that need to be picked up or turned over to the successor.

It is common in existing call centers to find that there are reports produced that are not used by some or all of the recipients. A report may have been developed to meet a demand from a former manager or to track a situation that was resolved months ago. Therefore, it is a good practice to review the reporting and communications plan at least annually and determine if each report is still relevant and useful to all of the recipients. Cutting down the distribution list may be appropriate for some if the report cannot be totally eliminated. Perhaps the data provided is not at the right level of detail for the current environment. A new report may be needed based on a new technology implementation or a change in process or products/services provided. The annual review will help to ensure that the reports serve a defined purpose and are worth the time needed to produce them.

Communications Channels

Part of the communications plan includes determining the best channel to be used for the report or communications. Some information is best delivered in writing and other communications are better provided verbally and in person. There are many options to consider:

- *Face-to-face* – A human-to-human interaction done face-to-face is typically vocal but may be accompanied by a paper-based document to reinforce and memorialize the verbal statements. Face-to-face communication is typically the best choice when delivering bad news or counseling an agent on poor performance, but may also be the ideal choice for delivering praise and recognition. However, most vocal communication on individual performance should also be documented in a paper-based medium.

- *Paper-based* – This includes any printed or hand-written report including a pre-printed form, graphics, tabular numbers, printouts from systems, and/or text. The document can be any length from a partial page to many pages. This is the best medium to use when communicating a large amount of detail, a complex concept, an ongoing analysis that will be amended on a regular basis, or any analysis that requires charts and graphs to be effective. It is also appropriate when a conversation needs to be documented for future reference.

- *Telephone* - Another simple form of communications is via telephone. A telephone call may be placed to inform another party of a performance result, and this telephone communications may be accompanied by a paper-based document or email.

- *Email* - Email is more and more common and often used inappropriately when face-to-face communications is really required. However, email is a good choice for routine updates and unemotional information. Call centers use email to communicate minor changes in product or pricing or the marketing focus of the day, for example. It is best for small amounts of detail at one time rather than large documents.

- *Internet or intranet* - The Web must also be considered an electronic communications channel that can be an effective or destructive mechanism for disseminating both information and misinformation. This includes both the company's intranet and the external Internet. In multi-site call centers, an intranet site is often used as a central repository for performance data and information that needs to be accessed by personnel at all sites.

- *Real-Time Display* - Another electronic form of communication in the call center is the real-time display that may be on a wall-mounted light board, a TV screen, or displayed at the agents' desktops on the phone or PC. This channel is typically used for information that is only seconds old and continually updated. For example, the display may provide information on the number of calls in queue or the latest problem that agents need to be aware of to properly handle customer calls arriving in the next few minutes (such as the location of a power failure for a utility provider).

- *Formal presentation* – Delivery of a formal presentation is generally a combination of a face-to-face communication with written supporting documentation. Presentation graphics, slides, or other charts may also accompany it. This may be used in the call center in weekly meetings with teams or in training programs, for example.

- *Grapevine* – The informal communications channel uses the ever-present grapevine of rumors and generally verbal information passed from one person to another without a formal plan. As the information is passed along, it tends to be modified and may lose any resemblance to the original information as each person adds or subtracts based on his/her interpretation and personal biases. While it is possible to use the grapevine as an effective communication channel, it is generally avoided due to the lack of control over the quality of the information and the people who will hear it.

Communications to Agents

Communication with agents involves not only the information regarding job performance metrics and achievement of goals, but daily operational data and the constant barrage of changes that must be assimilated each day. Ensuring that agents on all shifts receive the important data, along with those who may be absent on any given day, is a challenge that requires a thoughtful plan and consistent execution.

Operational Communications

One of the most frequent and important communications with agents is the data regarding the schedule. Each agent wants to receive her assignment as early as possible to allow plans for childcare, appointments, and transportation arrangements. Changes to the schedule may be required by the center to adjust to varying call load and staff availability, as well as daily trades of schedules between agents. Keeping the agents and the center informed of all of these changes is a constant challenge. Setting up a process to manage schedule exception reporting is a key task since there can be hundreds of schedules exceptions a day in a large center.

Another constant flow of information is the change data that agents need to be up-to-date on the latest product features, pricing changes, marketing campaigns, and technical problems that may come up on interactions with customers. Distribution of this information can be done verbally, on paper, via email or even voice message. The most effective method depends in part on how long the information is valid and whether it is simple to remember and apply or complex. Pricing changes may require written documentation but the alert that new pricing data is available on the intranet site may be all that is required in the distributed communications. A temporary system failure may be communicated to the agents via a wall-mounted display since it is usually a simple message of limited duration.

Performance Communications for Agents

There are many performance measures that apply to the call center as a whole, some that apply to teams, and those that apply specifically to the agent. The measurements that apply to an individual agent include both quantitative measures as well as some measures that are qualitative in nature.

There are some measures over which the agent has little or no control. It is essential to consider that aspect of each measurement so that agents know whether a measure is within their control and how it can be affected. While it is useful to share other measures with the team to ensure broad focus on the bigger issues, it is not reasonable to hold agents responsible for them. For example, one metric that agents have little control over is the service level or ASA. If the agents are adhering to their schedules and available when they are meant to be, they cannot be responsible for an unusual call volume or the inability of the WFM team to produce an accurate forecast. The agents need to know how well the center is performing against that goal since it is important to the center overall, but it should not be a metric on the agent's performance expectations.

Communications to Teams/Supervisors

Communications and reporting to teams and supervisors generally include summary results for the agent group that is included in the team. The supervisor needs to see the individual results for each member of the group, and the group averages to make comparisons. In addition, it is often useful to have a report that shows the team's position relative to the overall center goals and to other teams, especially when some competitive spirit will encourage improved performance.

In general, group summary reports are not sensitive and are less likely to create an emotional response than the individual reports that are used to communicate individual agent performance. Since the individual performance of each person is buried in the totals for the team, no one will be singled out as a great or poor performer. Therefore, these are commonly communicated electronically or posted for all to see either on an intranet or printed and posted on the wall of the center. In some centers, it is accepted practice to post the reports with the agents' names and individual data, while in others a code is used so that each agent can find his or her own data and see how it compares to the other individuals in the group, but everyone's privacy is protected.

It is also appropriate to share center-wide information with the supervisors and teams to indicate how well the center is doing in achieving its overall goals. These might include speed of answer, abandon percentage, cost/revenue per call, and customer satisfaction survey results. While individual agents should not be held responsible for these goals, each person plays a role in ensuring that these goals are met. So keeping everyone informed about how well the center is meeting its overall goals helps to build the spirit of teamwork that is essential to the call center's success. To the extent that an entire call type or work type is controlled within a single team, it is especially appropriate to provide the summary data on that work to the supervisor for that team.

Communications to Management

As the reporting and communication process moves to the overall call center level, the data that was provided in detail for teams and individuals is summarized one more time. The data may be sorted in a number of ways including by call or contact type, by shift, by day, by supervisor, and so on. The manager will see the reports sorted with an overall summary for each team or data type and the totals/averages for the entire center. In multi-site operations, the director may see each center separately and rolled-up into a system-wide view. At this point, trend analyses with charts are generally useful to give a graphical overview of the data in a quick-to-read format since tables with lots of numbers are hard to analyze at a glance. Trends over a 12-month period are common, but daily data may be needed to ensure that the details are not buried in the averages. If a change has taken place that will affect the statistics (such as implementation of a new technology), the change should be noted on the reports to ensure that the impact can be correlated with the trends.

A useful report for managers is one that summarizes what the drivers are that cause customers to contact the center. This kind of report can be produced when the agents use either an ACD or data system feature that categorizes each call based on what the caller requested. For example, the ACD feature called "activity codes" allows an agent to key in a number during the call that indicates what the agent did for the caller or why the customer called such as billing question, relocation of service, technical support, product inquiry, place an order, etc. The ACD can then produce a report sorted by activity code that indicates how many total times that code was chosen for the category. Since an agent could choose more than one code on a single call if the customer needs more than one kind of help, the total number of codes may exceed the call volume. These kinds of reports are very useful in tracking down the root cause of customer calls so that unnecessary ones can be avoided and revenue-producing calls can be increased. For example, if there is a sudden surge in billing questions, the call center manager needs to alert the accounting department regarding the increased volume and try to determine what has prompted it. If a new bill format is being used, or a change in some kind of calculation has shown up on the bills, the center can coordinate with the accounting group to ensure that the proper explanations are given to callers and any change that might more effectively communicate the new data to customers is found so that calls can be reduced.

At the center level, it is appropriate to report accessibility goals such as call blockage, hours of operation effectiveness, and self-service option availability/usage. In addition, speed of answer goals such as service level or ASA, delay percentage, and longest delay before answer or abandon are appropriate reports on a center-wide basis.

Overall speed of answer, delay experiences, and abandon percentages are typically reported at the center level, but for each call or work type separately. As more centers take on electronic work such as emails, response time on these transactions will be tracked in much the same manner as the call service levels are today. While call data is readily available from the ACD, report information on email, web chats, and other media are often more elusive. If an integrated queue management system is used, the reports may be fairly easy to obtain, but if email is managed in a separate system, that will be the source of data on these contacts instead. Tracking work such as faxes and correspondence tends to be a manual process.

Profitability concerns for the call center overall go beyond the revenue and cost per call data. The center will track its overall compliance with the operating budget on a monthly basis as a minimum, and capital budgets will be tracked to ensure that the projected return on investment (ROI) results are actually achieved. Many centers track their head-count in terms of full-time equivalents (FTE) to ensure that the center is operating within budget since this is the single biggest component of cost in the center. This involves calculating a forecast of workload for several months into the future and analyzing the utilization of full-time, part-time, contract, and outsourced personnel, along with potential for overtime. Determination of the number of staff on vacation and the overall shrinkage estimates are included in the headcount analysis along with forecasts of training classes and the workload that they may be able to handle.

Self-service utilization is generally tracked at the call center level to determine the trend of IVR and web usage as these are both technologies designed to off-load some of the work from the agents. However, these system reports are also generated in the IT/Telecom department in many organizations since system utilization is more in their purview. It is useful to correlate the shift in work volumes as these self-service tools are used to see the impact it has on the average handling time of the calls that agents handle.

Communication to Executives/Other Departments

At the level of reporting needed for senior executives, summary charts and graphs are generally appropriate. Trend analysis on measures that are directly tied to the corporate mission and vision will be of most interest. However, the call center manager should be prepared with the detailed data that backs up any graph, as it is not uncommon for a senior manager to take an unexpected interest in some statistic.

Key performance indicators are often chosen as the report data that is provided to senior management. Development of customized reports such as "dashboards" can be very helpful is seeing the important elements of the data quickly.

Monthly communication through paper reports will generally meet the needs of most senior managers, but the call center manager should ask the executives what level of data and frequency is preferred. Some will want an email while others will appreciate a printed copy. An occasional formal presentation with slides and flip charts may also be appropriate, especially if there is something unusual going on or anticipated. As a rule of thumb, information should be contained on no more than two pages, with backup available upon request. This is enough to allow the executive to "put a finger on the pulse" of the call center without spending more than fifteen minutes at a time.

As far as communications with other departments is concerned, there is no standard to guide the process. Each department that obtains data from the call center needs something different and will expect to see it in a format that can be integrated into the normal flow of information in that department. For example, marketing may want to see how many callers responded to a specific advertising effort and need that data on a daily basis so an ineffective ad can be pulled and another tried. Product development needs to hear the kind of product enhancements that customers are suggesting, but may only be able to really use the data during specific product cycle points. Since the call center is often the intermediary for these other departments in listening to the "voice of the customer," determining what these departments can use, when, and in what form, is an important process to ensure that the call center is as effective as it can be as an internal resource.

Communication to Other Stakeholders

The sections above have addressed the needs of agents, teams, supervisors, managers, senior executives, and other departments within the company. The remaining stakeholders are the customers and the stockholders or other owners of the company.

The call center needs to communicate continuously with customers in a variety of ways. As a minimum, the center may need to inform callers that the call may be monitored or recorded for quality control purposes. This meets the legal requirement for two-party notification where needed. This is typically done via an announcement in the IVR or in the first point in the call flow at the center as the caller is entered into queue for an agent.

The customer needs to be informed if the call center is experiencing long queues and subsequent delays for callers. This is often done through a special announcement that the callers hear as they enter the queue. The announcement may make an automated prediction about how long the caller will wait, or may simply let the caller know that the wait is unusually long at that moment. If the center is shut down due to some emergency, of course, customers need to be informed and offered another time to call back or another way to interact with the company. Most customers are very forgiving of unusual situations and appreciate being informed if the situation will affect them.

In some cases, the service that the call center provides is a direct response to some kind of situation that may affect a small number of people or nearly every customer. A technical support center may want to add an announcement informing callers that a major data function is out of service and when restoration is expected, for example. The power company can assist callers and itself by having a similar announcement when a major power failure is experienced that tells callers what area of town is affected by the outage and when the power is anticipated to be back in service. Many of the callers will abandon after hearing the message since they are now assured that the company is aware of the problem and is working to resolve it. This improves customer satisfaction and reduces the workload for the agents.

Customers also need to be solicited for feedback on how well the call center and company are serving them. Customer satisfaction surveys can be done through a variety of media and give the customer a chance to let the company know if there are problems in the service delivery process.

Summary

Reporting and communications serve a wide variety of purposes and provide information to everyone from the agent to the stockholders. There is an incredible amount of raw data available within the call center environment. Quality monitoring and customer satisfaction surveys provide qualitative data to add to the mound of quantitative information. With all of this possible information, the call center needs to develop a plan for what to communicate, in what form, when, and to whom. A framework for reports and communication will help to make sense of all of the data and place it into the form that will effectively support decision processes.

Delivery of the information to the recipient must be in a format and via a channel that is appropriate to the kind of communication involved. Some communication can be handled in an email or via a paper report, but sensitive information or any communication that may be emotional must be communicated in person. Documentation may support the verbal interaction to memorialize the conversation, but it is the discussion that is the key to an effective interaction.

CHAPTER 11: MANAGING STAFF PERFORMANCE

Introduction

Performance management is the key to business success. And in the call center, managing performance means looking out after two areas of performance – that of the call center overall and that of the individual staff members.

The process of individual performance management begins with defining performance goals and expectations and communicating those to the staff. Both quantitative and qualitative performance should be measured on an ongoing basis in order to evaluate current performance levels versus desired performance. Any performance gaps that are found during this review should be addressed through coaching and performance counseling.

This chapter provides an overview of the performance management process to shape individual behaviors and performance. These steps are most often carried out by frontline supervisors in the call center and are addressed in much greater detail in the book *Call Center Supervision: The Complete, Practical Guide to Managing Frontline Staff,* available from The Call Center School Press.

Performance Management Model

Everyone has values and beliefs that shape perceptions of others. Because individual perspectives cannot be trusted to be objective, supervisors and managers need to make sure they are looking at performance of individuals with an objective, unbiased perspective. A performance management model can provide this structure. Without a model or process, members of the call center management team may not always interpret what they are seeing the same way. A model provides a guideline to ensure a true performance picture is seen and a structured process is followed in approaching a performance problem or irregularity.

One way to explain how the performance management process works is to use a metaphor to present the concept. The metaphor for this concept is a visit to the doctor and an attempt to diagnose a medical problem. There are many similarities between the performance management process and the medical diagnostic process, including:

- A set of standards exists to define what is "healthy" or desired performance. Just like there are medical standards that describe what is healthy, there should be standards of performance defined for the call center that describe desired behaviors and performance.

- Symptoms alert someone to the possibility of a problem. Just as medical symptoms may alert a doctor, there may be undesirable behaviors or performance scores by call center staff that alert the supervisor of a performance issue that needs to be addressed.

- A process is used to analyze symptoms and determine cause of the problem.

Just as a doctor would not treat symptoms without knowing the cause, the supervisor in the call center should seek out the root cause of the performance problem to determine how best to address it.

• A plan or method of treatment is established. Once root cause of a problem has been identified, then a treatment or improvement plan can be discussed.

• The diagnostic procedure begins with small tests and builds to more complex (and expensive) ones depending upon severity of the problem. Some performance issues and their causes will be obvious, while some situations will require more research and testing to determine the problem and best course for improvement.

• Progress is monitored and corrections or adjustments in treatment are made if/when necessary. Some medical problems require little to no follow-up while others require constant monitoring, and the same is true in the call center. Some performance issues require only a minor correction, while other performance issues will require rounds of counseling and perhaps ongoing corrective action to shape the desired performance.

Setting Performance Standards

In order to objectively evaluate how an agent is performing, it is critical to first define both qualitative and quantitative standards and desired performance. The key to effectively defining the measures is to describe each measure of performance in terms of specific behaviors the agent is expected to display in each area.

For example, one customer service competency that an agent may be expected to have is to "portray a positive corporate image." When listening to calls to observe whether or not an agent is performing satisfactorily on this criteria, it is important to have specific behaviors to look for in order to tell whether their performance is meeting expectations or not. Two different people monitoring the same call may have very different opinions on whether an agent "portrayed a positive corporate image." Therefore, this competency must be described in terms of specific behaviors that show whether the performance is acceptable. Examples of positive behaviors related to corporate image might be using the company name in the greeting and closing, or use of the word "we" when referring to company policy. On the other hand, using "they" to refer to the company or saying something negative about a company policy would be viewed as negative behaviors. By describing specific behaviors to look for and being able to check "yes" or "no" as to whether the desired behaviors occurred, the call center can remove much of the subjectivity of the monitoring and scoring process, ensuring consistency and fairness in performance evaluation.

Measuring Performance

Once performance expectations have been defined and key performance indicators have been outlined, it is time to measure actual performance to compare against the goals. There are a variety of reports that can be generated to provide information related to the agent's performance. These various types of information are discussed below. The most common reports are generated by the ACD. Additional information can be found in contact management systems related to specific cases and resolution, quality monitoring systems, and workforce management software.

Quantitative Performance

The ACD system provides statistics related to call center, team, and individual performance. From an individual standpoint, call volume and AHT can be reported, along with a more specific breakdown of talk time, wrap-up time, and on-hold time. A short calls report can be generated that shows the number of calls that were handled in less than some number of seconds (perhaps disconnected calls) and the percentage of transferred calls.

The CRM system can provide a consolidated look at which agents are most successful at up-selling or cross-selling, as well as track the completeness of customer demographic information entered into the system. The CTI system (or middleware) can provide information that is gathered from the telephone such as the DNIS and ANI. Once the customer responds to prompts from the IVR, the CTI system can gather requested account information, payment information, and other customer account status and provide a summary of the transactions when queried by reporting modules.

The contact management system can provide information about the history of a customer account or problem, including which agent handled the call and the degree to which the contact was handled and closed successfully. Querying this system for customers that require multiple contacts for a problem resolution can help to identify agents that are having difficulty with the problem-solving process or resolution steps.

Finally, the workforce management system that forecasts calls and schedules staff can provide a wealth of information in terms of agent performance statistics. Historical and real-time adherence to schedules can be tracked and reported, showing those agents that are not complying with their assigned work schedule. Other modules of these workforce management systems can provide other statistics on agent activity and productivity, such as showing all agents that spend longer than average in ACW state or had shorter handle times than average. They can also provide exception reports on those agents who are consistently out of adherence with their work schedule.

Qualitative Information

Another way to measure agent performance is by some form of monitoring. This monitoring can be simple one-to-one observation, or may involve sophisticated remote monitoring of both telephone calls and screen activities.

Side-by-side monitoring is used when the supervisor sits next to the agent and monitors the conversation. The best procedure to accomplish this task, with minimal disruption to other agents, is to have the supervisor "double-jack" into the agent's telephone set. A double-jack refers to the agent's telephone set having dual headset connections that enables the agent and the supervisor to connect directly into the same telephone set using two separate headsets. The supervisor's headset will be placed in a "mute" position to enable the supervisor to hear both sides of the conversation, without the customer hearing any additional noise from the supervisor's headset. The biggest disadvantage of using side-by-side monitoring is the potential for the agent to be more nervous since the supervisor will be observing all conversations from the beginning to the end. Some agents are more comfortable without someone "watching over their shoulder," so the side-by-side monitoring procedure should be combined with one or more different monitoring procedures. The advantage to this approach is having the supervisor there at the agent's side to provide "on the spot" coaching and guidance.

Quality monitoring may be more sophisticated and include the remote monitoring and recording of the calls. This monitoring and recording function is accomplished through the use of a quality monitoring system. The quality monitoring system typically is programmed to record randomly, sampling each agent at different times of day and days of week throughout the period to ensure a fair sampling. Generally, the programming calls for a specific number of calls or number of minutes to be recorded per agent. Optionally, the system may also record the data screens and entries the agent performs during the calls so that the supervisor can see exactly what the agents saw on the screen and what keystrokes they entered as they processed the call. This information will be displayed on the supervisor's terminal as the call is reviewed so that the supervisor can determine if the agent is using the data systems in the most efficient way, making appropriate notes in the customer files, and accessing the right information to solve the customer's problem. With a quality monitoring system, valuable information is stored to assist in the coaching process and the agent can also see exactly what was done right or wrong in the review.

Performance Analysis

Performance information will likely be gathered from a number of sources. Quantitative data from the ACD, contact management system, and workforce management system will be compiled. It is important not to focus evaluation of performance too much on quantitative information simply because it is more readily available. This quantitative information must be combined with qualitative scores from observation and the quality monitoring process. Once all the information has been assembled, the next step in the process is to analyze the results.

Some of the performance results will be analyzed and viewed from a call center or team perspective. Other information will be evaluated on an individual basis to determine if an agent is performing as expected, or if there are performance gaps that need to be addressed. A performance gap is the difference between how the agent is actually performing versus what the performance should be. A gap analysis determines the gap between the current proficiency versus the desired mastery performance.

The gap analysis involves comparing actual performance against existing standards and objectives of the center. Once the gap has been identified, the next step is to diagnose the root cause of the performance gap and to determine how to address it with the individual.

Diagnosing Performance Problems

There are three basic reasons behind all performance problems in the call center or in any other work situation. Each performance problem can be attributed to one of these reasons:

- *Don't Know* – The first reason for undesirable performance is that an employee is unaware of performance. He may be not performing up to speed in a certain area because he doesn't know what the performance expectation is, or perhaps he's aware of the expectation or goal, but is unaware that his own performance is not meeting that goal.

- *Can't* – Once the possibility of the "don't know" aspect of the performance problem has been eliminated, it may be that performance is due to the fact that the employee "can't" perform. The employee may lack the training required to do the task, or there may be barriers that are preventing him from completing the task as expected.

- *Won't* – The last reason for performance problems is where an employee knows the expectations, knows his performance level, knows how to do the job, and all barriers have been removed. In this case, the employee "won't" perform. She may have decided not to perform due to a lack of consequences for performance or non-performance, or she may simply not be motivated to perform.

Supervisory Strategies

Once a performance gap has been identified and has been attributed to one of the don't know, can't, or won't categories, the supervisor needs to create a plan for intervention. If performance problems fall into the "don't know" category, the supervisory strategy is to enlighten. The supervisor would first ensure that all employees know what is expected of them and then provide consistent and timely feedback so every agent knows where he/she stands in terms of meeting the goals.

If performance problems fall into the "can't" category, the supervisory strategy is to enable. For these employees, the supervisor would ensure agents have the proper training to complete the task and remove any obstacles that are preventing them from performing.

The supervisory strategy for the "won't" category is to empower. In this situation, the supervisor would need to evaluate the consequences in place for the employee. Once the review is completed, the supervisor would change or implement the proper consequences for the agent's performance. If it is determined that the agent isn't motivated, it is a great opportunity for the supervisor to provide motivational coaching. Supervisors should be continuously monitoring progress and creating a plan to assess the agent's progress. If the original intervention fails, the supervisor should be prepared to try other action plans. This process is part of a successful performance improvement plan.

After the root cause analysis has been completed, a conclusion will be reached. The following questions should be asked to determine whether the conclusion appears valid and will lead to improved performance:

- What data was collected to determine that there was a problem?
- Is the root cause that was identified within the agent's control?

- Does the root cause have a high impact on the agent's success?

- Is it likely to result in improved performance if a plan is created to address it?

- Is the root cause stated in specific enough terms so that the solution can be precisely defined to address it?

Once the root cause has been identified and a conclusion has been reached, an action plan will need to be designed and implemented.

Coaching and Counseling

Coaching is the process of instructing, directing, guiding, or prompting employees as they work toward desired outcomes. When coaching, the supervisor should strive to maintain the self-esteem of the employee and to listen and respond with understanding. The supervisor shouldn't always be the first to offer a solution. Successful coaches ask the employee for help in identifying and solving the problem.

Coaching is about focusing on developing and encouraging each employee's potential. When coaching, the supervisor will develop a plan detailing actions that need to be accomplished by a specific date. Coaching has two challenges: 1) making sure performance standards are met, and 2) providing feedback aimed at helping agents take on the task of self-development and improving in their job performance.

A successful coach will encourage and reward constructive behavior and will try to influence behavior, rather than to change personality. Coaches also accept responsibility for their team's performance and avoid placing blame for issues that negatively affect the team. Successful coaches lead their team to improved performance by providing feedback and recognition. Other characteristics of a successful coach include the following:

- Encourages cooperation, openness, and self-confidence

- Provides immediate recognition of the achievements of employees

- Establishes facts using a pragmatic approach

- Adds public praise to private words

- Asks the employee open questions that encourage honesty

- Provides opportunities for employees to express their true feelings

- Keeps asking questions until they understand what the employee means

- Assists employee in realizing long-term goals and aspirations

- Leads from the front and sets a good example

Corrective Measures

There are many different coaching approaches and the call center should evaluate different approaches to see what works best. Two common practices used in coaching are outlined below – the FOSA model for providing feedback and a progressive discipline model for addressing performance problems.

FOSA Model

Documenting employee performance throughout the year and giving timely and ongoing feedback helps to complete an accurate and effective appraisal of performance. One common approach to the documentation process is use of the FOSA model. FOSA is an acronym that stands for:

- Facts to identify, qualify, or define problem
- Objectives targeted to resolve problem
- Solutions to help reach objectives
- Actions to be taken if problem is or is not corrected

Progressive Discipline

Successful call centers formalize the disciplinary process to ensure it consistently and systematically warns employees when their performance falls short of the expectations. The formal disciplinary procedure is usually coordinated by the human resources department to make sure that each step in the process is implemented properly, and according to company and government regulations.

Intervention as early as possible is the recommended approach when an employee's performance or workplace conduct doesn't meet the company's expectations or standards. Most disciplinary procedures include the following four components:

- **Preliminary notification**. This is the first step in a progressive disciplinary procedure. During this phase, employees are notified that their job performance or workplace conduct does not meet the company's standards and expectations. The first notification is usually accomplished in a one-on-one meeting between the employee and the immediate supervisor with the message being delivered verbally.

- **Second notification.** During this phase of the disciplinary process, notification is given to employees that problems identified during the preliminary notification stage have not been resolved and that performance or workplace conduct have failed to improve or have worsened. This notification is again accomplished with a one-on-one meeting between the employee and the immediate supervisor, but in addition to verbal notification given to the employee, the manager will include a written document that outlines specific areas of performance or workplace conduct that need to be improved. The document should indicate how the employee's performance or conduct has a direct impact on the success of the team or the center. It should also include a plan of action for the employee to follow that gives the employee the opportunity to improve. In some call centers, employees may be asked to sign the document used during this phase to acknowledge their understanding of problem and the steps required to improve performance.

- **Final notification**. This phase is the most formal phase of the disciplinary process with employees receiving notification from a senior call center executive or human resources executive informing the employee that if the job performance or workplace conduct problems continue, the employee will be subject to further disciplinary action up to and including termination. This document used during this phase is most often called a corrective action plan or a performance improvement plan. The document provides specific steps that must be followed along with associated disciplinary actions such as suspension, mandatory leave, or possibly a demotion.

• **Termination.** The final phase in the disciplinary process is termination. This step is taken when all other steps have failed to resolve the problem.

As the call center management team reviews the progressive disciplinary process, it is important to remember that the above steps serve as general guidelines. If there is any doubt about legal implications, the management team, in conjunction with the human resources team, should seek legal counsel immediately.

Positive Reinforcement

Positive reinforcement should be used often since rewarded behavior is repeated behavior. If the call center supervisor wants to encourage agents to adhere to their schedules, then when an employee demonstrates the behavior, the supervisor should reward it. A simple, inexpensive positive reinforcement is all that is needed in most circumstances. This positive reinforcement provides visible recognition affecting the self-esteem of the employee in a positive way. If possible, the rewards should be visible ones to communicate to others that positive behavior will be rewarded.

Ongoing Performance Appraisal

A formal method of evaluating performance and providing feedback to employees is the performance appraisal process. The performance appraisal process is an ongoing exchange between the employee and supervisor throughout the year. During the exchanges, the supervisor has the opportunity to recognize good performance and provide coaching and feedback when performance is not meeting the expectations. The performance appraisal process not only evaluates performance, but also offers a means for employees to develop their performance.

A successful performance plan can be used effectively to identify superior employees as candidates for promotion, acknowledge and encourage good performance, identify and motivate average employees to achieve excellence, acknowledge and correct poor performance, and identify substandard employees as candidates for corrective action/discharge.

Performance appraisal forms are an integral part of the performance management model. A performance appraisal form is the tool used to evaluate how well employees perform their jobs compared with a set of standards. When appraisals are completed correctly and consistently, they should provide employees with what they are expected to do, identify if they are meeting their goals, identify their strengths and weaknesses, and provide suggestions for improvement.

Agents and supervisors sometimes focus too heavily on the use of evaluations in connection with poor performance. Good performers need encouragement and acknowledgment to sustain and improve good performance while poor performers deserve to have an assessment of their performance as well as an opportunity to improve it. A supervisor's ability to develop "star" performers is as important as their ability to identify and eliminate poor performance.

The performance review period should begin with the agent and the supervisor meeting to set goals for employee performance in the coming period. These goals are related to the overall goals of the call center as well as to the specific assignment of the agent and his or her stage of professional growth. Both the agent and the supervisor must agree to goals.

As the year moves forward, the supervisor should frequently let the agent know how he or she is doing. Praise is important as well as constructive feedback. References to the mutually agreed upon goals should be a regular part of these conversations. If necessary, adjustments should be made in the performance standards and goals as time goes by.

The supervisor may need to take on a greater role in the agent's achievement of his or her goals if the agent's performance has not been satisfactory. If progress has been good, both can enjoy the success, and presumably the call center's goals are being met as well. Quarterly or annual reviews should be routine meetings and few surprises should arise. If feedback is constant (even daily, in some cases), these more formal reviews are typically used for adjustment (up or down) of the goals and performance standards for the agent.

Supervisors should maintain performance files on agents who report to them. The files should contain notable and specific examples illustrating an employee's job performance or results and should also include instances when the supervisor provided feedback to an employee. These files serve as a source of information from which to track performance and provide feedback and should include any information strictly related to performance

By tracking performance and maintaining records of feedback provided throughout the year, over time a supervisor will accumulate a file filled with detailed examples of an employee's work contribution. These examples can be drawn upon to support and give credibility to performance ratings on the performance appraisal form.

Any development plan should be a joint initiative between the employee and the supervisor. The employee should be asked to complete the development plan based on the development needs or interests from the employee's perspective. The supervisor should schedule a planning session with the employee to discuss the plan. The employee should be prepared to discuss his interests and the supervisor should be prepared to offer suggestions for development opportunities based on business needs and/or career interests of the employee.

Employee Performance Improvement Plan

The development plan should be a joint initiative between the employee and the supervisor. The agent should be asked to complete the development plan based on the development needs or interests from the employee's perspective. The manager should schedule a planning session with the employee to discuss the plan. The worker should be prepared to discuss his or her interests, and the supervisor should be prepared to offer suggestions for development opportunities based on business needs and/or career interests of the employee. A template for a development plan is included as below.

COMPETENCY DEVELOPMENT PLAN			
Note the competency areas where training would improve the employee's knowledge or skill level. Be as specific as you can as to what company-sponsored development programs, outside seminars, or individual or group activities would accomplish the development objective.			
Development Objective	Development Activity	Resource	Target Date For Completion
1.			
2.			
3.			
Employee Signature and Date:			
Manager Signature and Date:			

Performance Agreements

In many call centers, a formal agreement exists that outlines what performance is expected and what consequences will be if performance does not meet objectives. This performance agreement may exist between an individual employee and the call center, or may be in place for a call center serving an organization's needs such as in an outsourcing arrangement.

To prevent ongoing misunderstandings about what is expected in terms of attendance and adherence, as well as quantitative and qualitative performance, it may be useful to have a written contract with each call center employee outlining the scope of work he or she will be expected to do, and what performance objectives are. This contract can be as simple or complex as desired, and can be presented for signature either upon hiring or sometime during the training process. Having such a contract in place can help eliminate confusion about what performance is actually expected on the job at various stages of an employee's development.

Summary

There are many performance measurements that are used to gauge the efficiency and effectiveness of call center staff. The main purpose of these performance measures is to ensure that every individual is performing up to potential and supporting the goals of the call center and the overall organization.

The first step in managing staff performance is to clearly define performance standards and expectations. Once these goals and expectations have been set, the next step is to gather information about actual performance versus desired performance to identify performance gaps and problems. There are many sources of quantitative information from which to draw, while qualitative information comes from observation and monitoring to ensure adherence to the proper behaviors and actions. Analyzing performance results involves a variety of methods and tools to identify performance trends and pinpoint opportunities for performance improvement. Upon identifying performance gaps, the next step is to diagnose problems and determine the best course of action for improvement. Systematic coaching and performance counseling will help to shape the desired behaviors and performance.

CHAPTER 12: BUSINESS PROCESS IMPROVEMENT

Introduction

Performance management is all about measuring current performance and comparing against performance goals to gauge success of the operation from a number of different perspectives. The last chapter discussed managing the performance of individual staff and this chapter will address managing the performance of the call center as an entity.

It is useful to think about measuring performance in terms of what each of the primary call center stakeholders cares about most. The most important stakeholders are customers and there are many different performance measures in place to ascertain whether the center is meeting customer expectations. Many of these expectations are quantitative in nature, such as speed of answer or first call resolution rate, while others are more closely related to how well the call was handled. When defining performance measures related to the customer, it's important to get systematic feedback on what the customer expects and how well the center is meeting those needs. Defining and updating these measures should be done through a process of systematic customer surveying.

Employee satisfaction is also important to achieving not only an efficient call center, but one that consistently meets customer expectations as well. So surveying the employees about their issues and concerns can help focus call center management on areas that may be affecting the quality of the customer's experience, including provision of well-trained, tenured personnel.

Feedback from customers and employees, as well as internal productivity measurements, may point to performance problems in the call center that need to be addressed. Correcting performance problems and ensuring ongoing quality and productivity in the call center requires ongoing efforts in the area of business process improvement. This chapter will briefly outline different techniques used for process improvement and how these are commonly applied in the call center.

Defining Customer Expectations

The key to call center success lies in listening to what's happening within and outside the operation and identifying what customers care about and how well the organization addresses those needs. Simply taking internal measurements of the operation may tell a company how *efficiently* it is using its resources, but listening to customers is key to learning how *effectively* those resources are being applied.

Gauging effectiveness in the eyes of the customer is a critical step. Customers consider a number of factors when assessing service delivery and these factors relate to the points where the call center interacts with a customer. So it is important to regularly survey customers about these interactions and "touch points" to ensure that expectations are being met or exceeded.

Every customer interaction or event has an outcome, and the customer will have a perception about the call center's performance based on that outcome. This perception of performance will contribute to an attitude that a customer has about the call center and the company in general. This attitude then drives future behaviors to stay with the company, make future purchases, and so on.

Acting on the results of regular customer surveys will improve customer perceptions and attitudes, leading to a return on investment of increased loyalty and retention. And the survey process has an added benefit of being a public relations tool in itself. Many customers will have better attitudes toward the company simply because they were included in the survey process, and attitudes may improve significantly if customers get feedback that changes were made based on their input.

Many types of surveys can be used to define customer expectations and gauge customer perceptions. These types of surveys are generally defined as one of the following:

- *Specific purpose surveys.* A specific purpose survey is designed to answer a limited set of targeted questions. For example, the survey may ask questions related only to the call center's hours of operations or self-service alternatives.

- *Transaction surveys.* A transaction survey is related to a specific transaction and typically occurs within a short period after the actual interaction with the customer. The survey questions are related to the effectiveness of the transaction itself and may address perception of the agent handling the contact, call resolution, efficiency, quality, and so on.

- *Periodic surveys.* A periodic survey is distributed on a regular basis and typically addresses a variety of issues, some related to recent transactions and some related to perceptions and attitudes about the call center and the organization.

The Survey Process

There are five basic steps in the survey process:

1. Project planning
2. Instrument development
3. Survey administration
4. Data analysis
5. Reporting and action

Project Planning

Planning a customer survey includes defining a statement of purpose, the required resources, a project budget, project schedule and deadlines, and actual survey content development.

The first step in planning a customer survey project is to develop a statement of purpose. This statement of purpose will answer the following questions:

- *What is the motivation for the study?* It should be clear whether the survey is meant to identify current strengths and weaknesses or to gather scores to show the value of the call center to the organization.

- *Who is the target audience?* The study group should be defined based on the purpose of the study. It should be determined whether all customers will be surveyed or whether a particular subset of customers will be targeted. Study groups might be defined by demographic, by number of purchases, transaction value, and so on.

- *What results are needed?* Any survey should be conducted with an end result in mind. It should be determined what answers are needed to identify opportunities for improvement in client relationships.

- *What actions will be taken with the information?* Before beginning any survey, a plan for data analysis and action should be in place. Some might argue that the only thing worse than not doing a survey is to do one and not use the information.

Resource Requirements

An important step of the planning process is defining the resources that will be required to conduct the survey. The most significant resources to be defined will be the personnel involved in the project. These personnel might include a project manager, who would have overall responsibility for the project, as well as project team members, who would participate either full-time or part-time. It is also useful to have a project sponsor, a person with enough authority to command resources and solicit participation from other functional groups as needed.

Defining needed personnel resources may also involve identifying outside resources. In the survey instrument design phase, the company may wish to use focus groups to develop and fine-tune the survey process, and the numbers and types of customers to be recruited will need to be identified. Likewise, outside consultants and specialists may be used during some or all parts of the survey project, and the scope and cost of their services should be carefully planned.

Other resources to be identified include the physical facilities to be used, including meeting rooms for focus groups, or an area for calling for a phone-based survey project. And depending upon how the survey will be administered, the company may need to acquire specialized software or hardware for the project.

Project Budget

Items to be included in the survey project budget include the salaries of the project manager and members of the project team. The service fees from outside consultants and specialists will also be included in the overall budget. If the survey is to be paper-based and distributed via mail, there will be printing and mailing costs to calculate. For a telephone survey, the cost of telephone usage should be considered, along with any additional phone lines that may be needed. Regardless of the type of survey administration, there will be costs associated with the analysis of results and perhaps printing and distribution of results.

Some survey projects include the use of incentives to encourage participation from customers. These incentives may be discounts or coupons for purchases, actual monetary compensation, or some sort of prize.

Project Schedule

The project schedule should accomplish two things—outline the amount of time needed to do the work and state the milestones and deadlines for all stages of the project. The phases typically included in a project schedule include initiation and project planning, instrument design and preliminary testing, survey distribution and data collection, data analysis, and reporting.

Content Development

Defining the content of a survey project is an iterative process that involves research on the front end to define what should be included to accomplish the project's goals and objectives. The basic content should be defined before any survey instrument design begins. When defining the content of the survey, it is important to query the management team for their concerns and interests, as well as identifying customers' concerns.

It is important to do a preliminary survey of customers to identify all the potential topics that should be included and addressed in the actual survey itself. In other words, the project team should conduct a "survey before the survey" in order to ensure the survey questions really reflect the customers' primary concerns.

Many organizations refer to this preliminary survey as a "critical incident study" in which customers are asked to recount their actual call center experiences. In this type of questioning, it is important for the interviewer to focus on incidents that help shape and define both positive and negative customer perceptions and attitudes. These interviews can be done as personalized, one-to-one interviews or as focus groups. The focus group option is particularly useful for stimulating ideas, providing a structured discussion, and gathering much feedback and information in a relatively short period.

Survey Instrument

In designing the survey instrument, it is important to keep in mind the purpose of the survey and what is needed in the final report. Design of the instrument is an iterative process and is easier with an "end state vision" in mind. In his book, *Customer Surveying,* Fred Van Bennekom suggests the specific questions to include in a survey are best determined by the needs, concerns, and issues as defined by the customer base. He offers the following service quality dimensions as a potential organizing theme:

- *Reliability*—Delivering on promises, such as speed of answer and accuracy of problem resolution
- *Responsiveness*—Willingness to help, time on hold, efficiency of agent
- *Assurance*—Inspiring trust and confidence through competency and knowledge, courtesy and phone etiquette, honesty, and forthrightness
- *Empathy*—Treating customers as individuals, communications skills

Once the types of questions have been determined, the next step is to select the format and rating scales to be used. Then the questions are drafted, tested, and revised as necessary to finalize the survey instrument. It is important to devote enough time to the design of the questionnaire so that customers will take time to complete it and will be able to complete it correctly.

The introduction of a survey, whether written or oral, should have many of the same elements. It should include information on who should complete the survey, the time required to complete it, what to do when finished with the survey, and deadlines for completion, as well as any other specific instructions.

Part of the written definition or oral script may need to include definitions or clarification of terminology as it relates to the call center. For example, speed of answer may mean one thing to the call center and something else entirely to the customer. The initial questions should be easy ones to get the respondent started and interested in the survey. It is not recommended to include demographic questions early in the study, since they typically do not engage the respondent and many people may find these questions invasive and choose not to participate in the study.

A critical design question is what data type will be used in the survey. Some surveys may be purely textual and unstructured, with the burden on the respondent to provide full answers. While this type of survey may elicit useful responses and information, it is harder to tabulate and analyze than a structured survey with categorical data choices. In creating a structured survey, there are a variety of options for responses:

- Multiple choice/single response (check one)

- Multiple choice/multiple response (check all that apply)

- Binary choice (yes/no, true/false)

- Adjective checklists

There are several options for structured response scales, as outlined below:

- *Nominal*—A design with nominal responses (i.e., A B C D) allows the data to be sorted easily. Nominal data does not provide a rating of choices, but simply a frequency distribution of the various responses.

- *Ordinal*—A design with ordinal data asks respondents to rank choices in terms of value or importance. This ranking implies a relationship among the survey choices. It may help to think about ordinal responses as the way in which Olympic skaters are judged. They are not only given a score, but each judge also determines what order ranking the skaters have.

- *Interval*—A design with an interval scale enables the respondent to assign a rating of some sort to the variable in question. This type of design thus enables an indirect comparison of variables being evaluated.

Some of the types of interval scales are shown in the exhibits that follow. The first example shows a Likert scale, which ascertains agreement with a statement. The second example is a verbal frequency scale, which indicates the frequency with which something happens, typically on a scale from "never" to "always." The third example illustrates a comparative scale.

Likert Scale

Listed below are several statements. Please indicate your level of agreement with each by selecting a number from 1 to 5.

	Strongly Disagree				Strongly Agree
I was on hold for a short time.	1	2	3	4	5
The service agent was courteous.	1	2	3	4	5
The service agent was competent.	1	2	3	4	5
My problem was resolved satisfactorily.	1	2	3	4	5

Verbal Frequency Scale

Listed below are several means of submitting a request for service. Please choose a number to indicate the frequency with which you use each when contacting our company.

	Never				Always
Telephone call	1	2	3	4	5
Email	1	2	3	4	5
Fax	1	2	3	4	5
Written correspondence	1	2	3	4	5

Comparative Scale

You have likely had many customer service experiences with a wide variety of organizations. Compared to the BEST call center experience you have had in the past 6 months, please rate our call center service on a scale of 1 – 5.

	Very Inferior				Very Superior
Speed of problem resolution	1	2	3	4	5
Courtesy of support reps	1	2	3	4	5
Self-service alternatives	1	2	3	4	5
Competency of support reps	1	2	3	4	5

It is important to note that several types of scales will likely be used within a single survey. In particular, organizations will want to measure customer perception about a certain area, but will also want to measure how important that particular item is to the customer. It matters little if ratings are high on areas about which customers care very little. Care should be given not just to ratings, but also to the relative importance of each area to the customer.

As illustrated in the comparison chart below, areas with a high rating on importance but low satisfaction scores are most worthy of attention. Variables receiving a high importance rating and a high satisfaction rating are areas to simply maintain. Areas with low importance and high ratings may be receiving too much attention and resources now, while areas with low importance and low satisfaction ratings may need attention, but not immediately.

I M P O R T A N C E	Area of concern	Maintenance
	Less concern	Potential over-emphasis

SATISFACTION

During the question and scale creation process, it is important to stay focused on the main purpose of the survey and not be tempted to put in additional "nice to know" questions. The survey should have enough questions to maximize information to the company about how to maximize the customer relationship, but not so many as to overwhelm the respondent. To minimize respondent burden and to ensure maximum participation, the survey should be visually pleasing, use simple wording and grammar, and not feel like a "test."

Once the survey instrument is complete, it is important to test it several times with a pilot group. Regardless of the way the survey is ultimately going to be delivered, it is useful to deliver the survey in person to a pilot group in order to have one-on-one interaction with the respondent. The survey administrator should time how long the survey takes, look for visual cues such as puzzled or frustrated looks, and be ready to address any questions or issues that are confusing. Several of these test sessions should be carried out to fine-tune the survey document before it is implemented widely.

Survey Administration

While the validity and reliability of a survey are linked to the design of the survey instrument, the precision and accuracy of a customer survey depend on how the survey is administered.

One of the key decisions to make in any survey project is how the survey will be administered. There are many options from which to choose, with each method having distinct advantages and disadvantages. These methods are hard copy via the mail, telephone interviews, email surveys with attachments, web surveys, and IVR-based surveys.

Mail Surveys

While the response rate of paper-based mail surveys is the lowest and the speed is the slowest, there are some advantages of this format. The cost is typically low, with printing and postage costs being the primary costs to consider. In many cases the combined cost of printing and postage can be lower than a dollar per survey.

A mail survey provides the opportunity to ask detailed questions, providing definitions and detailed descriptions if needed. It also has the advantage of giving the respondent control over the survey process in terms of finding a convenient time to do the survey and proceeding through the survey at a comfortable pace. There is also little opportunity for interviewer bias, and the respondent can retain anonymity.

Many companies address the low participation rate of mail surveys by offering incentives to complete the questionnaire. Also, telephone calls to announce the arrival prior to a survey and a personal request to fill it out will also yield a higher response rate. However, the low response rate of many survey projects necessitates an extremely large number of surveys to be sent out initially in order to reap a valid sample of returned responses, wiping out some of the cost savings associated with this approach.

Telephone Surveys

Doing surveys by telephone is more expensive than by mail, but the costs are sometimes justified given the higher response rate and personal interaction with customers. Sometimes the telephone survey may be preceded by a introductory call or perhaps a letter with the actual questionnaire enclosed so the customer will have a visual reference during the call.

Doing a telephone survey involves development of a script for the telephone interview in addition to the survey instrument. This script helps guide the interviewer down different paths the survey might take depending upon answers to certain questions. Some call centers use their regular phone staff to do telephone interviews. However, it is important that these interviewers be trained specifically in interview skills.

Telephone surveying is one of the fastest surveying approaches, with the speed dictated by the sample size and length of questionnaire. Another benefit is that when the predetermined number of surveys has been completed, the surveying can simply be stopped.

Telephone surveying also allows any shortcomings in the survey to be circumvented by a skilled interviewer. Questions can be clarified and additional comments gathered, which may be useful in later analysis.

A drawback of telephone interviewing is the lack of anonymity that the respondent may feel in talking to a company representative. Using a third party to do the surveys will help address this issue, but there may still be reluctance to be forthcoming with opinions in a telephone interview.

Email Surveys

Surveying by email is growing in popularity and simply involves sending out the survey document as an attachment to an email message. Responses are generated in electronic format, making them easier to tabulate and analyze later. The response rate is typically about the same as with paper-based mail surveys.

The cost of performing a survey by email is low, given that printing, postage, and telephone costs are eliminated. The only cost associated with this mechanism is typically the software package(s) used to create the survey, administer it, and tabulate the results. An email survey is faster than a mail survey, as mail delivery time on either end is eliminated and people generally respond to an email survey within a very short timeframe if they are going to respond at all. Therefore, data analysis can typically begin within one to two weeks of sending out the final email notifications.

Another benefit of email surveys is the willingness of respondents to provide additional comments to questions. As the population becomes more computer savvy and adept at typing, people are more likely to type in a response than to write one by hand. Typing in the response via email is also faster than relaying it to an interviewer by phone and having the interviewer write or type the comment.

Disadvantages of email surveys include the perceived lack of anonymity by the respondent (since an email address will accompany their response) and the inability to clarify questions or use a series of complex questions.

Web Surveys

Another method of electronic interviewing is the use of web-based forms and surveys. A survey is created in HTML format and posted on a web page where the customer may access it, make entries on the form, and submit it. The response rate on these types of surveys is generally lower, since the customer has to take more initiative to go out and find the form in order to complete the survey.

The cost of web surveys, like email, is quite low. There are no printing, postal, or telephone charges. The only cost incurred is likely to be the cost of a programmer's time to create the interactive Web pages. Turnaround time is generally fast, with most customers responding within the same day of the email or mail invitation to take the survey on the web.

Due to the flexibility and range of options with HTML programming, the complexity of questions and branching paths can be accommodated fairly easily. This format also accommodates customer comments quite easily. But while the perception of anonymity is improved with a web survey versus an email or telephone survey, many users are still skeptical about what "cookies" have been sent to their hard drive as they complete the survey.

IVR Surveys

Another surveying technique popular in a call center environment is surveying via interactive voice response (IVR) systems. Many organizations have an IVR system to provide self-service options to customers, and these same systems can also perform some simple surveying tasks, either at the end of a call or as a separate transaction. The cost of the transaction is low, since the only cost is typically a toll-free telephone call, assuming there is already an IVR system in place.

Sampling Considerations

After deciding on the survey mechanism, the next step is to select a sample size. The population should be identified, and then a decision is made about whether a census or a sample will be needed to represent this population. A census occurs when everyone in the selected population is surveyed, and the sample equals the population. Taking a census is a possibility when the population size is relatively small, especially if the organization uses one of the electronic surveying methods where cost per survey is very low.

If only a portion of the population is to be surveyed, then a sample must be used. When surveying a sample, the best means of selecting respondents is to select them randomly from the population as a whole. Random selection helps ensure that there is not a bias in the sample, meaning that the sample properly represents the population as a whole. Many of the survey automation packages will generate a random sample from an imported customer list.

In determining the appropriate sample size, keep in mind that a large enough sample must be used to get a statistically viable result. Determining the sample distribution size is affected by the number of responses needed and the expected response rate.

$$\text{Sample Distribution Size} = \frac{\text{Number of Responses Needed}}{\text{Expected Response Rate}}$$

The expected response rate is the percentage of respondents who will likely respond to the survey and may be estimated from past surveys with the customer base. It is dangerous to use "industry averages" here, as the response rate will be affected by the administration mechanism, strength of customer relationship, incentives, survey quality, and a number of other factors.

The sample distribution size is calculated by dividing the number of responses needed by the expected response rate. So, if a 10% response rate is expected, and a organization needs 200 responses to achieve the desired confidence level, then 2,000 people should be sent the survey.

The number of responses needed depends upon whether the key questions in the survey produce numeric data (from interval scale questions) or proportions (from categorical data). The number also depends upon how much variability there is within the sample. If there is little variation from one extreme to the other, then a smaller sample size can be used with confidence, where the number of responses needed will be larger if variability in responses is high.

Survey Administration

Performing customer surveys is both an art and a science. In addition to understanding the math of statistical sampling and effective survey instrument design, there is also work to do in terms of survey administration to maximize response rate and eliminate survey bias.

A key to effective surveying is to get the survey noticed, opened, read, completed, and returned. Many organizations use a pre-survey notification by either email, mail, or phone to alert customers that the survey is coming. This notification can be sent to the entire population or to the survey sample. This notification, used to motivate the customer to participate in the survey, typically includes an explanation of why the survey is being done, how it will benefit the customer, how results will be communicated, and what incentives may be provided for participation.

It is important to be aware of survey administration problems that could cause survey bias and prevent the results from being as valid or as useful as possible. Care must be taken to avoid administration bias related to the sponsor, targeting the wrong population, or introducing respondent group bias by the sampling procedure. For example, targeting a survey to only those customers who have contacted the center recently may include customers with particularly strong feelings and not account for the ones with neutral attitudes. Another type of bias that should be avoided is administrator bias, which comes from inconsistency in administrative skills and styles, a particularly common problem in telephone surveying.

Data Analysis

Once all surveys have been received, the next step is to analyze the data. A univariate or descriptive statistical analysis might be done, summarizing what respondents think. A more complex analysis might involve bivariate or multivariate analyses, which help explain the relationships in data and why certain attitudes and perceptions may exist.

The data analysis will typically include some analysis of central tendency, looking at the average responses from the respondent group. It is important to look beyond averages, however, and evaluate distribution as well. The analogy of a person with his head in a stove and feet in the refrigerator having an average temperature shows how important it is to look at the dispersion of results and not just the mean or median numbers.

In looking at distribution measures, standard deviation is the most commonly used measure of variation and distribution of results. It shows how results are clustered around the mean. The two sets of data in the sample below both have the same average result, but this example clearly shows that there is a wide range of responses yielding that average result—perhaps a wide enough range to warrant further investigation.

	Low 1	2	Med 3	4	High 5	Mean	Standard Deviation
Sample 1	15	0	5	0	15	3.0	1.88
Sample 2	2	5	21	5	2	3.0	0.87

Reporting and Action

The final step of a survey process is the reporting of results. The report from any survey project should include the following sections:

- *Purpose*—Why the survey was performed

- *Methodology*—The steps and process of the survey
- *Item results*—The specific findings for each question or scale
- *Overall results*—The overall findings and highlights for the whole survey
- *Recommendations and actions*—Next steps and follow-up

The survey results will likely be shared with the call center and related management teams. Some or all of the results should be shared with the frontline agents and supervisors. And some of the results should be communicated to customers as well, indicating any proposed actions to be taken as a result of the survey findings. These actions may be simply to do additional research or to address specific problems and issues uncovered as part of the project. Informing customers of the issues discovered and the organization's plans for dealing with them plays an important role in strengthening every customer relationship.

Measuring Employee Satisfaction

It should be noted that a performance review should go two ways. Not only should the agent's performance be reviewed, but their satisfaction with the job and the work environment should also be evaluated on a regular basis. Completion of a regular employee satisfaction survey can provide valuable insight into the current perceptions of the staff. This is a process that allows and encourages the employee to assess the management, environment, job, training, and career opportunities within the center. If there is dissatisfaction with some recent change or process, it is important to find that out as dissatisfaction plays a role in how the agent performs.

The survey is typically done in writing with employees providing feedback on an anonymous basis. This ensures an honest feedback opportunity without fear that the employee will be identified as the one who gave negative input. There are usually 10 to 15 questions that can be answered with a scale of choices and a few free-form text fields as well. A sample Employee Satisfaction Survey is provided on the next page. This survey assesses the satisfaction of the employee and asks the employee to grade the effectiveness of the department in serving its customers. The latter part of the survey provides an interesting comparison to a typical customer satisfaction survey that might ask many of the same questions.

This type of survey for employee satisfaction should be done on a regular basis with trend analysis to ensure that the performance and satisfaction is moving in the right direction. Where performance is below expectations, doing a survey every quarter may be needed, while a stable operation may want to survey semi-annually. It is also important that the results be shared with the employees so that they know that their input is being heard. Specific suggestions by employees should be addressed and management's response shared with all employees. This is somewhat like monitoring in that asking for the information and then doing nothing with it is worse than never doing a survey.

Sample Employee Satisfaction Survey

Your feedback is important to us. Please rate your satisfaction on the following items on a scale of 1 to 5— with 5 for very satisfied, 3 for neither satisfied nor unsatisfied. and 1 for very unsatisfied.

Scale Definition: 1—Very Unsatisfied, 2—Unsatisfied, 3—Neutral, 4—Satisfied, 5—Very Satisfied

1. Tools available to do job   1 2 3 4 5
2. Reference materials available   1 2 3 4 5
3. Training provided by company   1 2 3 4 5
4. Industry certification requirements for the job   1 2 3 4 5
5. Escalation process within group   1 2 3 4 5
6. Escalation process to other groups   1 2 3 4 5
7. Schedule you are assigned to work   1 2 3 4 5
8. Process/procedure documentation   1 2 3 4 5
9. Fairness of treatment by management   1 2 3 4 5
10. Career development opportunities   1 2 3 4 5
11. Coaching by management personnel   1 2 3 4 5
12. Peer support / coaching   1 2 3 4 5
13. Team spirit within group staff   1 2 3 4 5
14. Fairness of workload distribution in group   1 2 3 4 5
15. Willingness of management to assist with questions   1 2 3 4 5
16. Overall job satisfaction   1 2 3 4 5
17. Likelihood of staying with company > 1 more year   1 2 3 4 5

Grade your view of the overall performance of the call center.

Scale Definition: 1—Very Unsatisfied, 2—Unsatisfied, 3—Neutral, 4—Satisfied, 5—Very Satisfied

1. Speed of resolution of problems   1 2 3 4 5
2. Quality of resolution of problems   1 2 3 4 5
3. Technical skills   1 2 3 4 5
4. Helpfulness to customers   1 2 3 4 5
5. Consistency of service provided   1 2 3 4 5
6. Handoff of problems to/from other groups   1 2 3 4 5
7. Overall performance   1 2 3 4 5

What could be done differently to improve the call center's performance and service?

What could be done to improve your satisfaction with your job?

Please return completed survey to _____. Thank you for your feedback.

Business Process Improvement

As shown in the example below, process improvement begins with evaluating whether performance is on target or not. If not on target, a root cause analysis is performed. Once the root cause of a performance problem has been identified, a systematic process improvement plan should be implemented to address the problem and move performance to desired levels.

Process Improvement

There are several different approaches associated with process improvement planning in the call center. These process improvement methodologies tend to change over time as trends change and new business approaches are introduced.

One approach that has gained popularity in many organizations in recent years is known as Six Sigma. Six Sigma is a data-driven approach and methodology for eliminating defects, improving quality, and maximizing performance through consistent processes and procedures. It is widely used in the manufacturing world and has recently gained popularity in the service part of the business as well, particularly in call center operations. The methods of Six Sigma support a continuous improvement mission to measurably improve quality, service, and operational performance.

The most effective Six Sigma initiatives measure the direct influence a process improvement has on bottom line results such as customer satisfaction scores or operating costs. Any Six Sigma improvement process is carefully defined to be closely linked with the organization's top level business strategies so that the resources invested in the project will yield the highest return.

In some cases, the mandate to implement a Six Sigma analysis and process improvement plan comes from above with senior management directing the call center to perform the project. In other cases, an organization may take a "bottom-up" approach looking to the call center to directly identify opportunities for improvement in productivity and service at the ground level. Another approach ideally suited to the call center is to utilize customer satisfaction metrics to identify customer "pain points" upon which to focus changes in performance. Any approach will involve the identification of the biggest "gaps" in performance between goals and actual performance.

Six Sigma Step	Process
Define	Define the project scope. Identify the impact on the business. Determine the appropriate metric(s).
Measure	Refine the project scope. Select the output characteristics (Ys). Assess the performance specifications. Validate the measurement systems.
Analyze	Define the performance objectives. Document the independent variables (Xs). Analyze the sources of variability.
Improve	Screen the potential causes. Identify the appropriate operating conditions.
Control	Determine the process capability (for the Xs). Implement the process controls. Document what has been learned. Communicate results.

The Six Sigma process is made up of five distinct phases. While there may be some variation in this approach, most Six Sigma improvement programs follow these specific steps.

Definition

During this initial phase of the performance improvement process, a project team will determine and document the nature of the project. The specific performance gap is defined, along with how it impacts the organization. The business impact may be defined in terms of dollar operating costs, hours of service delay, and so on. This stage also includes the definition of the baseline metrics that will describe the problem and increments of improvement.

Measurement

During the measurement phase, the process output measurement is defined, output is tracked, and the resulting data is validated for accuracy. For example, if the output being measured is customer satisfaction, surveys would be implemented and satisfaction scores tracked to ensure validity and reliability of the measurement process.

Analysis

In this phase, the data is reviewed in search of relationships and variability. Using the data gathered on each key input (X) and output (Y), an analysis is done to see what correlations may exist between X and Y and what variability there may be in various cases of X. Various cases of X are analyzed to determine the ones that have the most impact on the output of Y, and those that are found not to have a significant effect are eliminated.

Improvement

Once the critical inputs controlling the outputs have been identified, designed experiments are run with key factors to determine the relative impact of each. Those variables affecting customer satisfaction the most are evaluated in a controlled environment to carefully measure the results of changes.

Control

Once processes and procedures are optimized to get the maximum output, a process control plan is implemented to manage the process from that point on. The processes are documented, including who is responsible for measuring and maintaining new processes and output, and how results will be communicated to others.

Root Cause Analysis

A key element in any business process improvement process or technique is pinpointing what is causing a performance problem to occur. Performance issues or "gaps" should be analyzed carefully to determine the root cause of the problem. It is important to not just treat the symptoms of a problem or the problem may worsen. Just like picking the yellow flower of a dandelion will remove the surface weed, treating a performance problem on the surface may momentarily address a problem. But if untreated at the root, the dandelion will not only be back, but be back bigger and stronger than before. The same may occur with a performance problem if the true cause of the problem is not identified and addressed.

There are several tools that are available to identify the root cause for almost any kind of call center performance problem. These tools include fishbone analysis, and flowcharting.

Fishbone Diagram

A fishbone diagram is a cause-and-effect diagram that resembles a fish skeleton, with the problem statement represented as the fish's head. A fishbone diagram provides a determination of all causes of a problem and can assist in identifying the root cause of a problem. Using a fishbone diagram is useful since it displays a visual image of the interplay between related issues.

Using a fishbone diagram allows the manager or supervisor to:

- Identify the possible causes of a problem by sorting and displaying them.
- Analyze the current process by reviewing all potential factors that may cause a problem in a process to occur.
- Identify probable and root causes of a problem.

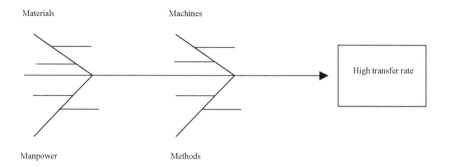

Materials

Machines

High transfer rate

Manpower

Methods

Sample Fishbone Diagram

Flowchart

Another tool that can be used to determine root cause of performance issues is a flowchart. A flowchart is a formalized graphic representation of the activities of a process. It is simply an outline presented as a box diagram, with lines that show the access routes among its parts. A flowchart can give shape and structure to any type of process and show where a breakdown in a process might occur.

To use a flowchart in the root cause analysis process, list all activities in the process and draw the flow of activities and the relationship of each step to the others. In standard flowcharting methodology, circles indicate the start or end of a process, rectangles show an action, and diamonds indicate decision points.

Regardless of the tool used to do the root cause analysis, once the presenting problem and its real cause have been determined, an action plan can be designed and implemented.

Summary

One of the most important aspects of measuring call center performance is determining how well customers are being served and their needs being met. One of the best ways to determine success in this area is to simply ask them. Carefully planned and executed customer surveys are critical to ensure satisfactory performance. Employee surveys are also important to ensure frontline agents are happy in their role and serving customers and the organization well. Once performance data and feedback have been obtained, a careful business process improvement methodology should be used to optimize staff and call center performance.

CHAPTER 13:RISK MANAGEMENT

Introduction

Managing risk in the call center involves identifying every component and what might potentially go wrong, and then developing a contingency plan that will prevent (or at least minimize) the effects of a disaster. When prevention fails, the disaster recovery plan goes into action to restore normal operations as quickly as possible, focusing attention to people first, and then to property. It is important to remember that the purpose of the disaster recovery plan is to minimize damages and restore the call center to normal working conditions as soon as possible.

Risk management also involves compliance with laws and government standards since failure to comply may have steep financial penalties. Inbound centers must ensure that monitoring is done within the state and federal regulations, while outbound telemarketing must comply with the Telephone Consumer Protection Act and Do Not Call legislation. All organizations must respect the legal and ethical requirements for protection of privacy, and those who operate overseas will find that there are local laws and regulations that must be understood and integrated into the operations.

Since the call center is often the "front door" to the organization for its customers, considerable damage can occur when that door is unavailable or the behaviors of the personnel within the center do not uphold the ethics and standards of practice that the company requires.

Risk Management Overview

A dictionary definition of risk is "the chance of injury, damage, or loss; dangerous chance; hazard." Protection from risk involves identifying and understanding what the chances and hazards may be, working to prevent injury, damage or loss, and finding ways to recover from such situations if prevention efforts fail. In many large organizations, there is a high-level executive in charge of risk management and this person often deals with matters of risk avoidance, insurance, security, contingency planning, and disaster recovery planning. The legal counsel has a role to play by writing the appropriate risk prevention and recovery language into contracts with both customers and suppliers, and maintaining an awareness of regulatory, legal and ethical issues that the company must address in its practices. Even the Chief Financial Officer has a role to play in hedging the company's financial position to prevent losses.

Another consideration for risk managers is addressing the opportunities that arise. No company wants to lose the chance to take advantage of an opening that will improve the company's profitability, brand image, or long-term market position. So awareness of opportunities is also a function of risk management.

There are a number of issues to consider under the category of risk management. For some organizations, a formal contingency/disaster recovery plan is in place, but for others it never quite makes it to the top of the priority list. When a disaster strikes close to home, there is typically renewed interest in ensuring that the company is protected. But the intensity of the concern dwindles rapidly in the day-to-day processes of running the company, and many plans are never finished. By the time the plans are written in many cases, the concern is low priority and competition for funding the prevention and recovery techniques often finds itself losing out to more immediate opportunities. However, there is no question that when a disaster actually strikes, the company that has a plan has a much higher potential for survival that the one that does not.

Contingency Planning

The contingency plan identifies potential risks and prevention techniques as well as potential opportunities and ways to seize them. A contingency is something that may or may not happen so it is easy to think that this effort is really wasted in negative thinking. But unless the risks are identified thoroughly, and the impacts that might occur are understood, there is no way for the company to decide if it should spend a specific amount of its resources on preventing them. And when opportunity knocks, the company has to be quick to seize it. For example, assume the company's largest competitor declares bankruptcy and charges of fraud are leveled against the executives. This is a chance to capture market share, but it must be done quickly and ethically to be effective. Having a plan in place for such a chance makes it more likely that the forces can be marshaled in time and the maximum advantage achieved.

The test of a good contingency plan is that the company rarely experiences any of the preventable disasters that befall others. When a local storm disables telephone service in the area to most businesses, but a center runs normally with a backup set of trunks provided by routing through another carrier, the contingency plan is doing its job. When an unexpected rush of calls comes in because the company's new product is the latest sensation, and the call center ships overflow calls to its outsourcer automatically, the contingency plan is making it possible. Many of the reactions that are necessary happen behind the scenes and it all looks like a normal day in the life of the call center. But without the plan and the alternatives it provides, stress would be high, revenues would be lost, and the brand image of the company tarnished.

Disaster Recovery

Planning for disaster recovery assumes that the prevention techniques in the contingency plan did not work, or the disaster is one that could not have been foreseen, such as the September 11, 2001 terrorist attacks. A disaster recovery plan must take into account even the risks whose causes may not be definable, but the results can be imagined. For example, the plan may need to address the loss of the entire building. It could be from fire, earthquake, tornado, or terrorism, but it really doesn't matter. The recovery processes for any of these total destruction situations need to be pretty much the same.

While total destruction must be considered, the reality is that most situations involve a partial loss. It could be a failure of electricity for an extended period, a fire that causes loss of part of the systems, a weather issue that keeps the staff from reaching the center, or a marketing campaign that no one mentioned to the call center in advance. Planning for such events is the primary role of the disaster recovery plan, because these are the problems that will be faced far more frequently than the major catastrophe. Identifying actions that can be taken on a short-term basis, the appropriate escalation steps, and the processes involved will make reaction to these events far less stressful on both employees and customers.

Regulatory Compliance

Lack of knowledge of the law is no excuse for non-compliance, and laws and regulations change continuously. Some industries have many unique regulations and compliance is carefully policed, with significant fines for failures. In the call center, for example, the outbound telemarketing industry is heavily regulated with hours that are acceptable to call, do-not-call lists, and so on. A requirement for notification to incoming callers that the call may be monitored or recorded for quality control is another example of a regulation unique to the call center environment.

Role of Insurance

Some risks are too great for a company to absorb individually, so insurance is designed to spread the risk across a large number of companies. The cost to replace the building and all of its contents in the event of a tornado is one that would drive most companies out of business. But the chances of it happening to any one company are remote. So many companies share the risk by paying a portion of the potential cost (the premium) to an insurance company who holds the money to pay out to the few that do suffer the damage. That way every company manages the potential risks at an affordable cost and the one that suffers the disaster will have the funds available to recover. Of course, the company that pays premiums but never has a loss may feel that the money has been wasted, but the peace of mind and potential to continue the business if a disaster strikes is what the money bought.

Hiring an outsourcer for overflow calls could be considered a form of insurance. The cost to ensure that the outsourcer is available when needed may be high for the few calls taken in the normal course of business. But when that huge surge of calls comes in and the outsourcer steps up staffing to handle them, the insurance money will be well spent. Insurance does not always involve traditional premiums paid to a third-party. Any time the company pays out something now to prevent a disaster later, it is essentially buying insurance.

Security Planning

Security is a growing concern for every company. This includes building security, protection of systems and data, security of personnel, and even protection of executives from kidnapping and other criminal attacks. Security is clearly a contingency process seeking to prevent losses. Wherever the company is concerned about people walking out of the building with the company's assets (like computer equipment), protection of employees walking through the parking lot in the dark, or a hacker breaking into the company's databases and stealing the customer information or company secrets, security planning has a role.

Even though companies implement security measures to prevent threats from outside the organization, there are additional concerns for the employees who remain inside the building. Violence in the workplace has increased dramatically over the past few years and security measures should be implemented to protect employees from their co-workers. When employees are terminated for performance reasons, the risk for violence increases. Some employees may react with physical violence, while others may retaliate with damage to the company's network and electronic data.

Due to economic changes, many companies are being forced to downsize their organizations by encouraging early retirement or by implementing a reduction in force strategy. When employees are voluntarily asked to leave a company, the security risk to the organization is lower than the risk of those employees whose positions are eliminated due to a workforce reduction. As with employees who are terminated for performance reasons, employees who do not voluntarily leave the organization pose an increased security risk to the organization. The safety of all employees must be taken into consideration to prevent physical harm or the destruction of corporate assets. Data security is a major focus for every company and is covered in more detail below. Risks from hackers and malicious viruses are significant and companies have suffered substantial losses in recent years from both pranksters and criminals, some aided by unsuspecting employees. There may also be risks in the event of a union strike in which the union personnel may sabotage the data systems and databases to make it harder for management to transact necessarily business.

Importance of a Contingency Plan

It is essential for every organization to have a contingency and disaster recovery plan. It is relatively common (although far from universal) to find such a plan developed and implemented for the Information Technology (IT) department. The impact of the loss of the data processing systems is huge. Recent studies suggest that two out of five enterprises that experience a full-scale disaster will go out of business within five years.

It is far less common to find a contingency/disaster plan that focuses on the unique requirements in the call center. Since this is the front door for many businesses, if this department is non-operational for any period of time, the impact on revenue and customer retention is likely to be significant. Where an IT plan already exists, expansion to include the center's needs can be accomplished fairly easily, but where no IT plan is in place, the call center may be the driving force behind the entire process.

Studies by Contingency Planning Research (CPR) over the last 10 years report that the biggest risks that companies face are those caused by Mother Nature. Storms, excessive rain, tornadoes, hurricanes, and other weather related situations, and the power surges and outages that often accompany them, are the threats that cause the most damage. While the events of September 11 focus our attention on the risk of terrorism, the likelihood of such disasters is small compared to the ongoing issues caused by weather.

A contingency/disaster plan needs to start with a focus on prevention. Every risk must be identified along with what steps would be necessary to prevent it from happening in the first place, since avoiding a problem is less expensive and less painful than fixing it after the fact. Another set of steps must be in place to minimize the impact when prevention fails. The plan must define the precise steps to take to recover as quickly as possible. The studies mentioned earlier focused primarily on IT and data system problems. Far less research has been done on what the business impact would be if the contact center as the main customer access point were to experience a significant outage so there is less data available to estimate the costs of losses and the potential solutions. Much of this will have to be developed by the call center.

Steps of Contingency Planning

There are a series of steps involved in developing a contingency plan. Following the steps leads to a systematic plan that can be presented to senior management for support and funding. In addition, the plan documentation will guide the staff through nearly any situation that can arise. The steps are:

1. Assemble the planning committee.
2. Identify risks and opportunities.
3. Detail the components of the plan.
4. Develop the impact analysis.
5. Identify prevention techniques and costs.
6. Identify recovery techniques and costs.
7. Determine exploitation of opportunity techniques and costs.
8. Develop the recommended plan for management.
9. Present the plan to management for approval and funding.
10. Create the detailed plan documentation.
11. Identify point of contact and responsibility.
12. Test the plan and adjust as needed.

Each of these steps is detailed below. Handling any disaster that may occur due to failure of the contingency plan or an unpreventable situation is explored in the disaster recovery planning section that follows.

Assembling the Team

The disaster recovery/risk management team should include representatives from every major discipline in the business. Obvious members are IT, telecom, and call center management. And don't forget to reserve a seat for individuals who influence call volume or depend on the call center. It probably makes sense to put at least one frontline agent on the team too. And if outsourcers are utilized, or are planned for use in the event of a disaster, a representative from the outsourcer organization should be included.

The following is a list of disciplines and support groups that should be considered for involvement in the team. However, care should be exercised in not getting the core planning team so large that it is unwieldy. Where possible, have the participants appointed in writing by senior management and job descriptions written to reflect this assignment on an ongoing basis.

• Information Technology

- Telecommunications
- Call Center Management
- Marketing
- Purchasing
- Human Resources
- Legal
- Facilities
- Engineering
- Safety and Environmental Affairs
- Public Information
- Community Relations
- Frontline Staff
- Outsourcers

As specific plans develop, it will be crucial to bring in call center technology vendors to help the planning team understand the full capabilities and options of the equipment and systems in place. It's important all fully understand how far the systems can be "stretched" in the event of a disaster, and what the costs would be to add backup or duplicate systems to keep the center operating in the event of an outage. Vendors should know exactly what the company expects from them in the event of an emergency and commit to making it happen so there are no surprises.

Other business partners should also be involved including service providers and suppliers, not to mention the financial institutions and insurance firms that the company utilizes. These organizations can provide useful services in the planning phase and in the recovery situation as well.

As the team is assembled, issue a mission statement, preferably from the CEO or site manager, to demonstrate the company's commitment to preparedness and planning. The statement should define the purpose of the plan and indicate that it will involve the entire organization, defining the authority and structure of the planning team. The planning process itself should have a schedule and a budget like any other project. Some budget dollars may be needed to cover research, printing, seminars, and consulting services.

Identifying the Risks

Identifying the potential risks involves taking a comprehensive inventory of all the components of the contact center. The team should "think negatively" about all the things that could fail and what the impact would be if they did. Consider each of the following components and what could go wrong: the physical facility, data systems, call center systems and applications, communications networks, electrical service, customer access points, partners, procedures, and staff.

Some important questions to consider are:

- What are the risks that could partially or totally disable the call center?

- What are the areas of the call center with the highest vulnerability?

- Which risks are managed partially or completely in departments such as IT?

- How can the call center plan link to the plans for other departments to ensure continuity and consistency?

- What are the potential ranges of failures?

- What are the interdependencies of systems, people, and processes within the call center and to others?

- What are the legal and regulatory issues that must be considered?

- What types of emergencies have occurred in the community, at this facility, or at other facilities in the area?

- What can happen as a result of the facility's location, such as flood, seismic activity, dam breakage, exposure to hazardous materials, or nuclear power leaks?

- What could result from a process failure such as an upgrade or replacement of a call center system?

- What emergencies could be caused by employee errors due to poor training, poor maintenance, carelessness, misconduct, substance abuse, or fatigue?

The best preparation against these potential threats may consist of a mix of internal controls and tools, and/or outsourced services that will meet the company's requirements for managing physical, technical, legal, regulatory, and human resources.

Look for the following documents to assist the team in developing the plan:

- Evacuation plan
- Fire protection plan
- Safety and health program
- Environment policies
- Security procedures
- Insurance programs
- Finance and purchasing procedures
- Employee manuals and handbooks
- Hazardous materials plan
- Mutual aid agreements

Set up meetings with government agencies, community organizations and utility providers. Ask about potential emergencies and their plans and available resources for responding to them. Sources of information may include the following:

- Community Emergency Management Office
- Federal Emergency Management Agency
- National Guard
- Mayor or Community Administrator's office
- Fire Department
- Police Department
- Emergency medical services organizations, including hospitals
- American Red Cross
- National Weather Service
- Public Works Department
- Planning Commission
- Neighboring businesses
- Public transportation authorities
- Hazardous material response organizations
- Utility providers for electricity, gas, sewer, and telephone service

Identify any federal, state or local codes and regulations that may apply to a crisis situation including:

- Occupational safety and health regulations
- Environmental regulations
- Fire codes
- Seismic safety codes
- Transportation regulations
- Zoning regulations
- Corporate policies

Rest assured that any risk that is not included on this list might be the one that strikes So be as thorough as possible and do not discard a risk from the plan because it seems too remote or small in impact to be worthy of the committee's time.

Detailing Plan Components

The following details some of the most common components that will be listed in the risk categories. While it is not comprehensive and may not cover unique challenges for a given call center, these items should start the thinking process as the planning committee begins to identify the risks and opportunities to be included.

Facility

Thinking about the facility risks must consider both the "black-hole scenario" of total loss of the building and its contents, and the wide range of partial losses that could occur. It doesn't take a major hurricane or tornado to cause a weather disaster. Various areas of the country regularly experience soaking rains with hundreds or thousands of businesses affected. A simple heavy rain can cause flooding in a localized area, disrupting power and potentially damaging equipment. Personnel may be unable to reach the office due to flooded highways and underpasses. The team should outline what can be done to prevent damage to the facility and the call center operations from a storm, including answers to the following questions:

- Can water seeping in the equipment rooms be detected before it is a major factor?

- Are tarps readily available to cover equipment and flashlights available to aid the process that must often take place in the dark?

- Is the main driving route to the call center a flood plain area or an underpass where a street may be inaccessible? Are alternative routes mapped out for employees to use in these situations?

- What types of emergencies could result from the design or construction of the facility? Is the building susceptible to structural damage or collapse?

Many other risks should be considered as well. Each of these can cause minor or major damage and affect call center operations significantly. Some techniques for mitigating each risk is listed, but this list should not be considered comprehensive.

- *Fire.* Install fire alarms as required by fire code and ensure that there are fire suppression devices in all equipment rooms that create the least damage to electronic equipment. While sprinkler systems may be required by law in areas where electronics are stored, installation of less damaging fire suppression devices may be an option.

- *Smoke, heat, and water.* Smoke detectors should be installed as required by code, especially in equipment rooms and storage areas where large amounts of records are held. Heat and water level detectors should be in every equipment room. Make sure these alarms along with all other environmental sensors are monitored on a 24 x 7 basis and that the monitoring personnel know what to do when these alarms occur. Shutting down a system can be better than letting it be totally destroyed by excessive heat or water. Ensure that there are floor plans for the building available showing where the shut-off valves are and that employees are assigned this responsibility if water becomes an issue.

- *Power loss or surge.* Surge suppression devices should be installed on all incoming power, especially power to sensitive electronic systems. Uninterruptible power supplies (UPS) should be provided for all major systems. This may be a battery backup system for telephone equipment or generators that will provide power if commercial power goes down for any length of time. One thing to consider is the length of time that the battery or UPS can power the current load of equipment. Often the systems have grown considerably since initial installation without consideration for increasing the capacity of the power backup systems. Where agent desktops have an integrated interface for the telephone functions instead of a separate telephone set (e.g., VoIP), be sure to back up the local PCs as well since the battery backup of the phone system would not power these devices.

- *Lightning.* Some parts of the country are more susceptible to lightning damage than others but damage can occur anywhere. All incoming telephone circuits should be equipped with lightning suppression systems. This includes all entries from the Telco, carriers, microwave links, and cables connecting multi-building complexes together. The potential damage from lightning is extensive when even an indirect hit is experienced in electronics, and a direct hit can melt the circuit boards.

- *Vandalism.* The best protection from vandalism is a good building security plan. No unauthorized personnel should be allowed to access the rooms where equipment is stored. Change passwords frequently, especially when a technician is terminated who might take revenge on the company by sabotaging one or more systems. Take this same precaution if the union workers for a vendor go out on a strike as it is not uncommon for the technicians to try to make work for the management by causing a high number of trouble calls.

- *Building.* Plan for evacuation for bomb threat, fire drill, chemical spill, detection of hazardous materials, etc. Ensure that the evacuation plan is well mapped out and all employees know where they are meant to exit and assemble. Most of these situations will be non-events, but everyone must be ready for the situation that is dangerous. Prepare for the possibility that the center will be inaccessible for a few minutes, a few hours, or even a few days. Consider employee options to work from home and rerouting calls to another site.

- *Endangered personnel.* Risks from intruders or even employees threatening employees must be considered in the plan. In addition, personnel can become trapped in a structural failure due to building damage or in a fire or other situation.

Consider the possibility that a "command center" may need to be established in a crisis along with a media briefing area, shelter areas, first-aid stations, and sanitation facilities. These should probably be planned for an off-site location in the event that the site is inaccessible.

Data and Voice Systems

The terrorist activities of September 11th wiped out major data centers and huge amounts of end-user equipment. As a result, many more call centers now use a "hot standby" center with a current set of customer data. These companies may consider shifting personnel to laptops or other remote systems or have a large quantity replacement plan in place with a vendor.

If call center employees will be working from home temporarily, it is important to ensure that there is enough remote connection capacity, backup desktop images and capability available for provisioning laptops and mobile devices, and ensuring th necessary "logical" security measures for employees to authenticate and be granted authorization in order to gain access to company data and voice communications from a remote site. This is the kind of remote access that is specifically excluded during normal operations to maintain network security, so these provisions will need to be overridden, at least temporarily.

One enterprising chemical firm made a cooperative arrangement with a local bank call center to provide backup facilities to each other. Both companies used the same kind of data system and core applications and the same type of telephone system for the ACD. Each agreed to wire up additional outlets for agent workstations all around the walls of the company cafeteria. Then if one suffered a disaster than kept it from accessing a site, the employees could come to the other company and bring their computers and telephones with them, plug into the systems in the cafeterias and go to work. Not long after the agreement was made, the chemical company has a spill in the plant and had to evacuate the call center for several days. The employees took their equipment to the bank, set up and were back in business in a couple of hours. This kind of creative solution is possible and can certainly be more cost-effective than either suffering the loss or contracting for a commercial hot-site provider.

Writing down the detailed procedures for backup restoration is extremely important since the backups may have to be installed by someone unfamiliar with normal operations. Some questions to ask in assessing system risks include:

If data is backed up off-site every specific period of time, what is the value of the data that could be lost if a catastrophic event takes place between backups? All systems should have a database copy running in the system, a copy that is rotated daily in the same room or another room on-site, and a third copy that is rotated to an off-site location as often as possible. Depending upon the importance of the system and currency of the data, that could be daily or even monthly. It is important to rotate the copies so that any corruption of the copy will be detected quickly and a new copy produced. Too many backup data files are useless when needed because the medium has become damaged or some other corruption has occurred undetected. The systems list to be considered include the ACD, IVR, workforce management system, quality monitoring, learning management system, and any other electronic devices used in the call center, in addition to the data systems, managed by the IT department. While it is common to backup the data on the ACD, it is also important to backup the voice recordings that support the center as well. These include greetings, queue announcements, voice message system, and the IVR voice prompts and responses that are critical to operations.

- If a major disaster occurred in your area, would the hot site provider have contracts to support more users that it could accommodate at once? How could priority be ensured? When companies tried to access the capacity for hot sites after September 11, some found that they had to relocate across country to find enough capacity to accommodate them for the period needed, and others found "no room at the inn."

- Are the systems in place to detect intrusion into data or voice systems? Hackers can produce mass numbers of website accesses and emails blocking the pathways to the company website, and other criminals can find ways to access the company telephone lines to make large quantities of long-distance and overseas calls on the company's bill. Proper toll-fraud protection processes should be in place to prevent the latter and these are often services that can be acquired from the toll-free network carrier.

- Do you have a printout of the current hardware and software configurations of all systems? This listing can save hours, if not days, in getting a new system manufactured and shipped to replace one that is destroyed.

Call center systems and applications

One of the most effective ways to prevent system failures is to provide redundancy. This includes duplicate processors, operating systems, backup databases, and other components that will work in a hot-standby or fail-over mode so that operations are totally uninterrupted in the event of a failure. Working with the vendors of the systems to understand the options for redundancy will reveal the cost and effectiveness of a range of potential solutions.

If an IVR fails, a call center must be able to provide a backup quickly or it will have to deal with the increased influx of calls to the call center staff. Or in the event of an ACD failure, it is important to know how calls would be routed to the staff. Call center management should keep in mind that what will be missing during the downtime is not just call routing (where a simple hunt distribution will work in the short term), but valuable management reports. In any disaster, all steps should be outlined to get the ACD up and working as soon as possible. Often ACD reports serve as evidence that's submitted for "loss of business" insurance.

Another option to consider is backing up automated systems with manual ones. Identify the necessary forms and process steps that would need to be distributed to employees to continue to operate when the telephone system is working but the data systems are not. For some companies, the manual processes would be relatively easy to implement and for others, nearly impossible, but an honest assessment of what could be done and how, will be useful to the assessment of options.

Ranking the capabilities that are needed in priority order will be necessary. Identify which systems and which capabilities within those systems that the center finds most important to basic operations. Basic telephone service is required, but is skill-based routing really essential to basic operations? Can the center operate without quality monitoring for a few days or without workforce management systems? How important is the IVR or the website in handling customer interactions? In a bank where up to 80% of the transactions are automated, it is very important, but in another industry, it might be a minor inconvenience. Which transactions are most important to restore first if the entire IVR cannot be restored all at once? The technicians will need guidance to ensure that the highest priority items are done first and the rest in rank order.

Communications networks

Redundancy cannot help if the failure of the systems is due to a cable cut between th

Telco central office and the site, or even a central office or carrier network failure. While these failures are not frequent, they do happen. The Hinsdale (Chicago area) central office burned down several years ago leaving the local area without service for many days. A battery failure in a New York carrier switching center left long-distance calling in the area out of service for hours while the batteries were recharged. And a farmer burying a dead cow in Georgia managed to cut the main fiber optic carrier cables, disrupting the calling of nearly every company and individual on the eastern seaboard for most of a day. These are failures outside the control of the call center but must be considered in the plan. Many companies have contracted for service from two providers, or at least from two different central offices for local service. But it is important to ensure that the cable routes to those different sources do not share any common pathways that might both be disrupted. Contracting with two long-distance service providers is also common now and a single 800 number can have calls transported over both during normal situations and only one during a network failure of one of the carriers. When these facilities also support Internet connections, contracting with multiple Internet providers may not provide the needed redundancy.

Another option is to provide the connections to the Telco and carriers on two different media. For example, one set of connections might be underground cable while another on microwave circuits. Using a mix of digital and analog trunking can also provide a backup for failure of one or the other, and cellular services can be connected to an ACD for trunking in an emergency as well as long as the necessary equipment is in place. As a minimum, routing calls to a recorded announcement in the carrier network that informs callers of the situation and expected time for restoration will be needed. If this recorded announcement function is in place and ready to activate when needed, it will provide a safety net for all of these network and cable cut situations.

Electrical

Lightning is one of the most serious threats to electrical equipment. But lightning can enter through a variety of pathways. The planning team should identify all the paths and put the necessary protection in place. There have been thousands of dollars of damage to ACDs from an indirect hit, and a direct hit can destroy it or another call center system completely. Grounding of equipment is essential to its proper operation during normal periods, but may spell the difference between a failure and a crisis averted in the case of a surge from lightning or any other cause. Have a qualified electrician ensure that systems are properly connected to the electrical feed and backup systems (batteries or UPS), and that the appropriate levels of lightning protection are in place and are grounded thoroughly. This is probably the lowest cost and most effective preventative measure a call center can take to guard expensive equipment.

Power failures can happen at any time as can "brown outs" when demand is at its peak. Preparation for these situations is essential since nearly every system in the call center is electrical. Some will run on battery backups while others will need to be connected to a UPS in order to continue operations. The UPS will require fuel so be certain that there is a ready supply of fuel kept at the site in a place that will not constitute a fire hazard. Battery efficiency degrades over time, so ensure that a regular test of the batteries is included in the contingency plan.

An inventory of the call center will reveal all of the devices that rely on electricity and some of them are at each agent's desktop. Identify those that are critical in a power failure and ensure that the outlets these devices are plugged into are connected to the UPS. The UPS cannot reasonably be expected to power everything, so prioritization is essential. Outlets to plug in fans in the equipment rooms are essential to provide cooling for these systems in the event of failure of the air conditioning system. The heat these devices produce is tremendous and the systems can be damaged by excessive heat in a matter of a couple of hours. If no cooling is possible, the systems should be shut down until the air conditioning is operational.

Prevention of power failure can be considered in today's marketplace since there are now many communities that have more than one power provider. Consider contracting with both to better ensure at least one of them is providing electricity during an outage. It is also possible to have a cable cut or car accident that takes out a power pole. Even weather can take down the overhead lines that feed the call center. Work with the power vendor and trace the path of the lines that feed the building to identify those that are underground and overhead and encourage the provider to bury overhead lines where possible, particularly the ones on the company's property. If contracting with two providers is an option, ensure that the cable routing is as diverse as possible.

People

A contingency plan should outline what would happen to service if a large percentage of staff suddenly became unavailable due to something more serious than typical Monday-morning absenteeism. Call centers should be ready to react if a major flu epidemic hits the community or the staff is otherwise affected. For those in union environments, the possibility of a strike or other job action must also be considered.

For companies that have multiple call center sites, routing calls to another site may be the best option to overcome a short-staff situation in one center. This can be done with network features or other third-party routing equipment. Having a preset allocation scheme in the network or in the router for these occasions will make it possible to activate the feature on a moment's notice. The call center with only one site that uses an outsource provider to handle overflow can activate the same options, assuming the contract with the outsourcer provides for such a situation or a special arrangement can be made at the time.

For centers operating in one site with no outside contractor to assist, other options must be found. This can be a function of asking staff to work overtime or seeking other employees to fill in temporarily. One company keeps a list of all personnel who have worked in the call center at one time and have moved to other jobs. When a crisis hits, they can tap this group to find temporary help who can function at a fairly high level very quickly. This requires a cooperative spirit among the various departments who will lose staff for these incidents, but if it is only activated on a crisis basis it can work very well.

Routing calls to employees' homes or cell phones may be an option if the call center site is unavailable. If the company has utilized home workers in the normal course of business, it will be easier to make this happen. The call center can keep a list of employees' personal cell phone numbers and ask them to use these systems on a reimbursed basis during the crisis rather than having to acquire large numbers of cell phones to hand out to employees.

Another option is to route all calls to a voice mail system and have off-site employees pick up the messages and return calls to the customers. This is not ideal but it is better than not responding, so have a voice mail box set up on the system that could be instantly activated for this purpose and make sure it has a huge capacity to handle the needed load. In fact, if there are different phone numbers callers dial, set up a different mailbox for each so that employees can pick up only the calls they know how to handle. Consider reserving this voice mail capacity in the network, in addition to having it in the on-site systems, so that regardless of the failure situation, it can be easily activated.

Sometimes a significant portion of the workforce will be newly hired or temporary staff with minimal training to react to an emergency situation. This includes personnel from other jobs in the company who are drafted to fill in as needed, as well as those that would be supplied by a temporary agency. There won't be time to give these people more than the most rudimentary training, so it is essential that there be written scripts for the calls and clear directions on how to access help when the employee has a question. Computer-based scripts can be ideal for this situation if the use of temporaries or very high turnover are the norm, but activating such systems for the first time during a crisis is not a realistic option. Printed instructions will probably be more useful.

One useful inventory is one that identifies the response capabilities that may be available from the existing staff. Some may have medical training or do volunteer fire fighting, while another speaks multiple languages or has essential engineering skills. These people are likely to be more than willing to help any way they can and knowing which employees can help will speed the response dramatically.

The plan should also consider the opportunity that might occur when the staffing is normal but the workload is unusually high. This could be due to the success of a marketing campaign, or the result of some error on the part of the company such as incorrect statements. Tapping into additional human resources will be needed to seize these opportunities or resolve these challenges. Identify the alternative sources for staffing, the outsource options, and other technological alternatives that will address these situations. If it is a true sales opportunity, the contingency plan must address how it will be seized for maximum company advantage.

Processes

Several recent disasters have forced call centers to do things "the old fashioned way" when their computer system was down for an extended period of time. Some were able to conduct business by manually taking orders and looking up information in paper-based documentation. Others simply couldn't function without automated systems in place. Assess the processes and procedures used by the agents in the call center to determine which of them or what portion of each could be handled manually.

It may be necessary to develop some standard forms for agents to use to track the calls that are taken while the computers are unavailable, and these may need to serve as the data-entry forms when the systems are back in operation. Having a small supply of the forms that can be easily duplicated will make it possible to react to the crisis quickly.

Some transactions will not be possible during a computer failure, while others that are normally handled electronically will need to be done via the phone (such as credit card processing). It may be necessary to do some tasks after the customer has disconnected that would normally be done while the caller is on the line, so it may be possible to off-load this work to a team who is not fully-trained for the calls but can do these tasks. Consider each part of a contact and determine which parts can be done, which cannot, and which could be done another way.

Customer access points

The percentage of customer interactions handled over the Internet is growing. If the company web site is down, the call center should be prepared to handle the calls that may come into call center staff as an alternative. Any point where customers access the business is a potential risk and could "dump" increased workload on the other channels or deny customers access to the company. Part of the plan should be to effectively communicate with customers who normally use the affected channel to offer them other ways to contact the business rather than calling a competitor.

Review all of the transactions that customers can do on the website and determine which are the most critical to restore quickly. That will help the technical team prioritize the restoration process. When even the most rudimentary home page is activated, it may be possible to include a message to call the company's call center while the website capabilities are unavailable.

In assessing the risks in this area, consider the following questions:

- If a website or online service is provided across multiple locations, how will service be degraded with the loss of one location? Two locations?

- How many of these locations can go down before the system cannot handle a normal load of users?

- Can rudimentary website capabilities be offered while more sophisticated functions are being restored?

- What will be the impact on the call center if the website is inactive?

Partners

Partners refer to other companies that the call center depends on or provides services to on a regular basis. For companies utilizing outsourcers, it is important to consider the possibility that the outsourcer will have a disaster, even when the customer-company is operating normally. This is clearly a case where the tables are turned and the company needs to come to the aid of the outsourcer in its own interests. Routing of calls to the outsourcer may need to be curtailed for a few hours, or at least reduced. The call center may need to activate the contingency plan for increased staffing to handle these additional transactions.

Companies who provide outsourcing services as their business need a contingency and disaster recovery plan too. Selection of a partner should include a review of the plans of both companies to ensure that the plan exists and covers the most likely situations as a minimum. Where there are gaps in the plans, negotiation of coverage may be required to ensure that all contingencies have been considered.

Vendors

The terrorist attack of September 11th provided a clear picture of the important role that vendors play in disaster recovery operations. Businesses displaced by the attacks on the World Trade Center found out fast that the effectiveness of their own disaster-recovery plans depended in large part on the performance of their IT vendors, and a valuable lesson learned was the importance of maintaining close communication with IT vendors about their roles in a business' continuity plan long before disaster strikes. Smart businesses are beginning to revisit their relationships with technology providers to ensure that their vendors will be at their sides even in less-arduous circumstances. The vendor who will take the extra effort to be involved in the contingency/disaster planning process and place the enterprise at the top of the priority list will generally not be the low-priced bidder, so be prepared to consider this in vendor selection and contract negotiations.

It is also important to consider that each of the vendors and their products are generally part of a multi-vendor network and all of the pieces must work together to provide the desired result. For example, the call center needs an ACD to provide basic telephony services, but also needs the local Telco to provide trunks for the network, the IXC to provide incoming and outgoing long-distance services, and a host of other vendors to provide the specialized systems such as workforce management, voice mail, and IVR that must be interconnected to the ACD. All of these vendors will be under extreme pressures with multiple customers demanding attention in a widespread disaster. Normally competitive teams suddenly work together to achieve the results needed.

There are situations where vendors simply cannot provide all of the protection that a company would like. In the aftermath of the World Trade Center losses, Verizon Communications suffered major damage to its central office at 140 West Street. This switching center provides services for 300,000 telephone lines and 3.6 million high-capacity data circuits, many serving the New York Stock Exchange, large financial institutions and other companies in lower Manhattan. A gaping hole was torn in a seventh-floor exterior wall, exposing and damaging huge communications systems. And while Verizon worked almost around the clock for over a month to restore operations at 140 West Street and service to its customers, the company indicated that significantly reducing the building's network vulnerabilities would require more time or money than Verizon is willing to expend This suggests that multiple vendors may be a company's best protection from the failures of a single network provider.

Developing a clear communications plan is the key to faster and less stressful recovery. The roles and responsibilities need to be clearly spelled out and the communication processes and contact points for both vendors and customer must be clear and up-to-date as well. The contingency plan should also consider the possibility that a key vendor will be lost due to a disaster of its own, bankruptcy, or other problem. This could mean disruption of services or loss of the maintenance and upgrade potential for existing systems. Analysis of the products and services provided by each vendor, the alternative sources that exist for those offerings, and the likelihood of the possibilities should be included in the plan.

Summary of components

The above list outlines just a few of the risks in each of the categories. It's critical that the contingency planning team brainstorm all the negative possibilities in each of the areas, determine what can be done to prevent the negative events from occurring, and formulate a plan of recovery if the worst happens. The team should also consider all the positive opportunities that would require crisis-management techniques in order to be maximized to the company's advantage.

Analyzing the Impact

Calculating costs is a big part of developing a contingency plan. It's important to understand and attribute a value to each contact so that the team can calculate the cost of being out of operation. Even in those centers that do not generate revenue directly, it is important to agree on a value for each answered contact to serve as a base. Then each measure of prevention should be evaluated to see if the call center could realistically afford each one. Sometimes the cost of prevention is much higher than what the cost of recovery or lost business would be. But more than likely, the cost of an ounce of prevention is less than the pound of cure that might be needed in the end.

The Federal Emergency Management Agency (FEMA) recommends an impact analy-

Vulnerability Analysis Chart

Type of Emergency	Probability	Human Impact	Property Impact	Business Impact	Internal Resources	External Resources	Total Score
	5 to 1	5 to 1	5 to 1	5 to 1	1 to 5	1 to 5	
Flood	1	4	5	3	2	1	16
Network failure	3	1	1	4	4	2	15

sis using the form similar to the one provided below:

To use the chart, list the types of emergencies identified down the left column. Estimate the probability of any risk that has been identified. While this is a subjective exercise, it will help in determining which risks to prioritize in the prevention process. Use a scale of 1 to 5 with 5 as the highest probability. For example, a flood has been estimated as a low probability and a network failure a mid-range potential according to the sample analysis chart.

Next assess the potential human impact of each emergency including the possibility of death or injury. Assign a rating of 1 to 5 with 5 as the highest potential impact. The sample shows a flood as having a high impact on people but the network failure has little or none.

Assess the potential impact to property in terms of losses and damage. Once again, use the 1 to 5 scale with 5 being the highest. Consider cost to replace, cost to set up temporary replacement, and cost to repair. The flood in this example would have a high impact on property and a network failure may have little impact.

Score the potential business impact including loss of market share. Assign the rating on a 1 to 5 scale with 5 as the highest impact. Consider business interruption, employees unable to report for work, customers unable to reach the company, company in violation of contractual agreements, regulations or laws, fines/penalties/legal costs, and lost sales. The impact of a flood at the business is scored in the mid-range in the example with the network failure rated high.

Look at the internal and the external resources for ability to respond. In this case, a low score is better. Consider the following questions for each type of emergency:

• Do we have the needed resources internally to respond?

• Will external resources respond as quickly as needed or will there be higher priorities for them to serve?

In the sample, the internal resources available to respond to a flood are considered higher than those to respond to a network failure. External resources are considered high in both cases.

The final step is to add up the columns. The lower the score is, the better it is. This ranking will help to prioritize the planning and funding of solutions in the effort that follows. The sample shows both the flood and network failure as being relatively equal in their impacts. Of course, the ranking that would be assigned by any planning team could be quite different from those in the sample.

Where potential opportunities have been identified, the team will need to estimate the impact of each opportunity and the techniques needed to exploit it. While some possibilities have low revenue potential, they may have significant impact on the company's brand image or position in the marketplace. Once again a score sheet similar to the Vulnerability Analysis Chart can be used to identify the opportunities, probability, potential impact on revenue, image, and long-term market position. These would be scored along with the ability of internal and external resources to respond to the

Opportunities Analysis Chart

Type of Opportunity	Probability 5 to 1	Revenue Impact 5 to 1	Image Impact 5 to 1	Long-term Impact 5 to 1	Internal Resources 1 to 5	External Resources 1 to 5	Total Score
Marketing campaign	5	4	3	1	4	1	18
Competitor bankruptcy	1	3	1	4	2	5	16

opportunity using a process like the one shown in the sample Opportunities Analysis Chart below:

In the analysis of opportunities, a high score is better than a low score (opposite of the Vulnerability Analysis Chart), representing a chance that is significant and has a high potential to be exploited by the company.

Identifying Prevention Techniques

Once the impacts and resulting priorities are known, the next step is to determine what the prevention techniques could be and estimate the cost of each option. The possibilities need to include changes of procedures and other simple options along with the more elaborate solutions such as dual vendors and major system enhancements. Management will want to see a variety of possibilities and the costs associated with them before authorizing funds for a solution.

The options should provide a range of prevention possibilities, with some fully preventing and others only providing partial protection. The team should apply a score to the potential for the prevention technique to mitigate the risks, and to be consistent with the impact analysis, a rating of 1 to 5 is reasonable with 5 being total prevention.

An estimated cost must be determined for each technique and when compared to the other options under consideration and the score for the prevention effectiveness, the best choices should become clear. A sample Prevention Options Analysis Chart is provided below. Of course, more columns may be needed for multiple options.

Risk	Impact Score	Option A	Option A Prevention Score	Option B	Option B Prevention Score	Recommended Option
Network Failure	15	$15,000 annually for dual carriers	3 – both available carriers share part of cable route	$138,500 initial and $15,000 for dual carriers and added cable construction	5 – protects from one carrier failure and cable cuts	A

Identifying Recovery Techniques

The planning team will need to consider the recovery options should the contingency plan fail. Once again, the recovery options will range from simple manual processes with minimal expense to complete building replacement scenarios. Recovery can be partial or full, in stages or all at once, and the techniques considered must cover the full range of options.

In this stage, scoring the recovery techniques for their effectiveness (partial to full recovery) should be done along the 1 to 5 scale with full recovery options scored a 5. This will be compared to the cost of each option and compared to other choices to find the best choices to present to management for consideration.

A sample Recovery Options Analysis Chart is provided below, but once again, expansion for multiple options is likely to be required.

Recovery Options Analysis Chart

Risk	Impact Score	Option A	Option A Recovery Score	Option B	Option B Recovery Score	Recommended Option
Network Failure	15	$7000 send calls to network Voice Mail and call back	2 – phone and outbound long-distance call costs	$15,000 per Reroute calls to outsourcer	4 – Handle they arrive but outsourcer not as effective in selling as in-house staff	B

Exploiting Opportunities

The techniques identified to take advantage of any opportunities that develop are equally as important as the disaster recovery and prevention techniques. These are the chances for the company to grow and prosper in normal times and are far more likely to develop for most companies that the disasters planned for in the contingency/disaster plan.

Analyzing the cost of seizing the revenue opportunity against the value of the opportunity is a bit more straightforward than analyzing the cost of prevention and recovery. But those situations that affect brand image and long-term positioning of the company will be a bit more nebulous to reduce to dollars and assign values. However, the process is essentially the same as the planning for the other contingencies.

Opportunity Options Analysis Chart

Opportunity	Impact Score	Option A	Option Opportunity Score	Option B	Option B prevention score	Recommended Option
Marketing campaign creates double normal call volume	18	Overtime for current staff - $4000 per day	2 – will only answer part of the calls and service will be degraded for all	Contract with outsourcer and use as needed - $8500 per day	4 – Calls handled as they arrive but outsource not as effective at selling as in-house staff	B

Assembling the Plan

Once all risks and the costs of prevention and cures have been identified, it's now time to present the plan to senior management for approval. Before the team can begin to implement the plan and put in place the equipment, systems, and procedures, there will need to be approval and budget dollars from the top to make it all happen.

In most cases, call center professionals find themselves with a limited budget and cannot implement everything in the plan at once. So it's important to rank the risks, options, and preventive measures in their order of importance to carrying on effective operations. The priorities may be influenced by government regulations that apply to the business. To remain in compliance, it may be necessary to address specific functions early that might otherwise be a lower priority. Select those options that seem to provide the best balance of value for cost and present those as the recommended options. But include an appendix that lists all of the options considered and the estimated costs of each so that management can see the full detail of the effort that has been undertaken and choose different options if desired. Using the impact analysis tables is a good way to guide the presentation.

In recognition of the limited budget, it may be appropriate to recommend that some efforts be implemented in stages. That will allow some of the prevention to be in place quickly, while the final solution may be some months or years away. However, it must be made clear in the presentation that failure to implement even the first stages of the recommended preventions will increase the likelihood of having to deal with disaster recovery instead.

Presenting the Plan

Prevention options and costs

Focus the presentation on the recommended options but be prepared to enumerate the other options that have been considered. Provide the estimated costs for each option as well. This estimated cost will probably need to be given in a range of possibilities since some of the due diligence needed to finalize the numbers will not be done until management approves proceeding forward.

Recovery options and costs

Once again, focus on the recommended options and have the details ready if asked. In this case, the estimated costs for each option will likely be a broad range of possibilities that cannot be finalized without assumptions about the scope and nature of the exact disaster being addressed. But provide the best information available and a range that covers the reasonable possibilities.

Recommended plan and priorities

The final part of the presentation should contain a summary of the risks and recommended plan to prevent them. The impact of the risks and the priorities of the implementation recommended for the prevention techniques should be clear. It may be prudent to consider phased implementations if some of the solutions are expensive or difficult to complete.

Next, focus on the disaster recovery options and align them with the assumptions that have been made in terms of the prevention techniques. If the recommendation was to establish a relationship with an outsource provider, then include the disaster recovery options and costs that work under that assumption.

Be prepared for discussion and for management to select other options that the team recommends. But if the team has done its analysis well, it will be relatively simple to see what the change of options entails in both prevention and recovery. When a final plan is approved, it is time to commit the details of the plan to a written document. Given the likelihood of changes at the executive level, it is not recommended that the team develop the detailed plan prior to approval of the general plan.

Creating the Document
Contingency plan

This portion of the plan focuses on prevention of disasters so it is important to include the identification of risks, the prioritization from the impact analysis, and the recommended techniques for avoiding the problems. Details of the options and the costs involved will now need to be completed so that the business cases for each of these can be approved. This is generally not the primary focus of the documentation as most of this will be implemented as new systems, upgrades, process changes, etc., and be built into the normal operation of the business.

Disaster recovery plan

The disaster recovery portion of the plan takes over when the contingency planning has failed to prevent a disaster. This portion of the plan needs to be in detail and contain the following elements:

- *Executive summary* – Provides a brief overview of the purpose of the plan, the company's policy on disaster recovery, authorities and responsibilities of key personnel, and where response operations will be managed.

- *Elements of the plan* – These elements that were described in detail above serve as the foundation of the procedures that will be followed to protect personnel and equipment and resume operations as quickly as possible.

    o Direction and control

    o Communications and contact information

    o Life safety and health protection

    o Property protection

    o Record protection (including evidence for insurance)

    o Community outreach

    o Recovery and restoration

    o Administration and logistics

- *Emergency response procedures* – This spells out how the call center will respond to situations. If possible, this should include a series of checklists that can easily be accessed and used by anyone needing them. Specific procedures might be needed for some kinds of situations such as bomb threats and tornados:

    o Warning employees and customers

    o Communicating with personnel and community responders

o Evacuation and accounting for all persons in the facility including con tractors and visitors, and special plans for disabled persons or those who do not speak English

o Activating and operating the command center

o Shutting down operations or equipment

o Protecting vital records

o Protocol for turning control over to an outside organization or agency including entrance to use, who they report to, how they will be identified, and who the company contact person will be.

o Restoring operations

• *Supporting documentation* – This includes all of the details that personnel will need to respond to a situation including:

o Emergency contact lists with phone numbers

o Building and site maps with identification of utility shut-offs, water/gas/electrical customers, location of fire extinguishers, exits, stairways, escape routes, and location of restricted areas, hazardous areas, and high-value items.

o Resource lists – providing a list of all major resource that could be needed and any mutual aid agreements with other companies and government agencies.

It is not possible to have too much detail in terms of the inventory of equipment, configurations of systems, database elements, restoration steps, and lists of contacts and their roles in the recovery process. Assume that the building has been totally destroyed along with everything in it and that the key personnel who know how to handle things are all gone. Make it possible for someone who is totally unfamiliar with the company and its operations to order replacement parts and systems, implement the applications and products, recover the off-site databases, and enable the company to operate as quickly as possible.

Plan distribution

Most planners recommend that the plan document be printed and distributed in three-ring binders with all pages numbered. Each individual who receives a copy should be required to sign for it and be responsible for replacing updated pages. When an employee leaves or changes position, the responsibility and the documentation must be passed to someone else who will sign for the book.

Some portions of the plan should be provided to government agencies or partners and/or vendors, but be aware that some sections may reveal company secrets or provide private information about employees and customers. Key members of the team should keep a copy of the plan in their homes and/or automobiles. Electronic copies of the full plan should also be kept in the company files and at an off-site location.

To the extent that the charts and databases that make up the inventory and contact lists are also used by the company for normal operations, there should be a data linkage to these documents so that updating one, updates them both. This will minimize the potential for the plan to become dated and obsolete.

Assigning Responsibilities

The effectiveness of the plan depends on the people who implement it. That includes the team who are the points of contact in any situation and who take responsibility for the plan processes. It also requires that the staff be trained on the purpose, processes and procedures of the plan and their roles in it.

The team consists of the people who will be responsible for the plan on an ongoing basis, scheduling tests, and providing updated procedures. But it also includes the names and contact information for everyone who has an assigned role in the process as a point of contact for others. This includes everyone from the technicians who know the systems to the team leaders who will escort the people from the building in an evacuation. It also includes the external contacts that will be needed such as vendor personnel, community resources, and regulators who may need to be contacted for guidance. Insurance company contacts should probably be on the list as well.

Once the plan is completely written and approved, training should be conducted for all employees. Responsibility for the training should be assigned to specific individuals. The need for training should not only include employees, but also contractors and frequent visitors.

Testing the Plan

It is important to regularly schedule a test and run through various elements of the plan to ensure that the plan is current, workable, and that the measures in it produce the desired results. This is painful for the company and requires the backing of senior management, but without it, the planning effort is wasted. As time passes without any significant crisis, the commitment to the plan tends to waiver. Regular testing will help prevent this from happening and ensure ongoing buy-in with the process.

A tabletop exercise with management and personnel who have key roles is a good review. In a conference room setting, describe an emergency scenario and have participants discuss their responsibilities and how they would react to the situation. Identify any areas of confusion and/or overlap, and modify the plan accordingly. It is important not to actually simulate a crisis in such a way that a real disaster could occur. For example, one state agency decided to test its plan by disabling its mainframe computer. It took three days to restore the systems online and return to normal operations. The tabletop exercise is a safe way to test the plan.

Conduct a formal audit of the entire plan on a regular basis, at least annually or in the event of a potential threat. Make sure the plan reflects any changes that have occurred to systems, personnel, procedures, building layout, etc. Make sure there are current photographs and other records of the facility assets for insurance purposes. Review the training process to ensure that all employees are receiving appropriate levels of training. Be sure to brief employees on any changes that take place as a function of the audit process.

Tests should be done regularly but at irregular intervals so that they are not expected. Each drill should exercise a different scenario to ensure that all elements of the plan are tested from time to time. Any gaps in the plan that are identified in the process must be filled by updating the plan documentation and distributing it to all registered plan owners.

Disaster Recovery Steps

When prevention fails and a disaster develops, it is time for the disaster recovery plan to be implemented. The first order of business is to establish a single point of control for the crisis so that everyone knows who is in charge and can receive direction on the steps to take next. This individual is responsible for declaring the disaster and identifying the scope of the situation, ordering evacuation of the building or shutdown of the facility or systems, interfacing with outside organizations and the media, and issuing press releases as appropriate. The "incident commander" must have sufficient authority and responsibility to:

- Assume command

- Assess the situation

- Implement the disaster recovery plan

  o Set up the command center as needed

  o Establish communications with employees on the job and off

  o Establish communications with community resources

- Determine the appropriate response strategies

- Activate the needed resources, both internal and external

- Decide who may enter the site and who may not

- Order an evacuation

- Order system shutdowns

- Oversee all response activities

  o Establish a logging procedure for each action taken and the time

  o Identify any deviations from the plan and the reasons for them

- Interface with the press and community organizations

- Declare that the incident is "over"

Assessing the Damage

It is difficult in the middle of chaos to take a look around and make an honest assessment of the situation, but that is an essential early step in the disaster recovery process. Over-reaction is common and counter-productive, so a clear head is needed to see things as they really are and ask the right questions to assess the scope of the problems. However, this is an important task that generally falls to the person designated to be in charge.

Setting Priorities

Protection of human life is the most important focus, followed by protection of property. Ensure that individuals do not feel the need to be "heroes" and place themselves in more danger than is prudent. Saving records is not worth someone running back into a room filled with smoke. Once again, every person should know what his role is and do it based on the training and documentation provided. It is better to evacuate the area when in doubt than not, and make sure that all personnel are accounted for before allowing anyone to reenter the area.

Establish an off-site meeting place where evacuated employees should assemble. In a situation like a fire, not all personnel may leave at the same time in an orderly fashion, and some may have been out of the area at lunch or on a personal errand. So knowing where everyone is to go to check in is essential to accounting for everyone who might be at risk.

After all personnel are accounted for, it is time to think about protection of property. Remove important documents, system disks, and other valuables if possible first. The disaster recovery plan should list the valuables in the order that they should be found and saved, location by department or floor, and identify the person who has first responsibility for each item, with a backup person listed as well.

Set up a controlled perimeter around the site with the assistance of the police or fire department if there is any risk of looting or theft of property. Have all items removed brought to the off-site assembly point to be inventoried and safely stored.

Ensure that system shut downs, utility disconnects, and other measures have been taken care of by assigning each to individuals and having them report to the control center when each task has been completed. Non-employees will do some of these, but they should still notify the control center when the task is done.

Communicating the Plan

The communications plan needs to include the listing of all personnel with all of the contact media options including telephone, cell phone, pager, PDA, home phone, etc. The command center will need to issue a directive to all employees on how to communicate during the crisis, but if a special telephone number and website URL have been established ahead of time for this purpose, there may be little need to reiterate it. Many community resources like police and fire have their own communications systems and two-way radios, so it is important for the command center to know how it will reach these personnel for coordination.

Communications with customers must happen as quickly as possible. Let them know the nature of the situation and how long it is likely to continue. Identify alternative ways to do business with the company. Customers are generally very forgiving in a crisis, but only if they are informed about the situation.

Interaction with the media must be controlled at the control center to avoid wild stories and rumors from developing. Ensure that employees know that they are not to talk to the press unless authorized to do so. Someone who is versed in public relations should be assigned the responsibility for this interaction.

Implementing the Plan

Once the situation is assessed, it is time to implement the plan. Refer to the documentation and follow the prescribed and tested procedures to the degree that it is possible. There are some situations that cannot be foreseen, and these may require some creativity in responding, but most will fall within the plan. A great deal of effort, thinking, and testing went into the plan, so use it.

Documenting for Insurance

Ensure that someone on the team is equipped with a camera to record the details of the disaster where appropriate. Prior to any restoration taking place, some record of the situation should be made that will support any kind of insurance claim that might be appropriate.

Returning to Normal

Once the crisis is under control, estimate the time it will take until the company can return to normal operations. That may be hours or months, but having an estimate can set the stage for the decisions to follow. For example, staff can work overtime to react to a temporary problem, and maybe even keep it up for a few days or even a couple of weeks, but it cannot go on for months. Once the duration is estimated, it is possible to determine what is needed to maintain function during the crisis, but also when it might be possible to return to normal.

As the crisis winds down, the team needs to plan the transition back to normal operations. It does not happen automatically except in minor situations, but must be planned to ensure that nothing is forgotten in the process. Communications is key to this phase to ensure that everyone knows what to expect and when, including employees and customers.

Revising and Updating the Plan

There is no test of the plan that is as effective as a real disaster. Things will not go as planned in every case and lessons will be learned. Once the "dust settles," take a long look at the documentation and the plan and make the necessary revisions to ensure that it meets the company's needs for the next situation that arises.

Standards Compliance

Every industry has rules and regulations that apply to the companies that work in it, and there are specific regulations that apply to the call center business. It is incumbent upon all managers to know the laws that apply and the implications of failure to comply. Since the laws change rapidly, it is also important to establish a trusted source that can provide updated information and interpret the new laws as they apply to the specific call center operations. In most cases, this will be the company's legal council.

Inbound

The primary statute that applies to inbound call centers is the Wiretap Act (18 U.S.C 2510, et seq. and 47 U.S.C 605). This act prohibits the use of eavesdropping technology and the interception of electronic mail, radio communications, data transmission and telephone calls without consent. The FCC has rules and tariff prescriptions prohibiting the recording of telephone conversations without notice or consent as do most states.

Where supervisors and quality monitoring staff will listen to or record calls, it is essential that the parties being observed be made aware of it. Agents should be required to sign an acknowledgement as they are hired. While not all states require both the agent and the caller to be notified, it is good business practice to do so on all calls. This is most easily done by including a statement in the recording that answers the calls that say something similar to "Your call may be monitored or recorded for quality control purposes." The announcement should be forced to be played on every call whether there is a queue for agents or not to ensure that every caller is notified.

Outbound

The primary law to be concerned about in outbound calling is the Telephone Consumer Protection Act (TCPA).

In 1991 President Bush signed into law the Telephone Consumer Protection Act of 1991 (TCPA), Public Law 102-243 (1991), which amended Title II of the Communications Act of 1934, 47 U.S.C. Section 201 et seq., by adding a new section, 47 U.S.C. Section 227. The U.S. Congress enacted it to reduce the nuisance and invasion of privacy caused by telemarketing and prerecorded calls. Congress ordered the FCC to make and clarify certain regulations, some of which are described below (47 CFR 64.1200).

The TCPA imposes restrictions on the use of automatic telephone dialing systems, of artificial or prerecorded voice messages, and of telephone facsimile machines to send unsolicited advertisements. Specifically, the TCPA prohibits autodialed and prerecorded voice message calls to emergency and health care operations. The TCPA also prohibits artificial or prerecorded voice message calls to residences made without prior express consent, unless it is an emergency call or specifically exempted by the Commission.

Facsimile machines may not transmit unsolicited advertisements. The TCPA also required that the Federal Communications Commission (FCC) consider several methods to accommodate telephone subscribers who do not wish to receive unsolicited advertisements, including live voice solicitations. The statute also outlines various remedies for violations of the TCPA.

The primary method offered is for individuals to ask to place their phone numbers on do-not-call lists at each company that they wish not to call them. Many states moved to enact state-wide do-not-call lists as well, and President Bush signed a law establishing a national do-not-call list in March, 2003. Calling a phone number that is on the list in any of these locations can result in a fine to the calling organization. It is the calling company's responsibility to have and use an up-to-date list. This legislation calls for stiff fines for calling people who have requested not to be called, and early enforcement has been rigorous.

The term "telephone solicitation" means the initiation of a telephone call or message for the purpose of encouraging the purchase or rental of, or investment in, property, goods, or services, which is transmitted to any person, but the term does not include a call or message:

1. To any person with that person's prior express invitation or permission

2. To any person with whom the caller has an established business relationship

3. By a tax-exempt nonprofit organization

In adopting rules to implement the TCPA, the FCC noted Congress' instruction in the Act that individuals' privacy rights, public safety interests, and commercial freedoms of speech and trade must be balanced in a way that protects the privacy of individuals and permits legitimate telemarketing practices. Congress pointed out that in 1990, more than 30,000 telemarketing firms, employing more than 18 million Americans, generated more than $400 billion in sales. But because unrestricted telemarketing can be an invasion of consumer privacy, and even a risk to public safety, Congress found that a federal law is necessary to control telemarketing practices.

Paper copies of U.S. laws and regulations concerning telecommunications can be ordered from the Federal Communications Commission at 1120 19th St N.W., Suite LL-20, Washington, D.C. 20036 (Telephone: +1 202 452 1422). More information about the laws can also be obtained from the Direct Marketing Association. The State Do Not Call List is available at www.the-dma.org/government/donotcalllists.shtml. It is important to understand that these laws change quickly and an updated list and specific legal language should be sought for those organizations involved in outbound telemarketing.

Collections Calling

For those organizations who generate outbound calls to consumers in an effort to collect debts due to clients (collection agencies), there are very specific laws that are defined in the Fair Debt Collection Practices Act. These are designed primarily to minimize harassment and abuse of consumers by the collection agencies, but the guidelines are good business practices even for business-to-business collections and other activities not specifically regulated by the Act. A copy of the Act can be found at http://www.ftc.gov/os/statutes/fdcpa/fdcpact.htm.

Summary

It is easy for call center managers to think that contingency planning and disaster recovery planning are not in their roles. However, there are a myriad of systems, components, and situations that are unique to the call center that will be missed if the call center is not represented in the planning committee that puts the company-wide or IT plan together. With the call center serving as the primary customer interaction point, and literally the front door to many businesses, it is essential that the risks in the call center be identified and managed. The contingency plan identifies the risks and works to prevent any damages from occurring, while the disaster recovery plan comes into effect when the contingency plan fails. Having a detailed plan that is well-understood by all employees will help to preserve human life and property and assist the company in restoring the business to normal operations as quickly as possible.

Compliance with laws, rules, and regulations is not optional, and lack of knowledge of the law is no excuse. The call center manager must be aware of the regulations that affect the call center's operation and ensure that compliance is achieved. Some laws that apply to nearly every call center include the wiretap laws that restrict monitoring without notice to those who will be observed, privacy laws, and the laws regarding restrictions on outbound telemarketing. Compliance with international laws will also be an issue for those call centers doing business overseas.

CHAPTER 14:
PRINCIPLES OF CALL CENTER LEADERSHIP
Introduction

Today's call center leader needs to have many of the skills and characteristics of any executive as well as special capabilities that are needed just for the unique call center environment. Exercising these capabilities will differ somewhat between the call center director, manager, supervisor and team leader, with each playing a leadership role for some portion of the team.

Personnel development is a key role of the leader and that includes developing staff as well as one's own professional development. Planning a strategy to reach a goal is the starting point, with identification of training, experience, and opportunities to develop the requisite capabilities and skills as the next steps.

Leadership Traits

Leadership is somewhat difficult to define. What works well for one person would not work at all for another. There have been many studies of what makes an effective business leader, but in the end, there is plenty of room for individuality. Some leaders are charismatic and others dictatorial. Some are financial geniuses, others are engineers, and still others are known for their marketing flare and public image. There are autocratic leaders who make demands of their subordinates with little input, and participative leaders who seek and encourage participation from their teams. In companies undergoing major changes, a transformational leadership style may be most appropriate in which the leader sees the current situation, the desired situation, and can help guide the team to achieving the vision.

Stephen Covey describes certain traits or habits of leadership in his book, *Principle-Centered Leadership*. These traits include service-orientation, positive energy, belief in other people, leading a balanced life, and engaging in new experiences as an adventure. Peter Drucker insists in The *Effective Executive* that leaders are not born, but develop through practice.

Another analysis of effective leadership is provided by Jim Collins in *Good to Great: Why Some Companies Make the Leap and Others Don't*. In the companies that have made the transition to "great" status, the leaders are operating at what Collins refers to as Level 5, in which they have all the characteristics of the first four levels and add the fifth:

- Level 1 – Highly capable and makes productive personal contributions
- Level 2 – Takes personal capabilities and adds them to the team effort
- Level 3 – Competent at managing other people toward objectives
- Level 4 – Leads by being a catalyst of commitment to a compelling vision
- Level 5 – Displays a paradoxical blend of personal humility and professional drive focused on the success of the organization over themselves

The need for humility is one that is also touted by Benedict of Nursia who founded the Benedictine order of monasteries that have survived through the ages based on the rules that he established for their management. In *The Benedictine Rule of Leadership,* it is noted that true entrepreneurship and leadership resolve do not come from the pride and ego, but rather from the personal passion to excel, to improve both the organization and the world around it.

Another important characteristic of a leader noted by Benedict is that the leader have a basic knowledge of each and every person who is within the managerial sphere. This meant that monasteries were kept to around 250 people or less. Being able to greet employees in the hall and ask some specific question about their job, their families or personal interests goes a long way toward making those people believe that their leader views them as important to the organization. Dr. Robert Hayes of TCS Management Group demonstrated this behavior. As the Executive VP, he made a personal commitment to learn the name of every employee and that of the spouse or significant other, even as the organization grew to over 400 employees. He greeted each employee by name at every opportunity and walked around the facility daily for the simple purpose of talking to as many staff as possible. Many who worked the phones would be on calls as he dropped by, but he'd wave to them and remember to try to catch them the next time. At company social functions, he surprised many spouses by greeting them by name often when he had never been formally introduced to them. The resulting loyalty that this process engendered in the staff was remarkable.

According to the book, *Growing Your Company's Leaders: How Great Organizations Use Succession Management to Sustain Competitive Advantage,* Bank of America defined five leadership competencies for their managers based on a study of best practices at GE, Citigroup, UPS, Allied Signal, 3M, Honeywell, Coca-Cola, Pepsi, and Wells Fargo. These five competencies and their related behaviors are listed below:

- Grow the business.
  - o Demonstrate deep and broad business acumen.
  - o Create competitive and innovative business plans.
  - o Build customer/client-driven environment.
  - o Institutionalize error-free quality processes.
  - o Excel at risk/reward trade-off.
- Lead people to perform.
  - o Align enterprise capabilities.
  - o Recruit and grow great talent.
  - o Inspire commitment and followership.
  - o Communicate crisply and candidly.
- Drive execution.
  - o Instill management focus and discipline.

o Build partnerships to achieve swift adoption.

o Demonstrate sound judgment and acts with speed.

• Sustain intensity and optimism.

o Constantly raise the bar.

o Display personal courage.

o Continuously learn and adapt.

• Live our values.

o Live our company's values.

o Put the interest of the bank ahead of his/her own agenda.

During the eulogies of former President Ronald Reagan, he was often described as "the Great Communicator." While not everyone agreed with his politics, it is hard to quibble with his ability to demonstrate leadership. A *USA Today* article written by Del Jones mentions the following seven characteristics of leadership that Reagan demonstrated:

• *Start with a moral foundation.* – Experts say most people forgive mistakes made by leaders who have both conviction and a good heart.

• *The vision thing matters.* – "Vision is the North Star for any organization," according to Wess Roberts, author of *Leadership Secrets of Attila the Hun*.

• *Take the heat.* – Great leaders are capable of making tough decisions. In Reagan's case, firing the air traffic controllers was one such decision.

• *Be comfortable in your own skin.* – The most powerful tool is the ability to make people feel like what they do matters, and leaders don't need to be mean to be tough.

• *Maintain a sense of humor.* – Even during the nuclear arms race when things were very serious, Reagan could joke about the little things.

• *Be a great communicator.* – It is not only acceptable but also desirable to show emotion and passion. Successful leaders take a simple message and repeat it endlessly.

• *Delegate.* – Reagan hired talented people, occasionally including former opponents, and then got out of their way to let them do their jobs.

The characteristics described above are generally focused on the requirements at the very top of an organization. While the call center manager or supervisor may not need to have all of these capabilities to be successful, it is clear that good leadership skills are helpful to be effective at any level of the organization.

There are some general skills and characteristics that are found in most successful leaders in the call center arena. These characteristics include:

• *Integrity* – A successful leader has unwavering ethics, must be honest and have the character to keep promises, be courageous, and to support the staff. Ethics are not situational and must be something that can be relied upon by all stake-holders.

- *Learning-oriented* – A successful leader must be able to inspire followers to grow, adapt, and continuously improve their knowledge and skills. In order to foster the growth of others, the leader must also be focused on his or her own development and learning.

- *Decisive* – A successful leader can and will be able to make a final decision when all the facts are known and the risks fully understood.

- *Big picture view* – A successful leader sees the influences and impacts of actions on more than the call center, and ensures that the call center is well-positioned within the enterprise to maximize its effectiveness overall.

- *Caring* – A successful leader realizes that managing a call center is a people business. The customers, the staff, and all stakeholders must all be satisfied for the call center to be successful. If the leader genuinely cares for all of these people, quality relationships will be built and teams can function well. Feedback will be provided in a constructive manner and discipline will be firm but fair. Employees will feel that the manager shows a genuine interest in the individual well-being and lives of each person, not just the company goals and financial position.

- *Focus on improvement* – A successful leader is able to step back from the day-do-day operation to see what is working well and what is not, accept the feedback of customers, employees and even outsiders, and to focus the operation on continuous improvement. Even an award-winning center that is working very well can always find ways to improve. That focus is not a destination but an ongoing journey.

The following chart shows examples of these leadership characteristics as applied to a variety of call center roles:

Leadership Matrix

Leadership Characteristic	Multi-site Call Center Director	Site Call Center Manager	Call Center Supervisor	Call Center Team Leader	Specialized Function Manager (WFM, QM, Training, etc.)
Integrity	Maintain broad personal commitment to enterprise integrity goals and assist subordinates in sorting through issues that fall in the "gray area". Support reasonable risk-taking within the operation.	Maintain broad personal commitment to enterprise integrity goals and assist subordinates in sorting through issues that fall in the "gray area". Support reasonable risk-taking within the operation.	Ensure that agents perform their roles in compliance with enterprise integrity guidelines. Guide agents in applying ethical resolutions within the boundaries of their empowerment.	Ensure that agents perform their roles in compliance with enterprise integrity guidelines. Identify any issues to supervisor as appropriate.	Maintain awareness of integrity goals and treats all stakeholders with integrity and respect. Identify any issues to supervisors or site manager as appropriate.

Learning-Oriented	Ensure overall budget includes sufficient funds for training for all personnel. Demonstrate commitment to learning through own personal development efforts. Ensure that staff have opportunities to develop both personally and professionally.	Plan training programs that address the needs of all staff and their career development, and ensures staffing is sufficient to allow training to happen. Look for opportunities within the organization to support development of new skills and knowledge.	Work with each agent on the team to identify career plans, training requirements, opportunities, and schedules agent as needed. Provide coaching to develop and reinforce skills.	Coach agents within the team as the training is completed to ensure skills are used effectively.	WFM analyzes optimal timing for training to ensure the balance of cost and service. QM measures the effectiveness of training to ensure skills are used and coaching efforts are guided.
Decisive	Using data provided by the site managers and others, analyze options and makes prompt decisions. Communicate the decision and rationale to site managers.	Using data provided by supervisors, specialty managers and others, analyze options affecting the site and makes prompt decisions. Communicate the decision and rationale to site personnel.	Using appropriate authority, make decisions on agent requests and contact handling changes to react to real-time issues after seeking input from team leaders and specialty managers.	Provide input to supervisor to assist in analyzing options and impacts of agent requests and contact handling strategies.	Provide data to support decision-making and analysis of options to site call center managers, supervisors and others.
Big-Picture View	Focus on the total role of the call center in the entire enterprise and its effect on all stakeholders.	Focus on the single site call center, but maintains a view of the entire enterprise.	Focus on the supervisory team, but maintain an understanding of the role of the team within the entire center.	Focus on the supervisory team, but maintain an understanding of the role of the team within the entire center.	Focus on the single site call center especially within the specialty involved, but maintains a view of the entire enterprise.
Caring	Champion the call center's role and contribution across the enterprise to ensure the appropriate resources are available and career paths developed.	Focus on the balance of agent and customer needs to ensure that agent needs are not sacrificed unnecessarily to meet customer needs.	Focus on the personal needs of each agent in the team and champions agent requests where they do not compromise broader call center goals.	Treat all personnel with respect and bring issues to supervisors that need to be addressed.	Manage the balance of personnel issues and functional requirements to meet call center goals in the application of the specialty role.
Focus on Improvement	Establish enterprise goals that are realistic but stretch the staff in meeting and exceeding company and customer expectations. Ensure that the resources are appropriate to make the goals realistic.	Translate the enterprise goals into site call center goals that are realistic and resources appropriately. Ensure that the "how to" is communicated to supervisors as well as the goals.	Coach team leaders and agents on their current and expected performance to identify gaps and opportunities. Ensure that creative solutions by individuals are shared across the team and center.	Coach agents on the team to improve performance as appropriate. Develop reports to aid the supervisor and site call center managers identify where skill gaps exist.	Perform "what if" analysis, identifies performance successes and gaps, and develops training to address gaps.

In addition to these characteristics, the successful call center manager should have the following skills and knowledge:

- *Organizational design* – The leader must determine the most effective way to design the organizational structure, assign roles, and create reporting relationships.

- *Strategic planning* – Developing the plan for the call center that aligns with the enterprise mission and strategies is a key skill to achieving the results that will provide the most value to the enterprise.

- *Finance* – The call center manager must be able to develop and manage to a budget, understand how to develop a business case with supporting financial analysis, and understand the overall financial statements of the enterprise.

- *Contract management* – Skill in negotiating and managing contracts is required for the acquisition of the products and services needed by the call center, but also for outsourcing agreements, contract labor, and even collective bargaining.

- *Survey techniques* – Assessing the satisfaction of customers and employees is an ongoing need and the skill to develop, administer, and interpret the results is important.

There are a myriad of other skills that would certainly be helpful such as understanding workforce management, call center technology applications, strategies and regulations involved in the management of human resources, and quality control techniques. These are all skills that can be supplemented with experts in the area who report to the manager/director, but a broad working knowledge of the principles is essential to management of the overall processes. Personnel in specialty functions and supervisory/team lead roles will need to gain these skills as they develop their careers.

Change Management

Change is the one thing that can be depended upon as a constant. The enterprise shifts to meet new competitive challenges and seize new opportunities, and the call center must evolve as well. It is also true that change is something that most human beings dislike. So the management of change is an essential skill for the call center leader.

Change must be driven by some requirement that is not now being met, so the plan to address the deficiency is the starting point of the change. Once the goal or the projected result of the change is defined, the specific steps for achieving the result can be developed. It is important for the change to be broken down into phases that can be easily assimilated into the organization. Involving representatives from all affected departments and all levels of the call center will ensure that the design of the planned change is balanced and workable.

Implementing a skill-based routing scenario is a good example of a process that can benefit from a change management methodology. The driving need may be that a company's CRM initiative and customer segmentation strategy requires the call center to treat some callers differently than others, with faster response times and with differing levels of self-service. The center may embark on a plan to segment the callers and the agent groups to match. The result that is the ultimate goal is a call center call handling strategy that is better aligned with the brand image and delivery of differentiated services to the highest value customers.

The development of the routing plan requires the aid of the marketing department to ensure that the segmentation and brand strategy are followed, the telecom department to ensure that the plan is possible within the current technology and that costs are well understood, and the call center training department to ensure that the agents can be effectively trained to provide the differentiated handling required. Involving frontline agents and supervisors will ensure that the process does not miss some important operational function and that there are champions to sell the concept internally when the implementation starts.

Once the plan is developed, it is anticipated that there will be phases of implementation. The final skill-based routing plan may be quite complex, but the likelihood of success will be improved if one small change at a time can be initiated, tested, and assimilated. If the change does not have the expected result, the process can be easily reversed and a new plan developed before it affects a large group of customers or employees. But if the entire complex plan is rolled out all at once, and if it does not work as expected, there is no way to tell which part of the plan is deficient. All that can be done is to reverse the entire process and start over and that is both expensive and painful.

The most important rules of change management are to measure the current situation, implement one change at a time, ensure each change works before adding another, and being willing to accept that the result is not as expected and that reversal is appropriate when needed. Change can not be accomplished without risk of failure, so willingness to accept reasonable risk and manage it is a key element of change management.

Ethics and Leadership

Ethics can be defined as the actions a person takes when he is absolutely certain no one else will ever know. It is the true character of the individual and the manner in which he relates to the rest of the world. The International Business Ethics Institute (www.business-ethics.org) defines business ethics as "a form of applied ethics. It aims at inculcating a sense within a company's employee population of how to conduct business responsibly."

Even within a religious order, Benedict's view of management ethics was not to preach ethical philosophy to his followers but rather to create the organizational condition for ethical behavior to be quite natural. The idea is to balance the natural desires of individuals and the imperatives of organizational action. Benedict spelled out ten action points:

1. The ethical values of the organization should always be explicit and consistent.

2. The value statements must be well thought out and limited in number. They are not political statements, but unbending standards that everyone must adhere to.

3. There needs to be a clear and easily understood explanation as to why these

are ethical values for the organization.

4. All employees must be regularly and formally reminded about the ethical values.

5. Values must be an integral part of screening, hiring and training.

6. Leaders must set the highest example of ethical behavior.

7. There must be unwavering equality in enforcing the rules and standards. No one is given an exception by virtue of rank.

8. There must a clearly understood enforcement process that is consistent, fair, and evenly applied. It is unacceptable to make an example of someone.

9. The leader must design the organization so that the benefit of community membership in the organization far outweighs the cost of violating its rules.

10. While organization forgiveness and second chances are important, ultimately the survival of the organization and the community must take precedence.

Organizations may state an ethical code of conduct that is expected of employees, but in the end, it is each individual who carries it out. While there is certainly a perception that many issues fall in the "gray area," in reality, very few decisions on ethical grounds are truly unclear. What appears to put them in doubt is the desire to gain from making an exception to the definitions of right and wrong. It is the role of the leader to clearly establish the ethical boundaries, resolve any questions about the perceived "gray areas," and support the difficult decisions that must be made to uphold the ethically right path.

This is clearly a case of leadership by example, not by what is said. When the tough choices must be made, the ethical decision must consistently be made, even when it causes temporary pain or costs more. The smallest compromises can begin to break down the moral fiber of the enterprise and lead others to make additional small departures, until the organization's behavior and its statements of ethics no longer match Personnel who are found to compromise ethically put the organization at risk and should be dealt with firmly and quickly, including termination where appropriate.

As an example, consider the manager who stretches the boundaries to include personal items on the company expense account. She feels justified because she spends so many hours at work and on the road away from her family, so a few dollars spent on gifts or family expenses seems like a reasonable exchange. The company views this manager as a highly effective member of the team and her departure would create a significant gap in the organization. However, there is no doubt that specific expense she has submitted are personal in nature.

The leader must confront the manager to let her know that the personal expenses are not acceptable, and that this behavior will not be tolerated. Repayment of the personal items must be made to reconcile the discrepancies. If that ends the practice, then the ethical problem has been solved, and may have been only a misunderstanding. But if further personal expenses are submitted, the company must take action, including the potential termination of employment. The cost to the company of losing and replacing the manager in real dollars is probably much higher than the total of the per sonal expenses over several years. But the tough decision must be made with an eye to managing the impact as much as possible. It is not necessary that any one else in the company know why the action was taken. However, if allowed to continue, it sets up a situation in which the compromise of ethics becomes known. Precedent is established, serving as further justification for others to follow.

Now apply the issues in the call center. Making an exception for one employee leads to more exceptions. Agents working with customers must also understand that the company requires them to do the "right thing" and employees must be empowered to do it. When agents are required to do things they find unethical or even in the "gray area," it places them in a compromised position. This often results in employee turnover when the agent determines that the things he is asked to do are not ethical in his mind. There is a narrow band of ethical behaviors. When employees cross over voluntarily, disciplinary action is in order. When employees are forced to cross over involuntarily, turnover is likely in both employees and customers.

Team Building

Another key leadership skill is the ability to instill a sense of belonging in the individual. One way to create a sense of belonging is to use teams. With a team structure, the team members assume responsibility, potential is recognized and fostered, trust and camaraderie develops. Friendships develop more easily in a team environment and people are more likely to look forward to coming to work each day if they feel a part of a group.

The overall challenges of leaders of groups or teams include:

- Provide for expansion of each individual's role so that participation in the team becomes more meaningful for the individual and effective for the organization.

- Create networks and groupings of a temporary nature that cross traditional divisions and promote cross-fertilization of knowledge and ideas.

- Enhance individual participation in management processes in order to enhance initiative and a sense of responsibility.

- Remove or minimize organization barriers to communication.

An interesting study done by the US National Aeronautics and Space Administration (NASA) in 1985 explored the challenges of group leadership and team dynamics associated with teams living together in a lunar outpost or space colony. While this is perhaps an extreme example, it demonstrates what is needed for a group in a micro-society when survival is incumbent upon team cooperation. These are some of NASA's recommendations for high-performance teams:

- While technical competence is needed, social compatibility is a key ingredient to maintain morale and performance. Team members should be selected and trained for desirable attitudes and skills, as well as different but complementary needs and skills.

- Groups with both sexes have the advantage of greater diversity, but could face some stereotyping and sexual harassment issues. Gender issues around leadership and command may need to be addressed as the team is formed.

• Multicultural groups also provide greater diversity, but require care in understanding differences in perceptions and communications processes.

• Team size is important. The team should be slightly understaffed so that people stretch themselves to perform (as long as there is no health or safety risk involved). If the team is too large for efficient decision-making, it may make sense to break it into sub-teams.

• Group cohesiveness results from the rewards and satisfaction of group membership. This can be as simple as the prestige of belonging to the team, or more tangible such as money or promotional opportunities.

• Performance can be affected by too much emphasis on group harmony and "group thinking." A certain amount of conflict in the group is healthy.

• Team continuity depends on the length of time the team will work together. In a long-term team situation, there must be strategies and methods for assimilating new members. This involves them sharing the group's history and knowledge base.

• High-performance teams strike a balance between the individual actions of members and the social influence of the group as a whole.

The overall process of team building requires that there be cooperation that trades off rival ideas and interests through negotiation. The ultimate results hinge upon the recognition of the common goals as well as the conflicting interests, and a desire to reach an amicable resolution to the conflicts. The view of conflict within the organization has evolved from the desire to minimize any conflict to one in which conflict is viewed as energy. If that energy is used properly, it can stimulate group action instead of boring conformity. It is helpful to identify different points of view and options and explore them thoroughly. Conflicting points of view can help identify more input, wider consideration of alternatives and improved solutions, but they must be managed to keep the conflicts at a professional level, not a personal one. When conflict is dysfunctional, it is often the result of one of four causes:

• Personal behavioral problems of an individual that have been projected on the group

• Social pressures, both internal and external to the group

• Incentive structures that reward non-cooperative actions

• Rules and procedures that are open to differences in interpretation and become inoperative or ineffective

The concept of teams suggests that decision by consensus is the norm. Therefore, the team must find a proposed solution to the challenge that is acceptable enough to everyone so that all team members can support it, at least to some degree. It may be reasonable to give every member veto power, somewhat like the Security Council of the United Nations, or perhaps a majority rules process will be more effective. Making consensus decisions requires that the team members all participate, take the time to consider all of the issues, and build mutual trust, respect and commitment. The following roles can be defined for members within a decision-making team.

Task Roles	
Initiating	Gives ideas and proposed tasks
Seeking information	Asks for facts and ideas
Giving information	Offers facts, ideas, and beliefs
Clarification	Clears up confusing
Summarization	Restates or offers conclusions
Testing for Consensus	Checks on the status of the group's position
Positive Roles	
Harmonizing/Mediating	Reduces tension and examines differences
Gatekeeper	Facilitaties the participation of the others
Support/Encouragement	Maintains a friendly, warm and accepting environment
Sets Standards	Helps in setting norms and testing limits
Negative Roles	
Blocker	Prevents movement or consensus
Dominator	Is hostile and talks over others
Joker	Uses humor and jokes inappropriately
Self-seeker	Oppresses other with personal needs
Withdrawn	Does not pay attention, is silent, or changes subjects of discussion

Overall, a call center is made up of many formal and informal teams. Ensuring that these groups work together effectively is a key role of the call center leader. Focus on the elements of teamwork that make it more effective and avoid the roles and situations that will diminish results. The result will be significant dividends in the overall performance of the call center within the organization.

Mentoring

At some point in a leader's career, he/she probably fell under the influence of a mentor. While many of these relationships are informal, some are arranged carefully to maximize the opportunity for a successful person to guide someone else who is "learning the ropes." As the career develops, the time will often come that the person who was the student will become a mentor to those who follow. And for some, they will be both mentor and student of another at the same time.

There is a distinction between the role of a leader and the role of a mentor. A leader is the individual who sets the direction, lets others know what it is, and inspires others so that they can follow. The leader may or may not be involved with individuals in their decision to follow or how they will do it. For example, a charismatic leader such as Martin Luther King, Jr. inspired many to the path of his vision. Many of those who followed him never actually met the man, but they followed nonetheless. Some who professed to follow did so in ways that were never defined by King. There were some who expanded on his vision while others focused on a tiny element or even may have misinterpreted his intent.

A mentor is not necessarily one who leads, but a person who provides encouragement and guidance on the options available and the potential consequences of certain choices. It is a one-to-one relationship in which the mentor can serve as a sounding board for ideas, a guide through the organizational politics, and a supporter when there is a risk to be taken. The mentor can help a person find the appropriate resources and opportunities needed for development and learning. A mentor can help a person through a personal or professional choice, not so much by supplying answers as asking the right questions. This can help a person figure out where his interests and passions lie, what his underlying values and core purpose may be, and which of optional paths may lead to the best result. So the mentor does not set the direction and expect to be followed as a leader does, but helps the person to set his/her own direction and make choices with full knowledge of the potential impacts and consequences.

Mentors can be within the direct reporting relationship with their students, or may be in totally unrelated businesses or departments of the company. It is often easier for the mentor to have no direct reporting relationship, since there may be conflicting priorities and business requirements. What is required is a framework for a totally open and honest dialogue. Discussion of personal issues, personality conflicts, ethical concerns, ambitions and fears must be possible without risk of recriminations or potential for this knowledge to put either party at any serious risk. So the mentor who is also a boss can be placed in a difficult conflict, but that does not mean it cannot work. Some of the most important mentoring roles are those performed by a boss who guides a subordinate through a difficult career choice, or ensures that assignments expand horizons or expose the person to the opportunities to learn skills needed for development and promotion. But to be successful, the boss/mentor must be able to put the student's interests first and guide him/her to the best options, even if it means that the team may lose an important contributor when the goals take that person into another job.

Professional Development

Developing personnel within an organization is one of the most important roles of leader. This includes developing staff, succession planning, and personal development. Creating a workplace culture that inspires employees to choose accountability for specific outcomes requires them to have information. For most companies, this demands a significant shift in thinking about employee capabilities and what's required for them to do their jobs. It involves developing learning practices that encourage experimentation, broad sharing of information, and transferring knowledge and expertise in a variety of ways. Providing these things inspires a culture of employee ownership and commitment.

Development of management personnel within an organization and the development of a successful succession plan needs to concentrate on the skills and knowledge that are needed within that enterprise. In general, that means asking the following questions:

•What processes and activities drive value in the organization?

• How do leaders affect those processes and activities?

The answers to those questions define the roles of leaders in the organization and the specific leadership requirements. The design of a development program includes new assignments, coaching, mentoring, training and more. However, these design components are best applied selectively as needed, rather than spreading them evenly across all participants. Define development needs according to the strategy and competency gaps of the specific leaders.

For example, if the organization's primary strategy is organic sales growth, and the key driver of growth is entering new markets, leaders will need to be capable of navigating through ambiguity and be able to thrive in a variety of cultures as the company expands markets to international settings. Even though there are unique local requirements for leaders in other countries, if managers are relocated internationally during their careers, it is critical to have some common leadership characteristics that serve as a compass for leaders to guide their behavior in any area of the world.

Personal development requires a commitment to a development strategy that is focused on the specific skills and experiences that are needed. The strategy might be to be the best call center manager possible, or to aspire to roles in higher management. Once the focus of the strategy is defined, working with a mentor to determine the skills, capabilities, and experiences that are required to attain that result can be identified. It is likely that some training/education may be required and it will be a personal responsibility to sign up for and complete those programs (with the potential assistance of the employer as appropriate).

Establishing a plan for acquiring skills and demonstrating them in the business setting is often a function of assignment to projects and roles that might not generally be considered part of the current job. Where this is the case, working with the mentor can help find those opportunities within the company, or even within the community. Volunteer efforts are often a good way to gain experiences that may not be readily available on the job.

For the call center professional, there are various types of certification programs that can be helpful. The Call Center Industry Advisory Council (CIAC) provides industry-recognized certification. This organization provides the testing and certification processes for call center managers and consultants, and may soon expand to including supervisory roles. Intermediary certification of specific skills can be obtained from various training organizations, but these generally focus on the student's attendance at a specific program and possibly completing a test on that content only. Whatever training route is taken, it is important that the program contribute to the development plan that the student has chosen.

Summary

The leaders set the tone for the operation of the entire call center. Good leadership can make it easy for the staff to meet the goals of the organization, while poor leadership can result in non-productive efforts. Leadership is needed at all levels from the call center manager or director to the frontline supervisors and team leaders. It is expected that the wide variety of personalities will manifest themselves in several leadership styles that impact the communications and decision processes in the center.

Leadership is a skill that can be learned and its principles applied in a variety of settings. These guidelines provide the most basic and essential ingredients for creating a truly sustainable organization, whether in the corporate world or public sector. According to The Benedictine Rule of Leadership, "Like an award winning pastry, the finest ingredients must be added with care, combined and stirred with proper technique, then appropriately baked with the attention and diligence of a master's eye. Even with the most solid of foundations, it still requires skill and subtle improvisation, appropriate to the time and place, to make a truly superior organization."